# Woodstock

# Woodstock

## From World War to Culture Wars

RICHARD HEPPNER

**EXCELSIOR
EDITIONS**

Cover Credit: Overlook Mountain (background) and sign at intersection of Woodstock's main streets (foreground) by Richard Heppner.

Published by State University of New York Press, Albany

Excelsior Editions is an imprint of State University of New York Press

For information, contact State University of New York Press, Albany, NY
www.sunypress.edu

**Library of Congress Cataloging-in-Publication Data**

Name: Heppner, Richard R., author.
Title: Woodstock : from world war to culture wars / Richard Heppner.
Description: Albany : State University of New York Press, [2024] | Series: Excelsior editions | Includes bibliographical references and index.
Identifiers: LCCN 2024009181 | ISBN 9781438499321 (pbk. : alk. paper) | ISBN 9781438499338 (ebook)
Subjects: LCSH: Woodstock (N.Y.)—History—20th century. | Woodstock (N.Y.)—Social life and customs—20th century.
Classification: LCC F129.W85 H47 2024 | DDC 974.7/34—dc23/eng/20240405
LC record available at https://lccn.loc.gov/2024009181

*To my grandsons, Henry and Elliott*
*Wherever life may take you in the years ahead,*
*Woodstock will always call you home.* — *"Pops"*

More and more, as I think about history, I am convinced that everything that is worthwhile in the world has been accomplished by the free, inquiring, critical spirit, and that the preservation of this spirit is more important than any social system whatsoever.

—Sinclair Lewis, *It Can't Happen Here*

# Contents

# Illustrations

# Acknowledgments

The pages that follow are the result of the generous contributions made by so many—and I am forever in their debt. Thank you to the Historical Society of Woodstock and JoAnn Margolis for being the careful guardians of Woodstock history. Great appreciation also goes to the Woodstock Library and Kim Apolant for their assistance in accessing the library's important collection of Woodstock newspapers. Thank you also to those who gave of their time and their knowledge of Woodstock history, including Ed Sanders, Karyn Bevet, Tobe Carey, Jim Hanson, Jay Sadowitz, Lorin Rose, Janine Fallon-Mower, Laurie Ylvisaker, Brian Hollander, Barbara O'Brien, WoodstockArts and Weston Blelock, Paul Van Wagenen, Matthew Leaycraft, Tina Bromberg, Emily Jones, Sarah Mecklem, Tom Unrath, and Michelle Slung.

Obvious appreciation must also be extended to Richard Carlin, senior acquisitions editor at State University of New York Press, for guiding me through the process and to the State University of New York Press staff who brought this effort to conclusion. Appreciation also goes to the town of Woodstock for providing me with the opportunity to serve as town historian for the last twenty-two years and to Bert Breitenberger, who instilled the love of history in his students.

To my wife, Deborah Heppner, thank you for your guidance, proofreading talents, and patience.

# Woodstock

## By Way of Introduction

Every Sunday, Florence Peper closed the front door behind her and made the short walk across Woodstock's Mill Hill Road to enter the Lutheran church directly opposite her family home. As the years progressed, though that walk was slowed by age, it was a rare Woodstock Sunday when her crossing did not cause cars to pause as she made her way to the church entrance.

An unmarried Florence Peper had grown into her old age living in the family home, which was next door to what was once her father's blacksmith shop. Born in 1892 and passing at the age of 92, Miss Peper, as she was fondly known, was a small woman, standing 5'2". And yet, her diminutive size belied the stature of someone who earned the respect of an entire community through her work on behalf of her Church and the local Red Cross, selling war bonds during World War II, freely sharing the bounty from the garden she planted each year, and extending care to those in need, as well as a chronicler of Woodstock life in a diary that spanned from 1914 to shortly before her death in 1984.[1]

Hers was not a lengthy literary style. Her diary consists of simple, usually one-sentence entries. That said, as the parade that was Woodstock everyday life passed by her living room window, little was missed. Births were noted, as were the many funerals she attended. Daily life, from winter blizzards to the seasonal butchering of hogs—"We butchered so much lard & grease I never saw. Worked till 9 o'clock in the evening"[2]—find their way into her recollections right below who got elected locally to events transpiring on the world stage: "Fri. 9/1—Germany Invaded Poland. Which means war."[3]

Because it spanned much of the twentieth century, Florence Peper's life speaks to a Woodstock many would not recognize today. Hers was a life couched in small-town existence, church suppers, lodge meetings, membership in the American Legion and Woodstock Fire Department ladies' auxiliaries, and conservative politics. (If Democrats are mentioned at all in her diary, it is usually by last name only: "Roosevelt" and "Truman.") It was a life, however, not far different from most born in her time. And yet, outside the very same window Florence Peper looked out upon the world, change had come—and would continue to arrive. From the early artists and their easels that dotted the Woodstock landscape throughout the first half of the twentieth century to the young people and musicians who followed in the 1960s and 1970s, the once remote lives of Florence Peper and those Woodstockers who found their way into her diary were to be isolated no more. An incremental transformation was underway, a transformation that brought eclectic lifestyles, division, progressive politics, and a new economic reality far removed from the self-sufficiency of Florence Peper's earlier days. It was a transformation that eventually propelled Woodstock onto the world stage, while leaving many Woodstockers, such as Miss Peper, wondering what had happened to the small town they thought they knew.

Community identity is typically drawn from the shared interests of its members. Such identity, however, does not come easy—or always accurately—when applied over time to a town such as Woodstock. Falsely known by many as the site of the paramount music festival of the 1960s, it did, however, play midwife to that tumultuous event. Once cited as the "most famous small town in America," the ingredients that gave rise to this idea are often shrouded within the mist that mixes history with nostalgia, a mix that can be increasingly distorted as time moves further away from the actual moment. Some will point to Woodstock's place in history as home to the Byrdcliffe Arts Colony established in 1902 by Ralph Radcliffe Whitehead at the base of Overlook Mountain. Others will note the town's importance by citing the long list of luminaries that have traveled the town's winding roads, from President Ulysses S. Grant to Bob Dylan. Some will, undoubtedly, hold up the attraction of Woodstock's physical landscape as the town's economy ultimately moved from what could be taken from the land to the beauty others saw in it. Or, perhaps, Woodstock can be best understood by the people who have crossed its stage: from cantankerous curmudgeons dispensing advice you should probably heed, to free-spirited eccentrics offering proclamations of prophecy and healing (proceed with caution), to well-intentioned citizens who occasionally make sense.

In many respects, Woodstock might be cited as a town built on paradoxes, layers not always in harmony with what went before. Today, for example, Woodstock is one of the most politically progressive towns in the region. And yet, for most of its history conservative politics infused itself into all that was governed. Today's liberal identity, however, rests upon the knowledge that Woodstock once knew the original sin of slavery, was no stranger to anti-Semitism and saw crosses burned on the side of its main road. For half of its history, art was what was found on a store-bought calendar until the day the very land that had been worked for over a hundred years became central to landscapes viewed through the creative eye. Long before music studios, the musicians that followed—and the young people who followed them—arrived in town, most Woodstock music bellowed from church organs on Sundays or was found in the fiddling that backed a caller at a town hall square dance.

At some point, the above contradictions were guaranteed to clash. When they have, much like a cold front that sweeps across the land in spring, both major and minor storms ensued. That too is part of Woodstock's identity: an identity that, at times, is actually embraced by its citizens as Woodstockers seldom fail to welcome a good fight.

The pages that follow attempt to unweave the various threads that have created the tapestry that was Woodstock through the middle of the twentieth century. While recognizing that no one period of a town's history is unhinged from another, the dichotomy of Woodstock's story finds ample illustration during this era. As the Depression years moved into the war years, as the boom of the fifties gave way to the challenges of the sixties and seventies, the building blocks of Woodstock's social, cultural, and political structure were challenged—and redirected—on multiple occasions. At the same time, brief glimpses of unity also appeared, as if to offer proof that a town infused with a diversity of strong opinions could indeed move ahead.

Unity in Woodstock, however, usually makes an appearance when there is the need to challenge authority and, though some of Woodstock's recorded history won't quite admit it, Woodstockers have always had an inherent streak of individualism built into their DNA. From its earliest days of settlement, Woodstockers have offered a clear indication that they might have some issues with authority. The Down-Rent War (1839–1845) is an early example. Also known as the Anti-Rent War, tenant farmers in Upstate New York, including Woodstock, came together to reject the feudal-type land leases—known as three-life leases—imposed upon them by wealthy landowners. Unable to secure the lands for themselves, no matter how many years they or their descendants worked or improved the land they leased, tenants, often disguised as "Calico Indians," hiding their identities beneath sheepskin hoods, began to retaliate against the onerous system imposed upon them. With the approach of any figure of authority whose purpose was to collect rent, horns sounded throughout the valley as a signal to gather, initiating attempts to interfere with the purpose of the unwanted visitor. The focal point of that interference was often the land agent employed by the wealthy landowner. Such was the lesson learned by one agent, John Lasher, on a March day near Woodstock's Cooper Lake:

> As soon as he was observed from across the lake there sounded the penetrating blow of a cattle horn calling out the "Indians," who before long, surrounded him . . . Lasher managed to run off as far as the shore of the lake before he was caught. Then the Indians turned to Peter Sagendorf's barn nearby and, finding some tar in a barrel, daubed it upon their victim and added chicken feathers from the hen house alongside before they allowed the unfortunate Lasher to get away.[4]

While less aggressive examples exist throughout Woodstock history, challenges to authority are a constant found in many chapters of Woodstock's story. One might say it's in the water, but even the water has provided a stage for Woodstockers to assert their independence. When the city of Kingston laid claim to Woodstock's Cooper Lake as a source for their drinking water, the powers that be in Kingston deemed it unacceptable for Woodstockers to swim in the waters exiting Cooper Lake and flowing into the Sawkill Creek—the same creek that offered Woodstockers relief in the heat of summer. Visitors from Kingston, as they passed over the bridge entering Woodstock, were horrified to witness Woodstockers—especially artists—enjoying themselves as they immersed themselves in the very water that would eventually flow from Kingston faucets. Complaints were made. The Kingston paper led with "Artistic temperament of transplanted Greenwich Villagers in Woodstock breaks out in a new form of 'self-expression' which involves bathing on city property and polluting city's water supply."[5] Even the district attorney got involved, issuing an injunction against swimming in posted areas.

Not taking Kingston's actions lightly, Woodstockers, in a way only Woodstockers can, organized the Great Swim-in protest of 1922. On a Sunday morning in June, one hundred Woodstockers marched from Woodstock's Village Green to the swimming hole near the golf course bridge, where, according to the *Kingston Daily Freeman*, "they swam or 'paddled' or just 'washed' according to temperament, age or degree of cleanliness in the drinking water of the city of Kingston, thereby asserting their rights to trespass on the property of the city and pollute the water supply of 27,000 people."[6] Eventually, the city of Kingston relented and installed a pipeline to carry the water downstream to their fair city and leave Woodstockers to worry about those artist types.

A community's evolution is seldom in a direct line. In 1902, however, Woodstock diverged greatly from the small-town norm. On a spring day, a man by the name of Bolton Brown emerged from the thicket near the summit of Overlook Mountain and looked down upon the expanse before him and the village that lay below. The former head of the art department at Stanford University in Palo Alto, California (he left his position after being reprimanded for employing nude models), Brown had been hired by Ralph Whitehead to seek out a physical location that matched Whitehead's dream for a utopian art colony. Believing on that March day that he had found the place in accordance with Whitehead's vision, Brown later wrote of that moment, "Exactly here the story of modern Woodstock really begins."[7]

As the son of a British industrialist, Ralph Whitehead came from wealth. And, though that wealth eventually underwrote the building of the Byrdcliffe Colony, a young Ralph Whitehead had come to disdain the dark side of industrialization and the inequality it fostered. Those underlying principles were further reinforced through his introduction to the concept of a utopian society centered on the arts while a student of social activist John Ruskin at Oxford University. Married to Jane Byrd McCall, who shared his interest in developing such a colony, early attempts by the couple in California and Oregon met with little success. Summoned by Brown to Woodstock, Whitehead, upon viewing the promise that Woodstock held, agreed to begin purchasing some fifteen hundred acres along the base of Overlook Mountain. They called their new enterprise, Byrdcliffe—a combination of the married couples' middle names.

Also employed by Whitehead at the time was Hervey White. Whitehead had met White in Chicago, where White, a Harvard graduate, was a part of Jane Adams's social service efforts at Hull House. Summoned to meet both Whitehead and Brown in Woodstock, White also agreed that Brown's "discovery" offered the promise that could fulfill Whitehead's vision. That agreement did not last long, however, as the two soon found differences in how each viewed operational structure within the colony (Whitehead was more authoritarian, White more freewheeling). Beneath their opinions over control within a creative environment, however, lay a more fundamental difference based on their backgrounds and the road each had taken during their earlier years. As Henry Morton Robinson, author and longtime acquaintance of White, later wrote for the Historical Society of Woodstock on the differences between the two men most responsible for introducing and growing the arts in Woodstock, "It can be said with perfect frankness that they were of different origins and backgrounds, separated by a whole world of economic difference, and destined, each in their own way, to work out the ideal vision he beheld. Hervey White has always been a poor man; he could not be Hervey White and be any other kind of man."[8]

Hervey White would leave Byrdcliffe and, in 1905, establish the Maverick Colony just over the Woodstock town line in Hurley, New York. While generously offering opportunity to a host of artists, musicians, writers, and actors over the years, it was White himself who blended the various creative talents and eccentricities that called Maverick home into a foundational prescription for the arts in Woodstock. In addition to his own creative work, White initiated a summer concert series known as the Maverick Concerts. Still active today, the Maverick Concerts represent the oldest, continuously operating chamber music series in the country. His Maverick theater productions attracted the likes of actors Edward G. Robinson, Helen Hayes, and Paul Robeson. And, in an effort to fund his colony, White introduced the word "festival" into Woodstock's lexicon by holding his Maverick Festival each year while, unknowingly, projecting what might come decades later. As Henry Robinson later described the Maverick Festivals, "The festival idea expanded enormously: became the only thing like it in America, a frankly bacchanalian rout at which the most ordinary inhibitions were slipped off, revealing the merrymakers as something the Greeks had plenty of words for. As many as five thousand revelers sometimes cooked their camp-fire dinners, saw Hervey's show and made the surrounding mountainside ring with the sound of their merriment."[9]

Though White's festivals eventually drew the ire of town officials and local clergy, forcing him to suspend the "merriment" at Maverick, he is still reverently recalled by Woodstockers for his generosity and service not only to fellow artists but also to many within the community, even Florence Peper. On November 5, 1918, Florence Peper wrote in her diary, "Will died at 11 o'clock a.m. Oh how sad we are. It doesn't seem possible."[10] Will was Florence Peper's brother and was yet another victim of the 1918 influenza epidemic that had swept the country. At his bedside, as he struggled to hold on to his life, was his nurse, Hervey White.

With the establishment of Byrdcliffe and the Maverick colonies and with the addition of the Arts Students League launching summer operations in Woodstock in 1906, new ways, new ideas, and new opinions were laid at the doorsteps of a townspeople not used to—nor that comfortable with—change. In the years that followed, a slow dance ensued as widely disparate views and lifestyles attempted to blend. It would not be an easy process. And, in many respects, it would take a world war to at least, temporarily, edge the town toward some semblance of harmony as Woodstock attempted to undertake a collective effort in support of the war effort.

And yet, even in the postwar years, the gap between what Woodstock used to be and what Woodstock was becoming once again began to widen as the attraction many saw in the art colony lured more outsiders to town along with the new businesses required to serve them. For a town whose needs had always been met through its own self-sufficiency, an economic change in service to tourism was a decided break with the past. Outsider access to Woodstock was further enhanced by forces beyond local control as, for example, the construction of New York State Thruway brought the Catskills and Woodstock within two hours of New York City. In addition, with the arrival of a new IBM plant in Kingston, sections of the community were looked upon as desirable locations for new home construction, construction that would meet the needs of arriving—and economically advantaged—IBM transplants. As a result of the changes that led Woodstock out of the postwar era and through the 1950s, debate grew over what progress should look like in a small town, debate that centered on such issues as the need for zoning laws, increasing concern over environmental issues such as water quality and land use, and expansion of educational opportunities for the town's children. As Woodstockers looked toward both the horizon and in their rearview mirror, many longtime residents were left wondering which reality was better.

This debate reached a crescendo as the 1960s brought to Woodstock unintended notoriety and association as a place where magic and music filled the air. As a link between the folk artists of Greenwich Village and

Woodstock began to establish itself in the latter part of the 1950s and early 1960s, the pace of musicians arriving in Woodstock accelerated with the arrival of Bob Dylan and his manager, Albert Grossman. And, while Dylan proved to be the name attached to the initial influx of young people seeking him out in Woodstock, in reality it was Albert Grossman who, much like Ralph Whitehead, fundamentally altered the course of Woodstock's direction in the years that followed. As Grossman built the stable of the musicians he managed—including The Band, Janis Joplin, Paul Butterfield, and more—he also developed his Bearsville properties to include Bearsville Studios and Bearsville Records. A man who enjoyed fine food, Grossman also ensured that he and the artists who arrived in town ate well through the establishment of two iconic restaurants in Bearsville. As Grossman's impact on the town grew and as more and more musicians began their arrival, a new road to Woodstock as an artist's colony was being paved.

Much as the artists in the first half of the century began to attract visitors to Woodstock seeking out a lifestyle different from their own, so too did the newly arrived musicians in town encourage others to begin to adopt a place where creativity seemed to spring from the physical environment. And, as the reputation of Woodstock grew through redefinition of what an artist's community might be, those who saw economic opportunity in the new wave, as well as those simply attracted to the association with freedom that was being projected, also followed. By the latter part of the 1960s, music resonated from multiple establishments in town. A series of music concerts held in a field under the name Sound-Outs not only reestablished the concept of Hervey White's original Maverick Festivals but also planted a seed in what eventually unfolded in Bethel, New York, in 1969. And, as the Woodstock name found its way into headlines around the world because of the Woodstock Festival, the earlier wave of newcomers grew to what some local citizens likened to an invasion of young people, an invasion that many believed was consuming the town. The hippies had arrived, and not everyone in Woodstock was pleased. One vocal resident urged at a town meeting that they should not only be arrested but also "deloused and have their heads shaved to clean them up."[11] In the days that followed, not all was going to be peaceful in the town of peace and love.

The impact of the name Woodstock as associated with the 1960s and 1970s is such that, even today, visitors arrive asking, "Where was the festival?" But Woodstock has always been more than a name attached to a specific event or a generation. Simply put, Woodstock history is not tied to tie-dye. To do so, would present a disservice to those individuals, groups, associations, and cultural innovators who have contributed to the course of Woodstock's unique journey. It remains important to continue to attach reality to that history, a reality that goes beyond nostalgia and reflects the day-to-day efforts of a citizenry that, despite certain forces that have impacted their lives, has worked to move a small town through its many years. It is not a perfect history absent scars and misdirection. No community is. And yet, such scars and errors can be a part of what informs a community and, in doing so, hopefully, aides in moving that community forward. More importantly, they do not eclipse the creative efforts and contributions those who have called Woodstock home have given to their neighbors and to the world beyond the shadow of Overlook Mountain.

In 1930, writing for the Historical Society of Woodstock, local historian Louise Hasbrouck Zimm posed the question, "Does Woodstock have a history?" In answering her own question, Zimm concluded that Woodstock possessed a history that is "anything but common."[12] As Woodstock has continued to fill the pages of its story in the years following Zimm's essay, Woodstock history has not traveled too far from her original assessment. While there are multiple roads to follow as one explores Woodstock history, there is perhaps one consistency that rings through the more than two hundred years of Woodstock's story: an inherent belief in independence, an independence first sought by early settlers in their opposition to unreasonable leases held on the very land they developed. It is the same liberty sought and practiced by a diverse population over the years, from Miss Peper's diary taking satisfaction in the election of Richard Nixon in 1968 to the six hundred marchers who later paraded past her home in protest over the war in Vietnam. It can be found in the creative and eclectic freedom seemingly unleashed by Woodstock's natural environment as found in the expressions of both artists and musicians over the years. It is witnessed in the disparate assemblage of Woodstockers— from artists to longtime residents—who rallied together in support of Woodstock's war effort at home and abroad during World War II. And, as the town turned hostile to the influx of young people during the hippie years, it can be seen in those who would move against local authorities and offer care to those without resources.

Woodstock has, for much of its history, attracted those who would see the world through a slightly different lens. As a result, Woodstockers, when honestly reflecting on their community, often take a degree of pride in the fact that they live in a town where debate and differences are an expected part of the journey. In many respects, conformity has not always been an option, and therein lies the true reality of what has been called the *Woodstock spirit*. In reflecting on the unique nature of his hometown, Dr. James Shotwell, Columbia professor, president of the Carnegie Endowment for Peace, member of President Wilson's contingent during the Paris Peace Conference at the end of World War I, and one of Woodstock's most eminent citizens, once offered testament to that spirit and the "uncommon" foundation of Woodstock history: "This is the amazing thing about the Woodstock community, that in all the changes of these changeful years, it still keeps in touch with its original purpose. There is nothing like it anywhere else in America for richness of content, beauty of form and color, and the irrepressible note of freedom."[13]

Welcome to an uncommon town.

# Chapter 1

# Setting the Stage

On Tuesday, June 27, 1939, First Lady Eleanor Roosevelt got behind the wheel of her Chrysler sedan and exited her Hyde Park home to begin a drive to Woodstock, New York. Making the trip alone and crossing the Hudson River by ferry, Roosevelt arrived in town just before 11:00 a.m. Her purpose that day was to lay a cornerstone for the dedication of a new workshop building at the fledgling National Youth Administration Center (NYAC), an element of Franklin Roosevelt's Works Progress Administration. With some ten buildings planned on land leased from the City of Kingston City Water Department, the NYAC was dedicated to teaching both young men and women vocational crafts such as woodworking, metalworking, and stonework to provide employable skills that could prove useful under the weight of the Great Depression. Those enrolled locally went on to assist in the construction of the buildings that would house the shops dedicated to the various training skills. The campus they aided in constructing along Route 212 eventually became home to the Art Students League and, today, the Woodstock School of Art.

After engaging in conversations with several young people from the center and a review of plans for future buildings, the First Lady was honored during a brief ceremony led by Woodstock artist and chairperson of the NYAC Advisory Committee Julia Leaycraft. Then, taking a trowel in hand, Roosevelt displayed, according to the *Kingston Daily Freeman*, "her skill as a mason" as she secured the cornerstone marked N.Y.A. 1939.[1]

From there, Roosevelt was off to the Woodstock hamlet of Lake Hill to assess the temporary housing occupied by members of the NYAC

Figure 1. Woodworking shop at the National Youth Administration Center. *Source:* Historical Society of Woodstock Archives/Woodstock Library Collection.

youth. Following her review, the First Lady of the United States climbed back in her Chrysler and began the return trip to Hyde Park.

The Great Depression, which had gripped the nation for a decade, had also crept quietly through the Catskills. While Woodstock's isolation brought little outside attention to the struggles that were occurring in the shadow of Overlook Mountain, self-sufficiency, always a part of Woodstock's DNA, had been increasingly called upon to stave off the absence of economic opportunity. Long gone were the tanneries that once crafted leather goods for the military. So too had the bluestone quarries that once stretched along the base of Overlook disappeared as cement began to claim dominance over natural stone. Still, Woodstock was home to many that were but the latest link to an ancestry that stretched back across almost two centuries. Most gave little thought to the hollow promises of a better life elsewhere.

Ironically, not unlike Woodstock during other periods of crisis—including the aftermath of 9/11 and, most recently, the COVID-19 pandemic—the overall population of Woodstock actually grew during the

Figure 2. Julia Leaycraft (far left) with Eleanor Roosevelt at dedication of National Youth Administration Center, 1939. *Source:* Courtesy Leaycraft Family Archive.

Depression. As historian Alf Evers noted, "People formerly employed in the cities decided to live year-round in their Woodstock summer places. Young people who had gone away to make their fortunes returned and lived with their parents. In an era without building regulations, some hasty and ramshackle building was also done. Additions were made to older houses and shelters were run-up to house returning families."[2]

Parents were not the only Woodstockers adjusting their physical space. Some, fortunate enough to possess the right size home or the ability to enlarge their home, turned to operating boardinghouses as the local economy began, out of necessity, to embrace the economic opportunity presented by what others saw in the land rather than what could be taken from it. Adding to the influx of newcomers and visitors were Hervey White's Maverick Festivals. Following the establishment of the Byrdcliffe art colony in 1902, White went on to establish the Maverick Colony in 1905. Unhappy with Whitehead's strict oversight at Byrdcliffe, the less-structured White imagined a utopian colony offering artists a rural environment in which they were free to create. To support the colony's concerts, theater productions, and multiple artistic endeavors, White, in 1916, launched his Maverick Festivals. Attracting thousands in its heyday and considered by many as an early seedling to the 1969 Woodstock music festival, the annual festival was, eventually, a victim of its own success, as the sheer size of the event—and the rowdiness and disorder often associated with it—brought complaints and concerns from the more conservative politicians and clergy that held sway in Woodstock.

And yet, though the Maverick Festivals would no longer serve as a singular attraction, Woodstock would remain on a list of destinations not only for the multitude of artists who arrived over the years but also for tourists that followed the same path. That appeal had been added to with the earlier arrival of the Art Students League and the number of young art students their summer classes brought to Woodstock each year.

As a result, even as the Depression took hold, Woodstockers, recognizing the impact the artistic community was having on their small town, also began to understand the lure it offered to the outside world. An economic lifeline was being offered as changing times brought a changing clientele to local businesses.

The end of Prohibition in 1933 also inspired hope in many of the owners of the town's restaurants and bars. Advertising from the era in the local Kingston newspaper demonstrated the various attempts by Woodstock establishments to lure patrons. The Colony Club on Rock City Road, for example, relied greatly on music as its prime attraction, announcing such acts as "The Sizzlers—NBC's Famous Band Hot from Harlem" or "Ruth Brewer and her RKO Artists—offering Sparkling Dance Rhythms and Close Harmony." The Colony's dinner special went for seventy-five cents with cocktails beginning at twenty-five cents.[3] Not far up the road, the Hungarian Club advertised dining and dancing "to the Tunes of an Inspiring Orchestra." Pledging, in a rather odd way, that "the reputation of our food remains the same," the Hungarian Club also promised an extended escape from the weight of pressing times by remaining open every night "until 3:00 a.m."[4]

Meanwhile, in the center of the village, the Irvington Inn under the ownership of Bill Dixon offered square and round dancing to the music of the moonlighting trio of Pardee, Allen, and Amarello. The Inn had opened in 1934 under the management of George Longyear, then passed to future town supervisor and New York State senator Ken Wilson, and finally in 1938 to Dixon. Thanks to its location, it was home to many of the town's prewar activities, including dances in honor of FDR's birthday; was headquarters for town fishing contests; was a favorite luncheon haunt for local officials; and saw appearances by the Cheats and Swings, Woodstock's preeminent square-dancing group.

Indeed, square dancing during the Depression years rose to great popularity in the town and seemed to be one activity that invited both townspeople and artists to come together—a feat not easily achieved over the years. Perhaps, as Alf Evers has suggested, it was a sense of returning to simpler days, when people could forget their differences and embrace the escape the fiddlers and callers offered. Whatever the reason, if square dancing was the one attraction that, even for an evening, brought artists and townspeople together, then the Cheats and Swings were often at the center of that conciliation.[5]

Finding their birth under the direction of Dyrus and Edith Cook at Willard Allen's Allencrest Hotel, the Cheats and Swings grew to become a prize-winning and in-demand collection of excellent performers. While the men dressed in waistcoats and tails, the women of the group donned the popular Woodstock Dress originally designed by Willard Allen's wife, Augusta. Born out of the necessity to create income for her family during

Figure 3. Cheats and Swings square dancers performing at Woodstock Town Hall. Women are attired in the Woodstock Dress. *Source:* Courtesy Allen Family Archive.

the Depression, Augusta Allen's dress was increasingly in high demand by women of the art colony. Made of cotton, velvet, taffeta, and other fabrics, its design allowed for wear at various occasions, both formal and informal.

Backed by a select group of local musicians, the Cheats and Swings were soon receiving invitations to entertain throughout the region and beyond. Following an appearance before the Roosevelt family at the president's Hyde Park home, invitations were extended to the group by the National Folk Festival in Washington DC and, in 1939, to the World's Fair in New York.

Despite their popularity, the Cheats and Swings managed, on occasion, to make headlines in other ways as well. During their appearance before the president and his family at Hyde Park, their caller and fiddler—having enjoyed the president's open bar a bit too much—fell into the president's swimming pool.[6] In addition, Dyrus Cook was known as a man who did not shy from expressing himself if a slight was detected. In a memorable letter to the local paper in February 1939, Cook unleashed a racist screed against the organizers—a nonpartisan political committee—that had arranged for a Harlem-based band of Black musicians to appear at the Irvington Inn for a presidential birthday celebration. Arriving at the Irvington in the latter part of the evening for an appearance, Cook found the musicians from Harlem performing before a scarce audience. Not happy with the arrangements, Cook wrote a letter to the *Kingston Daily Freeman* that not only revealed his own, deeply ingrained racial prejudices but also held a mirror to how many in town still felt about intrusion from the outside:

> At 10:30 our Cheats and Swings exhibition team and orchestra arrived at the Inn to bolster a dying show. As audience we had a score of Cheats & Swings members and admirers, and possibly a dozen who came to dance to the hot-spot music furnished by the imported night club colored orchestra.
>
> How come Woodstock couldn't have a fine "homey" sort of party and rallied the folk for a "folk dance" party? Haven't Cheats & Swings, Ulster County square dance champions been sufficiently publicized hereabouts for this committee to be aware that Woodstock is the cradle of a growing folk movement in this part of the state? Why should our folk of all political parties, who wished to assist a good cause, have been insulted by dictation from without—by the committee sending to us Harlem tooters?

He concluded:

> It is just too bad that county politicians should fail to observe that the Woodstock community has individuality, color, showmanship and abundant talent and spirit to put on any kind of show it wishes to promote and get away with it in handsome style. Shortly now Woodstock Township is going to dedicate its new town hall. I invite the members of this county committee to come to the exercises and get an eye-full. And if they've got a hot-spot hoocha orchestra in leash, tie 'em outside. For Woodstock is gradually emerging from the musical reign of terror.
>
> Indulgently yours.
>
> Dyrus Cook[7]

In many respects, despite changing times and attempts by the outside world to intrude on the town, Woodstock remained an isolated township in the Catskills. As a decidedly conservative, white, Protestant town, Woodstock's history, like many local histories in the rural north, often traveled the same road as our national story. As a fledgling town in the late eighteenth and early nineteenth centuries, Woodstock was no stranger to America's original sin of slavery. In the nation's first census, fifteen slaves were enumerated as part of the town's overall population in 1790. The 1800 census listed twenty-six, while 1810 noted nineteen slaves under the ownership of several Woodstock property owners. Even with the eventual outlawing of slavery by New York State in 1827, former Woodstock slaves and their descendants found little economic opportunity in Woodstock or surrounding communities. While many remained with their former owners, others found themselves under the auspices of the town's Overseers of the Poor, an early form of welfare whereby the town paid a community member to provide for the former slave or indigent person in exchange for their labor.

Even well into the twentieth century, attitudes toward race changed slowly. Local history notes that on the night of August 21, 1924, Woodstockers were witness to a cross burning on a field just outside of town heading toward the hamlet of Bearsville. Only a month later, in the inaugural edition of Woodstock's first newspaper, *The Woodstock Weekly*, local readers were greeted with the headline "Ku Klux Klan Gains More Members."

The brief article offered that the Klan had "held several public meetings in Woodstock and added new members to its organization."[8] According to Alf Evers, the efforts of the Klan locally included vitriol and contempt directed not only toward Blacks but toward Jews and Catholics as well. Evers further notes that, at the time, local Klan membership was made up of "Woodstock people of right-wing convictions, many businesspeople and descendants of early local families."[9]

While the majority of Woodstockers eventually began to push back against the activities of the Klan and their activities in the 1920s, deep-seated animosities toward those perceived as different did not die easily. Prior to World War II, for example, townspeople, fearing the takeover of local hotels by Jewish owners, worked to limit such opportunities. It was a period, described by Evers, in which "anti-Semitism, long present in Woodstock, now grew and expanded like a weed in a June garden."[10]

A certain level of animosity and distrust also ran through the core of many Woodstockers regarding many of the artists who had arrived in town beginning with the founding of the Byrdcliffe art colony. Despite the occasional respite from differences both camps found in local square dances and, for example, efforts at fundraising during World War I, the separation between artists and townspeople was an inherent part of life in Woodstock over the first four decades of the twentieth century. In large part, the differences between the two camps lay not only in the mere fact that the arriving artists were certainly of a different breed than longtime residents of the town but also in how Woodstockers viewed the changes the artists and those who followed were bringing to a small town where change was not easily embraced.

While the cornerstone of the original art colony, Byrdcliffe, had diminished in its impact on the town over the years, the young artists who flocked to the Art Students League as well as those who were drawn to the Maverick through its yearly festivals and Hervey White's benevolence brought with them new ideas, new ways of living, and, often, different political opinions. For a small town long set in its ways, it was a difficult proposition for established residents to see life through the same lens as the newly arrived artists. And yet, in at least one respect, both were connected through a common denominator—the land—as each drew life and livelihood from the same physical landscape that would find its way onto a multitude of canvases over the years.

Still, the relationship was not an easy one. Unaccustomed as they were to seeing nude models perched on rocks along streams that flowed through their land, local residents were leery of both the lifestyle and suspected promiscuity of their newfound neighbors. As a result, rumors of unspeakable goings-on among the artists flew about town. When the shirts of a few men were ripped in a burst of horseplay at an Arts Students League dance, for example, sheriffs were summoned from Kingston to investigate an alleged case of "nude dancing." In the meantime, righteous citizens continued to peep through the bushes that bordered Sawkill Creek in hopes of detecting and reporting instances of nude bathing.[11]

And yet, at least during the years of the booming twenties, many in the town held contradictory feelings about the newcomers. On one hand, older and more prominent residents of the town saw the continued presence of the artists as a constant reminder that this was not the Woodstock their forebearers had envisioned. On the other hand, the arrival of the artists had indeed brought new visitors and new life to the town's much needed economic fortunes. Old barns were being converted into studios, keeping local carpenters engaged. New shops began to spring up to cater to visitors. Boardinghouses were filled during the summer months, and real estate prices began to rise. In many respects, despite resistance by some town elders, the quiet town at the entrance to the Catskills was fulfilling the hopes of many that, perhaps, Woodstock did indeed have a future.

A significant ingredient in that optimism—even through the Depression—was the construction and opening of the Woodstock Playhouse at the entrance to the art colony. The reality of the Woodstock Playhouse had grown from the vision of Robert Elwyn. A descendant of one of Woodstock's oldest families, Elwyn had emerged as an actor, director, and theater manager under the watchful eye of Hervey White and the Maverick Theater. Desirous of a facility that could support more ambitious productions, Elwyn was determined to construct his own theater. In the spring of 1938, Elwyn turned to his uncle, Arthur Wolven, to construct a theater based on the design of architect A. E. Milliken. Though unique in its inception, both inside and out, construction was completed in just forty-eight days, permitting the opening of *Yes, My Darling Daughter* on June 30, 1938. So impressed with the new theater, *The Overlook*, Woodstock's weekly newspaper at the time, commented on opening night by stating, "With apologies to the actors and actresses, the play was of a secondary consideration. The first nighters came to see the construction wonders that had been wrought and if all the ooohs and aaahs that were uttered during the course of the evening were laid end to end, they would reach from here to the scene of the undeclared Sino-Japanese war."[12]

Figure 4. Interior of Woodstock Playhouse. *Source:* Historical Society of Woodstock Archives/Woodstock Playhouse Collection.

The town was indeed changing. And yet, as the Depression continued unabated, many of the newly arrived artists were pressed to direct their skills toward more practical endeavors. While several Woodstock artists had gained notice during the early years of the Depression—Georgina Klitgaard's "Winter in Bearsville" took first place at the San Francisco Art Association's fifty-fourth annual exhibition, and the Maverick's Carl Walters took honorable mention for his pair of decorative plaques at the Syracuse Museum—the teaching of art within the colony offered a possible means by which to secure a more predictable income. As a result, Alexander Archipenko made the decision to bring his successful Ecole d'Art class to Woodstock in the summers, while the sculptor Alfeo Faggi began instructing students in composition and drawing as well as sculpture. And, as the *Kingston Daily Freeman* noted in a somewhat overly optimistic assessment of changes in the art colony and the benefits accrued from such instruction:

> Many people are taking their art instruction seriously and . . . some well-to-do young men and women are studying art today where but a few years ago they were traveling and idling in the play-centers of the world. Thus, the few who have been

forced to give up their art for business occupations [sic], there are more to fill the gap, and the business of art instruction and of the creation of art goes merrily on despite the economic depression.

And, in the case of the Woodstock colony (and others) this condition gives an unusual impetus to the business of the local tradesman, hotel keepers, real estate dealers, and the lesser servants of the material life. Thus, Woodstock hardly feels the depression, for the colony fattens in summer on the success of artists from everywhere who congregate in the Catskill Mountain ateliers.[13]

Despite the sunny overview provided by a local newspaper, as the Depression dragged on and continued to impact the region, many of the artists who had adopted Woodstock as home found that the one tenuous lifeline they could grab on to was offered through President Roosevelt's Works Progress Administration (WPA) and its subsidiaries, the Public Works of Art Project and, later, the Fine Arts Project (FAP).

As the artist and onetime head of the Fine Arts Project in Woodstock Eugene Ludins noted, "With no industry and practically no jobs of any kind, the money the WPA brought here was crucial. More than fifty artists were employed at a salary of $18.50 a week. That doesn't sound like much, but it brought in about $1,000 to the town and was enough to keep artists and their families alive and working as artists."[14]

Still, even though the money brought in by WPA artists was spent locally, there was resentment from several townspeople over the fact that artists were, in effect, subsidized and they weren't—thereby impacting the split between artists and locals further. At one point, the artist Judson Smith, who would assume leadership of the project, sensing this resentment, felt the need not only to defend the little artists received from the government but also to push back against the perception that artists were apart from the community they too called home. Appearing before Kingston's Kiwanis Club, Smith told his audience, "Some artists had long hair because they couldn't afford haircuts," and some wore baggy pants "because they were cheaper than the well-cut variety."[15] Despite efforts by Smith and others to draw attention to the plight of artists during the Depression and to justify the project's efforts to bring art within the reach of everyday life, such a defense found increased questioning in a Republican town such as Woodstock as the Depression—and the Roosevelt administration—wore on. As Woodstock artist and WPA recipient Karl Fortess stated years later, "The community environment here, in this town, was very Republican, in fact [the dislike of President Roosevelt], . . . who was responsible for this pump priming, made people spit when they heard his name."[16] In short, many Woodstockers were asking, Why was there such spending on a select group when so many were hurting? Eventually that question found an answer arriving from Washington.

As the various federal programs both evolved and devolved throughout the Depression, several local artists grew increasingly unhappy when cuts in the programs eventually forced decisions about who would and who would not receive funding. Charges of favoritism, outright dishonesty, and inept management rose to such a level that a group of artists threatened the formation of a union and proceeded to conduct a sit-down strike in front of Judson Smith's home.

Although reduced funding to the Federal Art Project in 1939 began to foretell the demise of government support for many Woodstock's artists—and, by the same token, diminish its economic benefit to the town—artists from the colony had contributed extensively to the enhancement of art throughout the country. New York's FAP administrator Audrey McMahon called these artists "the most important group of artists in the country . . . the foremost artists of the time," and Woodstock's contributions were disproportionately greater than similar efforts across New York State, if not the country.[17] Indeed, as the decade of the 1930s closed, hundreds of prints by Woodstock artists "were allocated to libraries and public schools across the country," while a multitude of murals by such artists as Doris Lee, Wendell Jones, Anton Refregier, Ernest Fine, Georgina Klitgaard, and others had been commissioned by the Treasury Department's Section of Fine Arts.[18] Many can still be found on post office walls and in schools throughout the country.

Moving into 1940, Woodstockers continued to press ahead with life in a small town despite the increasing number of war headlines dispatched from Europe. In mid-January, members of the Woodstock Odd Fellows gathered for a winter dinner prepared and tended to by the Daughters of Rebekah. One week later, townspeople assembled to enjoy a dramatic comedy offered at the town hall to benefit the Woodstock Fire Department. Joining the evening's postproduction entertainment was Russian dancer, choreographer, and instructor Alexis Kosloff, while Woodstock physician and frequent performer at the Maverick Concerts Dr. Hans Cohn concluded the evening with a solo cello performance. Woodstock was still doing what communities do.

Figure 5. Charles Rosen (left) and Clarence Bolton collaborate on a Depression era mural. *Source:* Historical Society of Woodstock Archives/Jean White Collection.

As spring approached, however, Woodstock found itself in the midst of a measles outbreak. Noting that some of the cases were severe, the town's health officer, Dr. George Bassow, called upon the community to cancel all "social gatherings of children." And, with an eye on the summer and the local economy, the good doctor pressed for townspeople to act swiftly to contain the outbreak. "Woodstock is a summer resort," Bassow stated, "and it is highly desirable that the disease be completely eradicated from the section before the time when summer visitors are due to make their appearance."[19] Whether or not the town listened to Bassow is not totally clear. What is clear is that Woodstock was more than ready for visitors in the summer of 1940 and for any relief that might offer a glimmer of normalcy.

Writing for the *Kingston Daily Freeman* at the time, columnist Marguerite Hurter brought to her readers a Woodstock seemingly untroubled by the economic woes of the past decade and a town yet untouched by the rising peril an ocean away. Hurter, who began her career as a journalist following World War I writing for the *Chicago Tribune* and the *Chicago Herald-Examiner*, later moved on to write columns (e.g., "Women, Clothes and Figures" and "The Skirt") for *Variety*. Eventually, she parlayed her success into writing a syndicated column that was distributed to more than fifty newspapers nationwide. And, while how and why Hurter found her way to Woodstock in 1940 is not clear, her summer recollections of Woodstock and the columns she wrote reflected a Woodstock different than the one known to most of its longtime, more conservative citizens. Through her journeys about town, with access to the art world and her familiarity with the denizens of Woodstock's nightlife, Hurter portrayed an image of a town in contrast, for example, to the more traditional—and more sober—dinners served at the Odd Fellows Hall. As she wrote in August 1940:

> Tuesday night there will be an auction of great excitement in the Woodstock Art Gallery, when the composite picture which was painted last Friday night at the reception of the Woodstock Art Gallery's third exhibition, will go under the hammer.
>
> Peggy Dodds [artist and member of the Woodstock Artists Association] began the painting with the head of a rather bizarre lady. Someone drew a nude body. Frank London [artist and also an active member of the Woodstock Artists Association] added a skirt for politeness sake, and from then on it was a free for all. Nobody thought to give the lady a bodice, and some old ladies were shocked, but it was a heap of fun. Holley Cantine, the Saugerties paper mill mogul, waxed nautical and painted a boat in the background. We do not believe the young lady of the painting is dressed fit for a boat ride, but we wish we might win the painting. It is autographed on the back by more famous names than you could collect in an autograph book.[20]

Hurter was not above a little name-dropping in her columns as well. Making her way about Woodstock that summer, she noted:

> Gloria Vanderbilt and her sister, Lady Furness, have taken a house in Woodstock and beginning Saturday will establish themselves as regular summer members of the famous art colony in the Catskills.

Kitty Kelly, actress and Hollywood celebrity who played in Bob Elwyn's Woodstock Playhouse in "Something Gay," has won many friends in Woodstock. . . . Kitty is responsible for the Gloria Vanderbilt–Lady Furness visit here and during the run of the show sat each night in the front seat to cheer Kelly. They have all been staying at the Village Inn, and Mr. Allen says they seem to like Woodstock a lot.[21]

It was also not beyond Hurter to combine her connections to Hollywood with local lore, as she demonstrated that summer by connecting the local iceman with W. C. Fields:

This morning we met Clarkson Reynolds, the ice man. Reynolds is a character well loved in Woodstock, and we asked him whether he knew we once made up a song about him? It went something like this:

"Oh, the ice man!
He's a nice man . . .
He'll freeze you,
But Please you . . ."

It went on in the same silly strain and Bertie Shevlin [known for "whanging out popular tunes on the piano"[22]] sang it with a few special yodels one day when we were with J. P. McEvoy. Mr. McEvoy was doing a show for Flo Ziegfeld with W. C. Fields that season. One morning he telephoned us in excitement and asked us to sing the ice man song over the phone. We thought it was a gag but began to yodel. Imagine our surprise when he created the role of the ice man for W. C. Fields! Later Mr. Fields did the ice man stuff in a moving picture Mr. McEvoy scripted in Hollywood. About that time, we remembered that we never collected a percentage. The moral? Never yodel.[23]

By the height of the summer, however, despite a whistling in the dark approach by some within the colony, more concerned citizens began to finally turn their attention to what was happening overseas. On July 30, a collection of Woodstockers came together in support of pro-British policies to form a local chapter of the Committee to Defend America by Aiding the Allies. Meeting in the Zena home of newcomer Josepha Whitney, the gathering brought together a selection of long-standing community volunteers, including Mr. and Mrs. Alfred Hutty, Mr. and Mrs. Martin Comeau, Harriet and Elsie Goddard, and Mr. and Mrs. Louise White.[24] As part of their activity that evening, telegrams to be sent to both Franklin Roosevelt and the Republican standard bearer in the 1940 election, Wendell Willkie, were drafted, urging both to commit to providing aid to Britain and to undertake the "humane task of helping to evacuate British children to this country."[25]

Two weeks later—almost two months after the fall of France—a "gala fair" was held at the home of Alice Wardwell in support of the American Committee to Save Anti-Fascist Refugees in France. Entertainment for the event was provided through the music of Vladimir Padwa, pianist and musical director for the Woodstock Playhouse, and vocalist Gus Hovorka, a member of the Maverick Students' Theater. The featured speaker for the event was George Pershing, nephew of World War I general John J. Pershing. In his remarks, the younger Pershing spoke of the emerging threat facing anti-Fascist refugees who had fled across the German border into France. Under the armistice that had been signed following the fall of France, Germany had demanded that the French "hand over all German subjects indicated by the German government." According to the *New York Times*, those returned to the Germans would become, "marked men . . . men conveniently rounded up in French concentration camps as German subjects."[26]

On the evening of September 16, those passing by a newsstand in Woodstock could not help but notice the commanding headline in the *Kingston Daily Freeman* announcing, "LONDON POUNDED BY BIG BERTHA." Closer examination just beneath the headline revealed yet another story that hit closer to home. Pictured above an article titled "16,500,000 Americans Are Told to Register for Draft October 16" was an assembly of young men who had arrived that day at the 156th Field Artillery armory on Manor Avenue in Kingston to register for the National Guard and to commit to a year of "extensive training" at Camp Dix. Among those pictured were John Rowicki and William Hutty of Woodstock. The paper noted that those registering that day were given the "opportunity of spending the night with their families" but were required to report for duty by 7:00 a.m. the next morning. It also made clear that security had become a serious concern, as "Local guardsman armed with police clubs are on duty patrolling the grounds and no visitors are admitted except those on business. Every visitor is questioned before being admitted to the armory."[27]

On November 5, 1940, Woodstockers joined the rest of the nation as they went to the polls to cast their votes for president. And, while Franklin Roosevelt would prevail both nationally and in New York State, Woodstock stayed true to its Republican/conservative roots and overwhelmingly cast their votes for Wendell Willkie. It was more than forty years before those same roots began to give way and the town's political preferences turned.

Less than a week later, a ceremony at the Reformed Church in the village center redirected the town's attention back to the war when a service flag was dedicated to the sons of Woodstock who were in service at Camp Dix. Those honored included Willard Allen, William Hutty, Norman Dock, and E. R. Perkins Jr. It was estimated that 125 Woodstockers attended the ceremony led by the church's Reverend Harvey Todd. The following day, November 11, with the prospect of world war once again looming on the horizon and with patriotism on the rise, Woodstock held its first-ever ceremony in remembrance of World War I and Armistice Day. With the flag on the Village Green lowered to half-staff, a minute of silence was held at 11:00 a.m. Taps was sounded by Roger Cashdollar and Archie McCaw.[28]

At year's end, as Woodstockers gathered in the center of town for the annual Christmas Eve celebration, seasonal aspirations of good will still pervaded those in attendance. The tradition of townspeople gathering on the Village Green on Christmas Eve had begun almost a decade earlier, during the depths of the Great Depression. Originally staged by local shopkeeper Agnes Schleicher, the evening had evolved from one with decidedly religious overtones to one in which those gathered eagerly awaited the arrival of Santa Claus. Taking up his position beneath a lighted evergreen at evening's end, Santa proceeded to dispense gifts to the gathered Woodstock children. For many, it was perhaps the only gift they would receive as the Depression continued to cast its shadow over the winter landscape. And yet, in 1940, as carols were sung and children awaited Santa's arrival, dark clouds of a different nature loomed on the horizon. All too soon, as the calendar turned to 1941, a small town long sheltered by the gentle slope of Overlook Mountain would join the world in the unimaginable and unspeakable events wrought by global conflict.

Chapter 2

# 1941

## With Eyes on the Horizon

Memorial Day, 1941, would be different for most Woodstockers. Certainly, as had been the custom over the years, several activities and remembrances were planned throughout the day. And yet, many in the overflow crowd that gathered in Woodstock's town hall that Friday could not have escaped the feeling that the tide of war was slowly encroaching upon American shores.

Their anxieties would not be diminished that day as county judge J. Edward Conway approached the podium to deliver the keynote address. "It is mere quibbling to say that the United States is not now at war," Conway began. Referencing the perceived activities of the so-called fifth column and those who would undermine the nation's efforts as war drew near, he forcefully put forward, "If we are to turn and run we will get the shot in the back—that is the reward of the coward. The United States is not a coward nation and, by the grace of God, never will be. We must go forward, united loyal people, prepared to make any sacrifice necessary to restore peace to the world."[1]

Combined with worries about the approaching war, Woodstock had not had an easy year. Within two days in February, the town lost two prominent members of the community through suicide. On Tuesday, February 18, the daughter of William Terwilliger, unable to locate her father, contacted Dr. Hans Cohn, Woodstock's primary physician at the time. Terwilliger, who served as both treasurer and office manager of the Woodstock Country Club, was eventually found by Cohn lying in a woodshed at the golf course. Next to his body lay a .20 gauge shotgun and a "notched stick," which had been used "to pull the trigger of the gun."[2]

The very next day, at approximately 7:00 a.m., neighbors of the Hungarian Inn reported hearing a gunshot coming from its direction. When they looked out, flames had already begun to consume several buildings within the complex. As firemen began approaching the scene, they came upon the body of Julius Szalay lying next to an automobile. Yet another shotgun lay on the ground.

Troubles had plagued Szalay and his establishment despite efforts to make a go of it following the end of Prohibition. Prior to his death, the inn had been rented to various tenants, but financial success failed to follow. It was learned by investigators that just two days prior to Szalay setting the fire and taking his life the property had been sold through a bankruptcy court to the individual who held the mortgage. The local press reported, following the discovery of multiple notes left behind, that Szalay was depressed by his financial reverses and was "disgusted with life and the way things are being run today."[3]

As if the news in February hadn't been bad enough, March brought with it the announcement that, following the suspicious death of a dog in town, a rabies quarantine was in effect. The quarantine ordered that, going forward, no dog in town was permitted to run loose. The quarantine would not be lifted until the end of November.

Within the arts community, however, 1941 was getting off to a somewhat better start. In January, the Albany Institute of History and Art unveiled an exhibition of American drawings featuring several Woodstock artists, including Emil Ganso, Ernest Feine, Eugene Speicher, Peggy Bacon, and John Carroll. Meanwhile, well-known artists such as Doris Lee and Carl Lindin were featured in their own exhibitions. Walker Galleries in New York was host to Lee's paintings through the month of January, while, in March, Bard College presented a retrospective of Lindin's work featuring several paintings that had previously found their way into "the largest exhibits in the country."[4] That was the good news.

The bad news was that the Federal Art Project found itself in the headlines once again as organizations representing New York's war veterans called for a congressional investigation of "Communist activities" within the project. Specific attention was on the activities of the arts program director Audrey McMahon, a frequent face in Woodstock and the former director of the Ulster County Arts Project.

As alleged by veterans' groups such as the American Legion and the Veterans of Foreign Wars, the Arts Project in New York was under Communist control through a secret group that led to the dismissal or demotion of veterans "because they openly protested against Red activity." The veterans further accused McMahon of using her position as arts project director to appoint "registered Communists to key positions," while also allowing "radical demonstrations and activities" by Communist sympathizers to be "staged openly."[5]

The allegations of Communist influence and infiltration into the Federal Art Project and other WPA programs eventually led to congressional investigations. Though little was ever found to substantiate the allegations, the attacks on the program began to spell the end of the Federal Art Project and other Roosevelt era programs. Through funding cuts and artist layoffs, what remained of the program would, with war on the horizon, merge into creating camouflage for military hardware and designing military training manuals. With the program's eventual demise during the early war years, Audrey McMahon—having, as regional director of the program, overseen the creation of "8,742 paintings, 108 murals, 41,787 prints and 1,707 sculptures"—returned to New York City and lent her energies to fundraising efforts in support of various social agencies.[6]

Only a day after headlines in Woodstock's *The Overlook* first drew attention to the controversies surrounding the Federal Art Project, the *Kingston Daily Freeman* offered a seemingly innocent mention in its "social notes" column on Woodstock. The paper posted that Woodstock's Charles Pierpoint had been assigned to the USS *Meredith*. Meanwhile his twin brother, William Pierpoint, also in the Navy, was, according to the *Freeman*, resting "at home from the Navy because of ill health." He was expected to rejoin the Navy in July.[7] The twin brothers from Woodstock in the service of the Navy were unaware what the following year would bring—a year in which one would become Woodstock's first casualty of World War II.

As the Depression made the turn into the 1940s, Woodstock's economy had begun to improve, in large part due to an increase in summer visitors. That economy was fed not only by warm weather visitors to the galleries, shops, and restaurants but by an active winter scene as well, supported in large part by the development of a ski slope, toboggan run, and other winter activities on Ohayo Mountain.

Spurred on by the success and popularity of the 1932 Lake Placid Winter Olympics, the Catskills saw the rising interest in winter sports as a cold weather means to further increase tourism. As a result, in 1934, the Civilian Conservation Corps went to work in Shandaken's Woodland Valley, carving out the first ski slope in the area on land donated by the Simpson family in the name of Jay Simpson, a former forest ranger.

At about the same time, Konrad Cramer and Arnold Wiltz, along with several other Woodstockers, were at work in Woodstock forming the Winter Sports Association and initiating construction of a toboggan run and ski slope of their own on Ohayo Mountain. For a brief time, operations in Woodstock more than met expectations. In 1936, for example, more than two thousand visitors flocked to town to witness the first-ever Ulster County Toboggan Championship held on the site's half-mile course and featuring eighteen, four-man teams from Kingston, Shokan, Phoenicia, West Hurley, Saugerties, Mink Hollow, Rosendale, and Woodstock. The Woodstock team—Donald Jackson, Harold Shultis, Frank Barringer, and Marvin Wolven—according to a report in the *Kingston Daily Freeman*, "slid down the slope at the lightning like clip of 26.13 seconds average to take first place."[8]

At the time, as ski enthusiasts from the city became familiar with the recreational facilities offered by the Catskills during the prewar years, access to the Woodstock and Phoenicia winter sites was enhanced by the establishment of ski trains and ski buses. Trains would carry eager skiers from New York to Kingston and then on to West Hurley or Phoenicia. For people wishing to reach Woodstock, buses would meet the train in West Hurley and transport those seeking out the Ohayo Mountain facilities to the center of town. In addition to the Ohayo Mountain site, a ski slope with a rope tow briefly flourished in the Bearsville area near Cooper Lake.

As a result, at least for a few years, Woodstock pushed back against the effects of the Depression and became an active hub of winter activity. As the threat of war began to loom ever larger, however, and as successive winters of lackluster snowfall befell the area, the initial excitement generated by the efforts on Ohayo Mountain began to wane. As for the additional slope near Cooper Lake, the rope from the tow was eventually sold to the army in support of the war effort.[9]

Try as they might, as the calendar moved toward December 7, 1941, Woodstockers could not escape talk of war for too long. In August, a proposed debate over where the sympathies of local citizens lay regarding entrance into the war captured the headlines of the town's newspapers. In a wide-ranging interview given to *The Overlook*—and later quoted in the *Woodstock Press*—longtime Woodstocker Nancy Schoonmaker, who as a

Figure 6. Skiers arriving by bus in Woodstock. *Source*: Historical Society of Woodstock Archives/Winter Sports Collection.

proponent of "America First" and defiant against the prospect of sending "American boys to die on a foreign continent, in a foreign war," proclaimed to the paper that "Hitler can't touch us—ever."[10] Schoonmaker's voiced opposition to the war was not confined to Woodstock alone. In 1941, she would coedit *We Testify*, a collection of essays featuring the opinions of those who shared her opposition to entering the war, including Charles Lindbergh and Herbert Hoover.

Not long after the interview was published, Schoonmaker's sentiments against involvement in the war were countered by Josepha Whitney. Whitney, a part-time resident of Woodstock and a recent member of the Woodstock chapter of the Committee to Defend America by Aiding the Allies, asserted that not only were Schoonmaker's beliefs working in support of Germany but—going even further—the majority of Ulster County was, in fact, "pro-Hitler." To that end, through an exchange of letters obtained by the paper, Whitney challenged Schoonmaker to a public debate over the war with local attorney Martin Comeau serving as moderator.[11]

For a brief time, a ripple of excitement moved through the town over the possibility of such a debate between the two women. Certainly, Schoonmaker was not the only Woodstocker who opposed entry into the war, while Whitney's accusation that conservative Ulster County was pro-Hitler angered many who held firm to the belief that the mere mention of Hitler's name was worthy of denunciation.

Alas, the debate was not to be. In a disparaging letter responding to Whitney's allegations, Schoonmaker claimed to see no value in giving Whitney's beliefs a public airing while at the same time attempting to demolish her assertions: "You say in your letter—and I quote: 'It is well known that Ulster County is more pro-Hitler than any other part of New York State.' I should like here and now to challenge that statement. Ulster County is known as a stronghold of good old conservative Republicanism. By what trick of mind have you convinced yourself that Republicanism is identical with National Socialism?"[12] Continuing, Schoonmaker fell back on a dismissive charge that longstanding Woodstockers had, throughout the years, often used when it came to dressing down those who were relative newcomers to Woodstock: "I have owned a home and lived in Ulster County for almost twenty years. I have spent some ten additional summers there. I have visited every corner of the county. Yet I have never, to my knowledge, met one pro-Hitler person in the county. You have been in Ulster County in all probably less than one year. Yet you lay against it the wholly unfounded charge that it is pro Hitler."[13] While most Woodstockers would agree with Schoonmaker's assertion that the town and the county were far from being pro-Hitler, her America First beliefs were, at the same time, equally rejected by many town residents.

One person who would most assuredly object was Dr. James Shotwell, a longtime resident of Woodstock. A good portion of Shotwell's life had been spent on the world stage and in academia. Following World War I, he traveled with Woodrow Wilson to the Paris Peace Conference as part of Wilson's foreign policy team. His work with French foreign minister Ariste Briand helped lead to the Kellogg–Briand Pact, the ill-fated attempt between nations to outlaw war. A professor at Columbia, Shotwell also served as the president of the Carnegie Endowment for Peace and was in attendance in 1945 as nations of the world convened in San Francisco to draft the charter creating the United Nations.

As a result of his preeminence, Shotwell became a leading voice on the Woodstock home front in support of the war effort, lending his stature to fundraising rallies on behalf of those efforts. Shotwell—through his friendships with several world leaders whose countries would also take up arms against the Nazis and the Japanese—brought several preeminent voices to Woodstock. On one such memorable occasion, the Chinese ambassador to the United States, Hu Shih, addressed a Woodstock audi-

Figure 7. Dr. James Shotwell. *Source*: Historical Society of Woodstock Archives/
People Collection.

ence at the Woodstock Playhouse on behalf of a fundraiser for Chinese
relief. The event proved to be a major attraction as an overflow audience
of Woodstockers contributed $1,200 to the cause.[14]

As 1941 moved on, Woodstockers at times could not have helped
feeling as if they were fighting battles on two fronts. While the increasing
likelihood of war presented its own pressures on Woodstock families,
townspeople awoke on September 26 to the news that a case of infantile
paralysis had been discovered in a thirteen-year-old student living on
Rock City Road. As a scare went through the town, Dr. Hans Cohn, in
collaboration with the Board of Trustees for the Woodstock's School District
No. 2, ordered the public school in town closed. Cohn, while stressing
that that the "dangers of a pandemic" were unlikely, cautioned parents to
"keep their children close to home and away from crowds." In addition
to the closing of the Woodstock school, it was further advised that all
Sunday School classes also be canceled. Meanwhile, though the home of
the stricken child on Rock City Road remained under quarantine and

the boy was transferred to Haverstraw Hospital in New Jersey for further treatment, the case would prove to be an isolated one with the stricken child, according to Cohn, recovering "in six to eight weeks."[15]

Not more than a week following the polio scare, some brighter news relating to another child in Woodstock appeared in a letter to the *Woodstock Press*. A year earlier, following the local call to national leaders to aid in the effort to evacuate British children to this country, one family in Woodstock had taken the extraordinary step to be a part of the program. Writing from their home in Harpenden, England, the Blade family extended their thanks to Woodstock's James and Leona Montanye for providing for the safety and care of their daughter, Joy. Having made the difficult decision to send their daughter to the United States in January 1941, Hubert and Jocelyn Blade wrote ten months later:

> It became evident to us, from her early letters, that she had found a very kindly community in which to dwell, and her letters have particularly mentioned the kindness and hospitality of the Woodstock folk. Her own words are, "The church minister and his wife at Sunday and day school, and all Woodstock people are nice and kind to me and I like them."
>
> To the children of Woodstock we send our gratitude for the pleasure they have given her by welcoming her so readily into their midst.[16]

The following month, as war speculation continued to weave its way through town, even the astrologer for the *Woodstock Press*, F. Y. Hall, got into the act, predicting on October 4 that the nation would find itself at war "sometime in November." Though slightly off in his prediction, Hall also predicted that Mussolini and Hitler would have a "falling out" and that a "blowup" was in Hitler's future. The astrologer, however, stopped short of passing on to Woodstock readers what that blowup might be.[17]

On Wednesday evening, December 3, 1941, 150 Woodstockers made their way to Woodstock's town hall to attend the first in a new film series presented by the Woodstock Artists Association. Following introductory music played by Woodstock composer and instructor of music theory at numerous academic institutions William Ames, Julia Leaycraft, association president, introduced the two short films to be shown that evening—ironically, a collection of experimental German films. In her remarks that evening, Leaycraft noted that the series' next offering would have a more

American slant and feature such stars as Lionel Barrymore and Mary Pickford. By all published accounts, the evening's film presentation was the last cultural gathering of townspeople prior to December 7.[18]

Stunned as all Americans were by the attack on Pearl Harbor, Woodstock refused to let Christmas Eve on the Village Green go unobserved. While the event was briefly in question, a number of community volunteers rallied to raise the funds needed to provide the labor required to ensure the lighting of the town Christmas tree, the singing of carols, the reading of the Nativity, and Santa Claus's timely arrival on the Green—an arrival needed, perhaps, as much by the adults of the town as the children.[19]

Nor would Woodstockers let the year pass without one celebratory farewell to a year that had left all wondering what lay ahead. On December 28, Konrad and Florence Ballin Cramer joined their neighbors to attend the Waltz Ball held in Woodstock's town hall. The Cramers, both

Figure 8. Woodstockers gathered on the Village Green to await the arrival of Santa Claus. *Source:* Courtesy Mark Antman.

well-honored artists in their own right, were central to the Woodstock art scene and ready participants in Woodstock's social life, frequently joining parties and events where Konrad would invariably be called upon to pull out his violin and provide entertainment for the evening. With Vladimir Padwa, musical director of the Woodstock Playhouse Concerts; Byrdcliffe denizen Ben Webster; metal work artist Ned Thatcher; and others joining Cramer that evening, Woodstock's Waltz Ball, as Florence Ballin Cramer would later write in her diary, was both notable and rare when it came to a Woodstock event—notable in the number of Woodstockers in attendance yet rare in its "sober" nature as Woodstockers began to mobilize in response to a declaration of war.

> We didn't arrive until after ten. There were throngs of people, everyone in Woodstock almost, natives, artists, old and young, some in full evening and some in street attire, one or two in costume. There were three or four groups who provided music, they included musicians like Padwa who played with Dr. Hans Cohn, young Milton Wolven the butcher's boy who has spent two years at Eastman music school, then Ben Webster, Ned Thatcher, and Konrad. Ned did a good many monkey shines in the way of tricky playing of "the bones" and the crowd were so amused they wanted to watch instead of dancing. Ned kept repeating, "But why don't you dance!!!" They did dance finally, and the floor was closely packed with dancers and two rows of people sitting around the hall looking on. At a long table to the side refreshments were being sold. Fruit punch, sandwiches and cake. No liquor. As a matter of fact, there weren't any drunks about at all. Unusual at a party in Woodstock.[20]

Chapter 3

# The War Comes to Woodstock

Three weeks prior to entering her observations on the Woodstock Waltz Ball in her diary, Florence Cramer reflected on the news that had stunned all Americans, the bombing of Pearl Harbor. On December 8, 1941, Cramer picked up a pen (her typewriter was in the shop for repairs) and, in longhand, wrote, "At 12:30 today, the President gave a short but impressive talk. Immediately thereafter, both the House and Senate voted and war was declared within one-and-a-half hours by an almost unanimous vote. It is amazing how this sudden and cruel attack has unified the country and everyone seems ready to stand by the President."[1] Even as Florence Cramer was memorializing that moment in her diary, Woodstock had already begun to mobilize in response to the Japanese attack. World War II had come to Woodstock.

Air raid wardens were notified to be on the lookout for any suspicious planes and to report such sightings to Mitchell Field on Long Island, home of the Air Defense Command. Albert Cashdollar, Woodstock's town supervisor, was on his way to a meeting of the Ulster County Defense Council in Kingston, and Warren Hutty, serving as the temporary defense chairman for Woodstock, was at work calling a meeting of town officials to initiate defense plans for Woodstock and to find a permanent chairman who could lead those efforts during the difficult days ahead. Even Woodstock's American Legion post had begun mobilizing by initiating a town-wide "survey of all those owning firearms as well as those able to use them." In addition, the local post let it be known that they owned "several Army rifles" and that it was "considered probable that these will be put in readiness for immediate action should the need arise" and that live ammunition was being ordered.[2]

With war fever running high, less than two weeks following Pearl Harbor more than two hundred Woodstockers gathered at Woodstock's town hall to further organize the town's defense efforts. Not shy about expressing their patriotic feelings, the meeting began with all joining together to sing *America* and reciting the Pledge of Allegiance as led by Mrs. Arthur Peper.[3] As the meeting got down to business, the first order of the evening was to select someone to lead the town's defense efforts. That selection was quick—and unanimous—as Woodstockers called upon local attorney Martin Comeau. Comeau, married to Marion Eames, whose family oversaw a seventy-six-acre estate in the center of Woodstock, had grown in influence through his work on behalf of the town. Respected for his efforts as town attorney, Comeau was a veteran of the First World War, had served as a US marshal, as vice commander of the local American Legion post, and held numerous positions in support of the Woodstock Library, including president.

Figure 9. Martin Comeau would lead Woodstock's home defense efforts through-out the war. *Source:* Historical Society of Woodstock Archives/People Collection.

Rising to address those gathered, Comeau urged "that all persons—both male and female—between the ages of sixteen and sixty-five register to aid the home defense effort." To further that goal, Comeau announced that the town hall would be open from 9:00 a.m. to 8:00 p.m., Monday through Saturday, and on Sunday from 12:00 p.m. till 8:00 p.m. for anyone wishing to register. Adding a personal commitment to his call, Comeau also announced that he would donate the use of his own building on Tinker Street to serve as Woodstock's defense office.[4]

As defense chairman, however, Comeau knew he would need more than an office to succeed: he also needed committed individuals to lead Woodstock's efforts in support of the war. As the holidays passed, Comeau tapped several of his neighbors to oversee the efforts of the 317 Woodstockers who had followed his call to register to support the town's defense efforts. Reverend Harvey Todd of the Dutch Reformed Church was tasked with leading all air raid wardens in the village. Working under Todd were Reverend Lester Haws of the Woodstock Methodist Church and Reverend A. Walter Baker of the Christ Lutheran Church. While the initial choice of three ministers to serve as air raid wardens might have seemed odd to some, it was a decision based on practicality more than anything else. While Comeau hoped that air raid sirens, at some point during the war, might be installed to sound any alarm, church bells, for the time being, would have to do as Woodstock's early warning system.

Comeau was also mindful of the need for air raid coverage in Woodstock's outlying districts. To that end, he appointed Theron Lasher to lead the auxiliary police force, which included overseeing all air raid wardens outside the village proper. Lasher was well known to Woodstockers through his work as an integral member of Woodstock's Winter Sports Association as well as his efforts in support of Woodstock's popular midget auto racing track in Bearsville during the years prior to the war. To support Lasher's oversight duties, air raid warden appointments also went to long-time residents in each of the town's hamlets, including Newton Reynolds and Virgil Van Wagonen, Bearsville; Craig Vosburgh, Shady; Floyd Stone, Wittenberg; Egbert Shultis, Lake Hill; William Van Wagner, Willow; Egbert Shultis, Lake Hill; and Aurel Holumzer, Zena.[5]

Other assignments would follow from Comeau. Albert Cashdollar would continue as chief of the Woodstock Fire Department, with Reginald Lapo serving as assistant chief. Joseph Hutty, Woodstock's superintendent of highways, would serve as chief of the Public Works Service, with oversight of the newly created Demolition and Clearance Squad. Alice Henderson, representing Woodstock's Red Cross chapter, was selected as chair of the town's shelter defense efforts, while Dr. Hans Cohn would serve as health officer.[6]

In addition, as January 1942 neared its end, Comeau announced that a training program would be launched for those tapped to lead the town's various defense efforts. To comply with national regulations, Comeau advised that all auxiliary policemen, firemen, and air wardens undergo a detailed course of training before being considered qualified for their duties. No doubt, as Martin Comeau looked out from his office on Tinker Street, he could only have wondered how much more work needed to be done.

Albert Cashdollar, in his additional role as Ulster County defense chairman, was also busy filling numerous positions countywide. For one important appointment, however, he looked to his hometown and on January 9 announced the appointment of Woodstock artist Carl Lindin to the Ulster County Tire Rationing Board. Lindin—who beyond his preeminence in the art world served locally in support of the American Committee to Save Anti-Fascist Refugees, as a founder of the Woodstock Artists Association, and as member of the Board of Governors for the Woodstock Country Club—joined his fellow board members in confronting the unenviable task of doling "out the limited number of new automobile tires" allotted to Ulster County towns outside of the city of Kingston. As the Tire Rationing Board began the process of overseeing the disbursement of the 299 tires available at the time, Lindin and his colleagues determined that only seventy tires would be available to the public; the remaining tires were earmarked for distribution to heavy truck and bus operators. Under the established guidelines for a resident of Woodstock to receive a new tire, they needed a "qualified garage mechanic" to certify that "no more wear remains on the present tire or tires." And yet once that certification was obtained, there was no guarantee a tire would be forthcoming. The resident would then have to convince the rationing board that their vehicle was necessary for the local defense effort.[7]

As the new year took hold, a tale of two thermometers drew the attention of the town. During the first week of January, temperatures dropped to twenty below. To add insult to injury, the same sky that was attracting the attention of local air raid wardens dropped seven inches of snow on the town. Despite the onslaught of winter weather, a different thermometer could be found on the town's Village Green. Installed by the local chapter of the Red Cross, the thermometer display was erected to remind Woodstockers of the town's commitment to raising twenty-five hundred dollars for the county's war effort.[8]

By February 1942, blackout tests also became part of the Woodstock war experience. The first test came on Monday, February 16, with Woodstock receiving high marks (100% perfect performance) for its initial effort. During the test, fifty-one auxiliary policemen were on duty throughout the town. Just as in the movies, their purpose was to warn residents if any light was escaping from their home. As the local paper noted, "In the village square it was impossible for persons to recognize one another, even at short range, so complete was the blackout."[9]

Woodstock's blackout tests would become a bit more imaginative just a few months later, when on a Thursday evening during the first week in May, a "summons over the telephone to the OCD [Office of Civilian Defense] that the Bearsville Store had been hit by an incendiary bomb" launched Woodstockers into action. As part of the exercise, two ambulances were dispatched. In reality, they weren't really ambulances in the traditional sense. Rather, the vehicles that saw action that evening were a panel truck owned by grocer Fred Mower and a station wagon provided for the test by the Fitzpatrick family. Reaching the scene in just seven minutes, two "victims" were given first aid by volunteer responders Frielan Van De Bogart and Virgil Van Wagonen before they were transported back to the Woodstock Casualty Station, where Dr. Cohn and nurses Lilian Brinkman, Neva Shultis, and Edith Blazy waited.[10]

Woodstock, however, had never been known as a town of all work and no play and, despite a world war, resourceful Woodstockers managed to combine their social lives with efforts to provide for the common defense. In addition to the Waltz Ball attended by the Cramers as 1941 ended, a Valentine's Day Ball only six weeks later helped push the local chapter of the Red Cross toward its goal of raising twenty-five hundred dollars. The ball, chaired by local artist and author Marion Bullard, "attracted one of the largest crowds ever to assemble at Town Hall," and according to one account, "It was a gay party and those who attended pronounced it one of the best ever held." Noted children's authors Maud and Miska Petersham designed the program for the event, while the evening's entertainment reached a climax as Vladimir Padwa premiered his newest composition, the "Woodstock Polka."[11]

Figure 10. Program cover designed by Maud and Miska Petersham for the Red Cross Valentine's Day Ball, 1942. *Source:* Historical Society of Woodstock Archives/World War II Collection.

Yet another artist who called Woodstock home found his life redirected in a different way during the initial stages of the war. In an ironic twist, painter and lithographer Yasuo Kuniyoshi—despite his alien status due to his Japanese heritage—quietly began work as a freelance writer of American propaganda while also recording radio broadcasts delivered to the Japanese people via the Voice of America. Kuniyoshi also let his artwork speak for his belief in democracy by providing drawings depicting Japanese atrocities for use as propaganda by the government. Despite his wartime efforts on behalf of the United States, however, Kuniyoshi saw his bank account confiscated as well as his Leica camera and binoculars for the duration of the war.[12] As a result of the government's action taken against Kuniyoshi, 251 students from the Art Students League—as well as sixty-two of the country's ranking painters—authored a letter to President

Roosevelt expressing their firm belief "in the loyalty of our instructor and a great American artist, Yasuo Kuniyoshi."[13]

Forty years after it became home to one of the preeminent art colonies in the country, even the buildings encompassing the original Byrdcliffe Colony were considered for enlistment in the war effort. Though the colony's founder, Ralph Whitehead, had died in 1929, Byrdcliffe had endeavored to carry on under his wife Jane and son Peter. In May 1942, with the war well underway, the two were visited by representatives of the US Navy. Arriving at White Pines, home to the Whiteheads, were Rear Admiral Ralph Whitman, Captain R. Hayden, and Chief Pharmacist Durkin. The primary purpose of their visit, according to Peter Whitehead, was the consideration of "using the estate as a retreat for wounded and disabled sailors in the event the need for such a place developed during the course of the war." While seemingly satisfied with their visit, the officers returned to New York "to report to their superiors." Ultimately, no final decision was ever reached, and Byrdcliffe would go undrafted for the remainder of the war.[14]

Byrdcliffe also found itself in the news that summer as headlines broke that a Nazi spy with Woodstock connections had been arrested by the FBI. Maria Kerling, a housekeeper for Eleanor de Liagre Labrot—married to film and stage actor Brian Aherne and with homes both in New York City and at Byrdcliffe—was the estranged wife of John Kerling, one of several Nazi spies arrested after disembarking from a Nazi submarine along the coast of Florida. Though initially facing serious espionage charges that, if convicted, included the possibility of the death penalty, it was later determined that Maria Kerling had been separated from her husband for some time and, in fact, was involved with another man. Eventually, authorities dropped charges against the housekeeper although she was detained for the remainder of the war.[15]

As local men began to enlist and with 135 Woodstockers registered for the draft, Woodstock women let it be known that they were more than ready to assume whatever duties were required of them. Under the leadership of Julia Leaycraft and Woodstock artist and gallery manager Margaret Kenyon, a local branch of the American Women's Voluntary Services (AWVS) was formed. Patterned after a similar service in Great Britain, the local AWVS was designed to train women "to take over jobs of the men if needed in times of emergency." Included among the roles women would be trained for were such positions as wireless operators, truck and auto drivers when needed, and "every other phase of business and industrial life in which they could be of service."[16]

As the war progressed, Americans realized that resources once taken for granted would, at some point, be in short supply. Sugar rationing, for example, began on May 4, 1942. Less than two weeks later, cards were issued for gas rationing. Coming to understand this new reality, those who remained at home were forced to adapt and seek alternative solutions to sustain basic needs. One part of this effort was the establishment of so-called victory gardens. During World War II, according to the Smithsonian Museum, "nearly 20 million" Americans planted victory gardens, not only for their own consumption but also to allow "more food and materials [to be] available for the armed forces and programs that supported America's Allies."[17] Many Woodstockers were soon to be counted among the ranks of Americans who undertook their own efforts to produce fresh vegetables.

To oversee Woodstock's victory garden initiative, Martin Comeau appointed actor, author, and sometimes piano player for silent film screenings at the Maverick Colony Harrison Dowd to head the Woodstock Gardening Committee. With his appointment, Dowd wasted little time organizing the town on two levels: making parcels of land available for planting and, at the same time, securing seeds and vegetable seedlings. Within a short time of initiating the program, landowners throughout town began to donate parcels of land for use by their neighbors. Beginning with a plot of land donated by Martin Comeau running along Route 212 in Bearsville, the program expanded to include other sites. Byrdcliffe's Peter Whitehead offered a 100 × 60 foot plot of land on Glasco Turnpike for planting. Elsewhere, Miss Alice Wardwell made three-quarters of an acre available, while Margaret Kenyon offered a plot of land behind her home.[18] More community gardens followed.

Under Dowd's leadership, Woodstock also began to offer a seed and plant exchange. Several Woodstockers helped to get the program off the ground by donating young seedlings for distribution. Included among the early donors were herbalist Anita Smith and Victor Cannon. Cannon, who would later be honored by the town for his support of the victory garden program, also volunteered the use of his tractor (with an operator) to those making use of the town's community gardens. With a farm on Overlook Mountain known as Cannon's Ranch, Cannon, in addition to hosting school-children from time to time, also periodically exhibited his animals—including a one thousand-pound hog—at the Woodstock Library Fair.[19]

By all accounts, the victory garden program in Woodstock—including instructional lectures on effective gardening methods—was successful in meeting its goal of providing town residents with fresh vegetables made scarce by the war. And yet, while the main purpose of the program was to provide an additional food source for Woodstock tables, Woodstock's victory gardens, in the estimation of Harrison Dowd, served an even higher, more patriotic purpose. As Dowd urged his fellow Woodstockers, "Get away from the radio, the headlines, the rumor-spreaders, and see what the combination of seed and soil can do for you. We at home can fight the war our own way; not by armchair strategy, not by lying awake and speculating, certainly not by rumor spreading or listening, but by keeping one's mind and body fit for whatever may come. For this, gardening is the best answer."[20]

For Woodstockers, like most Americans, the rationing of tires and gas and the need to plant and grow victory gardens spoke to the demands of a war machine that, when directed at fighting a global war, drew supplies and material into it much like a black hole. As a result, Woodstock was impressed with the need to support the call for material that would assist in the continuous feeding of that machine. To do so, the Office for Civilian Defense appointed Reverend A. Walter Baker to head up a town salvage program. According to Baker, the importance of an effective salvage effort in Woodstock was threefold. First, a successful salvage effort offered "immediate value to munitions makers, by permitting the manufacturing of munitions more easily than having to draw from raw materials." Second, the recycling of salvage material would go far in alleviating anticipated shortages while, third, providing citizens with the "opportunity to do something towards winning the Victory." Most sought after were items containing iron and other metals. Also sought was rubber, paste, papers, magazines, rags of all kinds, burlap, soap, and toothpaste tubes.[21]

To facilitate the collection of items, two stall areas were set up in sheds near the Reformed Church just off the Village Green. Larry Goetz, a charter member of Woodstock's American Legion post and a World War I veteran, was appointed salvage master, with the task of sorting and bundling the material that would eventually be hauled to Kingston and sold. In addition, the town's athletic field served as a depository for material collected. Woodstockers unable to drop off items in the village were asked to have a neighbor deliver the material for them. Additionally, local grocers, including the Bearsville Store, Happys, and William Mower, offered, when delivering groceries, to pick up their customer's salvage material and drop it off on their return to town.

Unfortunately, in 1942, not every Woodstocker was content in seeing that "all" the donated scrap material went to aid the town's defense efforts. With the headline "Attention!! Traitors!!," the *Woodstock Press* let it be known that a certain individual or individuals had been seen stealing "metal from the scrap heap accumulating at the Athletic Field." Calling the individuals "the lowest kind of traitors," the paper warned that unless the material was returned, their names would be "turned over to the Salvage Committee." While no one was ever implicated in the theft and no names were made public, it appears that the warning from the *Woodstock Press* served its purpose, as further attention to any thefts failed to make headlines. It was, however, an act that was particularly galling to townspeople, knowing that the money raised from the sale of the salvage material was to be used to defray the expenses of the Civilian Defense Office, the Boy Scouts, and the local chapter of the Red Cross.[22]

On April 15, 1942, between two thousand and three thousand people gathered in Saugerties, New York, to see off a contingent of local draftees bound for Albany; among them was the largest single group of men to leave Woodstock for service in the US Army. Fittingly, the group's departure from Saugerties was not without ceremony. Following a parade through town that included, along with the inductees, the American Legion and a marching band, the large crowd gathered before the Saugerties Firemen's Hall. There, the name of each inductee was announced to the crowd. As each name was called and a cheer rose, "the prospective soldier stepped forward and took his place in one of the three buses bound for Albany."[23]

The story of Woodstock's home defense efforts would not be complete without attention given to the Woodstock Observation Post and continued efforts by Woodstockers to look skyward. Not long after the war began, to improve upon the town's spotting efforts the Woodstock Observation Post was established at Anita Smith's Stonecrop home on Meads Mountain Road at the base of Overlook Mountain. Appointed chief observer, Smith, an artist, herbalist, and early chronicler of Woodstock history, oversaw the building of an important element of Woodstock's defense efforts. Operationally, the Observation Post began simply enough as airplane spotters sat in a field gazing upward. A telephone nearby served as the means to report any sightings made. By the summer of 1942, however, through donations and fundraisers, a wooden tower was erected to provide relief from the elements for more than one hundred volunteer spotters. Staffed twenty-four hours a day, the volunteers dutifully noted every plane that passed overhead. As described by Gladys Hurlburt, who served as publicity director for the Post, the Woodstock effort was part of a "vast system of national Air Defense, now known as The First Fighter Command." Hurlburt also spoke of the importance of such an operation in Woodstock: "It is a mistake to think of Woodstock as remote and out of danger. As bombers fly, we are fifteen minutes from the heart of New York. When New York is attacked, the enemy planes will scatter. . . . They will get rid of their bombs wherever they are. When they try to get away from our planes, we go into action. We keep the army informed of the directions of their flights."[24]

While the nature of their work was of extreme importance, the life of a spotter at Stonecrop mixed brief flurries of activity with a great deal of time to simply ponder the war and life in Woodstock. In regular reports by Hurlburt in the *Woodstock Press* under the title "Looking Up," Woodstockers were kept informed of the Post's activities. In one report, Woodstock artist Allen Cochran described a typical early morning stint as a spotter in June 1942:

Figure 11. The Woodstock Observation Post at Anita Smith's Stonecrop home. *Source:* Historical Society of Woodstock Archives/Anita Smith Collection.

Twelve, Midnight:

I look at the bulletin board, "Special Instructions for reporting suspicious incidents." It brings the gooseflesh. Beautiful night. Hope it's as clear as this over Germany. "Go get 'em RAF!"

One A.M.: Everything under control. There goes a car. Good night, whoever you are! A rooster crows. At this hour? He must be cockeyed.

Two A.M.: Halfway mark. Coffee from my thermos. It's certainly quiet. A mouse in the wall sounds more like a cow. What? What's that? I hear a plane. I search the sky. A star moves. There it is! I report it. "Flash—to the east and going south." Man's voice answers from New York. Crisp but nice. Stillness again.

Three A.M.: Wonder where that plane was going? Wonder if anyone else is awake in the village? On nights like this, no one sleeps in Malta or Dover, or, I hope, in Tokyo. I hope Mr. Goering drops in here. Where's my pitchfork? "Flash! I wish to report Herman Goering plumping down on our meadow." Oh I wish it very much.

Four A.M.: Bruno Zimm takes over. I drive home in the first light of the morning. Strange hopes for today. I never thought I'd go to sleep saying, "God bless Stalin and Chiang Kai-Shek."[25]

Though the Observation Post was decommissioned two years later, it serves as a reminder—and as a representative centerpiece—of the dedication Woodstockers possessed during this time of sacrifice. Not only was it a place where townspeople and artists alike came together for a common purpose, it also symbolized Woodstock's connection to a wider world and the tragedies that were being visited upon others overseas.

In one of her more poignant recollections of the Post's activities, Gladys Hurlburt underscored that very connection while, at the same time, offering an image of Woodstock that many choose to remember. It is an image that provides an explanation, as if one were needed, for the commitment that Anita Smith and every volunteer brought to their task as the war continued to impact their lives. Upon hearing the news one morning describing the destruction by the Nazis of the small town of Lidice, Hurlburt wrote in "Looking Up":

This was to be a news column. It was to be gossipy and gay. About the new spotters, Engleburt Roentgen, Peter Whitehead, Margaret Wetterau, Clara Chichester, Mrs. Berlin and Mrs. Lerman of Library Lane. It was to be about the fine, great coat that Alan Waterous gave us. A "linesman coat" he called it. Football trappings enlisted for the duration. We were going to tell about the fireflies. How they bewitch us these nights. We watch a sky full of stars and suddenly they seem to dance! We close our eyes and look again. It's the fireflies. A firefly close to you has a green light like the taillight of a plane a thousand feet above us.

This was to be all our column until this morning we read about Lidice. When we got to the Post our youngest spotter was on duty. His name is Dan Randolph and he is twelve years old. He started as an assistant observer, but he was so good he was promoted. He knows more about the planes than most grown-ups. He is very proud of his job. At home he draws planes and studies pictures of enemy markings. When a plane flies over his house, he runs out to check it. He writes down slogans. He says his favorites so far are: "Keep 'em Spotted" and "Let's go Spotters!" That morning he stood out in the field looking up. He ran to the telephone when he saw a plane. His face was very serious. When his time was up he got on his bicycle and went home. His mother was waiting for him. She had his dinner ready. He was safe.

Lidice was a town in Bohemia as all the world knows. There is nothing there now. The homes have been burnt. There are no men. They have all been shot. There are no women. They have all been taken to "camps." The children have been placed in "suitable institutions." There is no Lidice today because not one soul would tell if he knew anything about the hero who shot the Nazi hangman. Heydrich.

As Dan went home to dinner our village was quiet. Women worked in their gardens. Men went about their business. The mail came in. The little Carey boy ran his fire engine up and down in front of his father's store. It looked like any summer day. But it was not. Something was happening to all of us. A rage was swelling in us as we thought about the children of Lidice crying for their mothers. Woodstock is about the same size as Lidice.[26]

Figure 12. Dan Randolph, youngest spotter at the Observation Post during the war. *Source:* Historical Society of Woodstock Archives/Anita Smith Collection.

That summer, Woodstockers gathered to celebrate the first Fourth of July since Pearl Harbor. As the crowd surrounded the speaker's platform on the Village Green, they were welcomed by the Woodstock Drum Corps, which, as the newspaper noted, "never played with more vim and precision." Reverend Todd served as master of ceremonies and Dr. James Shotwell offered encouraging words. But the highlight of the day was when the crowd surged forward to join Allen Waterous in the singing of "America," "God Bless America," and "The Star-Spangled Banner."[27]

Less than two weeks later, many in that Independence Day crowd also joined in a Bastille Day celebration held at the town hall. Organized by the Free French Movement in Woodstock, music again served to bring together those gathered. At evening's end, as Myrett Ponsella, a singer of Parisian street songs and a recent arrival in Woodstock, concluded her performance, she paused, raised her right arm, and proceeded to lead the entire gathering in singing the "La Marseillaise."[28]

In many respects, this was perhaps a more unusual time in recent Woodstock history than those assembled on the Village Green or in the town hall that July realized. Woodstock, it seemed, was becoming a united town. There was work to be done, and the debates and differences of the past seemed to matter little. And, as Woodstockers faced a collective uncertainty that the days ahead seemed to forecast, they did so with both resolve and questions, a mood captured that summer by Marion Bullard in her *Ulster County News* column, "Sparks":

> As we get down to three gallons of gasoline per week, the first jerk of it hurts but most Woodstockers seem to be cheerfully planning ways and means to get along. One woman called out as she walked down Tinker Street carrying her market basket, "I never thought I would enjoy this, but I do."
>
> Out of the attics and cellars are coming the baskets. Who knows what may be ahead if the war gets worse instead of better? So far we have our milk deliveries with the faithful driver setting down our milk bottles on the porch no matter what the weather. But just suppose his country needs his truck, his tires and his gasoline—what then?[29]

Figure 13. WWII gasoline rationing card issued to John W. Tyler of Shady for his 1941 Oldsmobile. *Source:* Historical Society of Woodstock Archives/World War II Collection.

For several young Woodstockers, however, milk deliveries were the least of their concerns as the war moved on. Draft notices would continue to arrive; others would choose to enlist. Whether departing by bus for Saugerties and, eventually, Albany or driven by a family member as they prepared to join in service to their country, each would go on to do their part. Soon, they would find themselves scattered across the globe, attacking and defending places they never knew existed. Perhaps on their way out of Woodstock, they instinctively looked back at the one place they did know and from which they could draw assurance: Overlook Mountain.

As the remaining months and years of the war cast its shadow over daily life in Woodstock, the town and its people took on what appeared at times to be dual identities. On one level, life in Woodstock carried on with all that was required of a small town. Schools opened their doors each morning, businesses served their customers, art exhibits opened, and local government functioned. On another level, a great deal of attention was focused on the war and what could be done at home in support of that effort. Over time, however, both elements of that duality would combine into a singular focus of everyday existence.

The schedule of town meetings and events noted in the *Woodstock Press* spoke to that duality as Woodstock moved through the first year of war. In printing the weekly schedule of town activities, for example, meetings involving air raid wardens were listed right next to the hours the Woodstock Library was open to the public. School trustees, according to the schedule, met at their regular day and time, while multiple first aid classes were offered to the public throughout the week. A front-page article in April 1942, under the headline "Record Trout Bagged Here," described a twenty-two-inch trout caught near the Woodstock Country Club bridge while, on the same page, a public plea from the Woodstock librarian called for the donation of books to be sent to those in the service.[30]

In 1942, the town knew sorrow and grief, as news of the first deaths of two young Woodstockers sent off to fight in the war arrived on its collective doorstep. In October, word came to the family of Charles (Buddy) Pierpoint that his ship, the USS *Meredith*, had been sunk in the Pacific. It would not be until Thanksgiving Day that the Pierpoints were officially notified that Charles had been declared missing in action. Despite hopes that all would be right, word finally arrived that Pierpoint had been killed when his ship was bombed by Japanese planes while attempting to deliver supplies to Guadalcanal.[31] A second death was reported to the White family, who learned of the loss of William in November. Having enlisted only a year earlier, William White was nineteen.[32]

Figure 14. Charles Pierpoint, first son of Woodstock lost in World War II. *Source:* Historical Society of Woodstock Archives/People Collection.

The Woodstock home front would not be without loss in 1942 either. Also in November, the Woodstock community in general—and the art colony specifically—had been stunned by the death of Carl Lindin following a short illness. One of the remaining Byrdcliffe originals, Lindin had received numerous accolades and awards throughout his years as a distinctive landscape and portrait artist. As one of Woodstock's leading citizens, he was also deeply involved in a variety of civic activities. A founder of the Woodstock Artists Association, he also served as a trustee of the Woodstock Public School District and as director at the Woodstock Country Club. With the outbreak of the war only a year earlier, Lindin began serving as a member of the Ulster County War Price and Rationing Board.

Following a funeral at the home he shared with his wife Louise, Lindin was carried to his rest by his friends—and art colony luminaries in their own right—Judson Smith, Henry Mattson, Bruno Zimm, Konrad Cramer, Miska Petersham, and Eugene Speicher.[33] He was buried in Woodstock's Artists Cemetery (formally, the Woodstock Memorial Society). Lindin's death represented to many in Woodstock the sad acknowledgment that the days of the original Byrdcliffe Colony and its founding members were beginning to recede into Woodstock memory.

In 1942 Woodstock also lost Larry Elwyn, a member of one of the town's oldest families. Elwyn was a bit of a legend around Woodstock. He was Woodstock's barber for more than fifty years, serving both old-timers and newly arrived artists alike with a dry sense of humor thrown in at no extra charge. His last shop operated at the corner of Tinker Street and Tannery Brook Road. Born in 1858, Elwyn, in his earlier years, pursued work as a painter and a decorator, while even trying his hand at quarrying bluestone. In the late 1800s, he ventured into local politics and was elected town clerk for two terms, serving from 1893 to 1900. An avid fisherman and hunter, Elwyn was known in the area as perhaps the best fox hunter of them all.[34] For many in town, the death of Larry Elwyn would also return thoughts to another era, an era when Woodstock was a far different community.

No doubt, similar sentiments echoed throughout the village a year later when Florence Peper's father, Henry Peper, also passed away. Peper was Woodstock's blacksmith, and his shop would later become Peper's Garage on Mill Hill Road. Far more than a blacksmith, however, Peper was a craftsman, as his iron work found its way into such establishments as the Overlook Mountain House and Morris Newgold's Colony Hotel on Rock City Road. In 1913, Peper joined other prominent Woodstockers, such as Ralph Whitehead, in establishing the Woodstock Club, an organization that was instrumental in the founding of the town library and a nursing service for Woodstock. A prominent member of Woodstock's Lutheran Church and the Woodstock Fire Department, Henry Peper was beloved by the town he served. As testament to the esteem in which he was held, businesses throughout the town closed their doors while his funeral service was underway.

One other loss—though not of a human nature—would have a major impact on the town as the war years progressed. In 1942, the *Woodstock Press* announced that it would, toward year end, cease publication. Connecting the decision to end the paper's run directly to the war, editor and publisher Donald McLennan stated in an editorial, "Advertising volume in every city and town in the country has been severely cut because of the war. Woodstock has been no exception." Noting further that the paper relied on advertising from out of town as a major source of revenue, McLennan added, "Gasoline rationing and the fears for the future of out of town business establishments have cut this source of revenue to the

Figure 15. Henry Peper. *Source:* Historical Society of Woodstock Archives/People Collection.

bone."[35] As a result, Woodstock was without a hometown voice for the remainder of the war.

Despite the losses Woodstock had seen, the war effort remained a central concern in town. Much of what had begun in support of the war effort following the bombing of Pearl Harbor continued throughout the years that followed, including salvage drives and additional fundraising in support of the Red Cross. In 1942, Woodstock participated in the Ulster County for Victory Salvage Harvest as part of a countywide drive to alleviate administrative costs. Through efforts headed by Woodstock volunteers Lamonte Simpkins, Reverend Todd, and Joe Friedberg, a total of 636 dollars was raised from the junk that was sorted and sold.[36] Later that year, a salvage drive specific to Woodstock and conducted prior to Christmas raised an additional 249 dollars. Much of the money raised would be directed to purchasing items organizers understood to be needed by those serving overseas. Items purchased included cartons of cigarettes, fountain pens, socks, candy, and subscriptions to both the *Reader's Digest* and *Time Magazine*.[37]

Wishing to continue supplying reading material to Woodstockers serving in the war, the local Boy Scout troop joined the Victory Book

Drive in February 1943. After encouraging residents to place unwanted books in various bins around town, the donated items were collected "with the help of Charles Cooper's horse," as Georgette Kenyon rode from bin to bin to gather the books. Noting that hers was only one of "many trips to empty bins," Kenyon promised to return, next time on "Miss Wilna Hervey's mule."[38] Precisely one year later, Kenyon would learn of the death of her husband, Lieutenant Eno Compton, as he engaged in action over Europe while serving in the US Army Air Corps.

Woodstock also continued its effort to raise funds in support of the countywide War Fund Campaign conducted by the Red Cross. With the thermometer on the Village Green serving as a reminder of the town's commitment to the fund, Woodstockers pushed toward reaching its share of the overall goal. In the spring of 1943, with the addition of donations totaling three hundred dollars, Defense Chairman Martin Comeau announced that Woodstock had become only the second town in the county to achieve its set goal.

Meanwhile, support for America's allies continued to grow in town as local chapters of France Forever and Russian War Relief and supporters of the Reformed Church's China mission actively worked to bring attention to their causes.

Beginning in 1940, the Woodstock chapter of France Forever celebrated Bastille Day. By 1943, it had grown to boast 175 members and, at the time, represented one of the most active organizations in the country. Led by chapter president Elsie Goddard, the 1943 celebration kicked off with Allen Waterous singing both "The Star-Spangled Banner" and "The Marseilles." Following Waterous, the Woodstock Town Hall gathering featured guest speaker Major Pierre Benedictus. Having seen action as a pilot in World War I—during which he was credited with shooting down four German planes—the start of World War II found Benedictus serving in France's air force reserves. As the Germans swept across Europe and into the Lowlands, Benedictus returned to active duty and was placed in charge of the airfield at Dunkirk during the evacuation of the British Expeditionary Force. His experience at Dunkirk and his descriptions of the bravery exhibited by French pilots as the Nazis attacked from the air formed the heart of his speech.[39] Following the presentation by Benedictus, tribute was paid to Caleb Milne of Woodstock, who was killed in Tunisia while serving with the American Field Service. At the time of his death, Milne was aiding in the rescue of wounded French soldiers when a mortar fell nearby.

In the audience that evening was yet another Woodstock connection to France that also began during the First World War. Philip Buttrick was on the battlefield in France on the eleventh hour of the eleventh day when the Great War came to an end. He was, perhaps, the most unlikely soldier to ever call Woodstock home. A graduate of Yale and an expert on cork forests, Buttrick found himself, in 1917, a member of the American Red Cross stationed in France. Unsatisfied with his work overseeing the construction of barracks, he was eager to join the fight on behalf of France. That desire, his love for the French, and a fear that the war would pass him by led him to the unique position as an officer in the French army. As a result, Buttrick found himself on November 11, 1918, in the unique position of overlooking the Meuse Valley as the guns of the "war to end all wars" fell silent.[40] For his service in the French army, Buttrick was awarded the Croix de Guerre for acts of bravery in the face of the enemy. Buttrick, who would later reside on Rock City Road with his wife Helen, continued his support for the French, becoming the first chairman of the France Forever chapter in Woodstock.[41]

Not to be outdone, several Woodstockers embraced support for Russia as well. As early as 1942, the Russian War Relief chapter in Woodstock hosted speakers to raise funds to purchase medical supplies for America's ally. Speaking at the town hall in September, a former officer in the Russian army, General Victor Yakhontoff, addressed the audience on the topic of the Russian front today. Promoted by the organization as "an authority on international affairs," Yakhontoff had similarly lectured at Harvard, Yale, Syracuse, and Smith College.[42] The following year, the Russian War Relief Committee went from a general to a prince, with an invitation to Prince Alexander Poutiatin to speak in Woodstock. With the claim that he was born in the Winter Palace at St. Petersburg and boasting a father who once held a prominent position under the former Russian czar Nicholas II, the prince spoke on a somewhat more forward-looking topic: present and postwar friendship with the Soviet Union.[43]

Later, as the war in Europe moved toward conclusion, the Russian War Relief Committee launched their own book drive in Woodstock in the name of promoting friendship between the American and Soviet people. With direction provided by its chair, Alexandra Padwa, the Committee announced several collection centers in town and urged townspeople to drop off "new and secondhand copies of the great classics of English language literature" at such locations as "the Woodstock Library, the post office, Cousin's store, Mower's store, Elwyn's store and Blazy's store."[44]

Figure 16. Fundraising booth created by the Russian War Relief Committee. *Source: Historical Society of Woodstock Archives/World War II Collection.*

Apart from the various efforts to support Woodstockers in service to their country as well as the nation's allies, individual stories also emerged throughout the course of the war as lives were redirected and scattered across the globe. For example, the Rose family gave three sons and a daughter to the war effort. While twin brothers Donald and Durand served in Europe, Malcom Rose served in the Army Air Corps in the Asian theater. Their sister, Muriel Rose, ended up outranking them all. Promoted to the rank of lieutenant junior grade, Muriel Rose served in the Navy Nurse Corps treating injured and sick service personnel.

Before bringing her remarkable talent as a folk singer to Woodstock in the 1950s, Sonia Malkine was a member of the French Resistance. Born in Paris, Malkine served as a courier for the underground at the age of eighteen. Among her activities, Malkine noted, "I transported papers, reports, money. Once in a while weapons but very rarely because that scared me to death. Every time I did, something would happen to scare me. Really. The least possible. The papers were bad enough. If I had been caught with them, I would have been shot or worse."[45] Following the war, along with her husband Georges—who had also been a part of the resistance and was an excellent artist in his own right—she brought their family to the United States and eventually to Woodstock.

Manuel Bromberg and Jane Dow were married in Woodstock just prior to the outbreak of the war. Shortly thereafter, "Manny" was on his way to Europe. Enlisting in the Army in the spring of 1942, Bromberg, who had studied at the Cleveland School of Art and the Colorado Fine Arts Center, was selected to serve in the War Artists Unit. From the invasion at Normandy and through the allied march across the European theater, Bromberg documented the war through his paintings, sketches, and photographs, several of which were published in periodicals and newspapers such as *Life* and the *New York Times*. For his wartime efforts, Bromberg was awarded the Legion of Merit, reading, "He has exhibited the qualities of a genius and an artist and has displayed unusual courage and initiative as a soldier by taking voluntary risks under fire in order to give a proper portrayal of our army in action."[46]

Though he didn't begin the war as a Woodstocker, future Academy Award winner Lee Marvin arrived in town after being wounded while fighting in the Pacific. Severely injured after coming under fire by a Japanese sniper during the Battle of Saipan in 1944, Marvin, following his return to the United States, began his recuperation at the Woodstock home of his parents. Eventually, though not for a lengthy period, he found work as a plumber's helper with Adolph Heckeroth of Heckeroth Plumbing.[47]

While news reports continued their accounts of a world gone mad and the deaths and lists of wounded mounted by the day, it was yet another death at home that left Woodstockers feeling a loss of a different kind. Hervey White, founder of the Maverick Colony, died on October 10, 1944. An art colony original, White had arrived in Woodstock with Ralph Whitehead and Bolton Brown at the founding of the Byrdcliffe Arts Colony. Following his departure from Byrdcliffe—and with little money—White went on to establish the Maverick Colony on farmland just across the

Woodstock–Hurley line. Sometimes described as Woodstock's first hippie, it was Hervey White who brought the original festival to Woodstock in the form of the Maverick Festivals while also producing remarkable literature that appeared in such celebrated journals as *The Plowshare*, the *Wild Hawk,* and the *Hue and Cry*. Working to construct a permanent concert hall, he succeeded in creating a building that still plays host to the Maverick Concert series today. It was under the rafters and roof of that very same building that Hervey White's life was remembered on October 23, 1944.

In addressing the large assemblage of mourners that day, Martin Schutze, a principal founder of the Historical Society of Woodstock, spoke of White's impact on the town:

> There is in the grief of us all who have known Hervey, a warm radiance of exaltation at the contemplation of the deep unity and purity of life. . . . We shall come to feel that Hervey's greatest achievement is this: where others who were endowed with all

Figure 17. Hervey White, founder of the Maverick Colony. *Source:* Historical Society of Woodstock Archives/People Collection.

the resources of wealth and position failed in similar projects, Hervey alone succeeded by the sheer force of his vision, integrity, and love of his fellows. He alone has furnished the final proof that the spirit is mightier than all the material forces.[48]

While Schutze's words were directed at White's life and legacy, his invocation in the belief that the human spirit can prove victorious over the material and powerful forces of the day would not go untested decades later in the town Hervey White was so instrumental in shaping.

As the war drew to a close in 1945, Woodstock began to account for what it had lost. At war's end, twelve sons of Woodstock did not return to the life they had known beneath the face of Overlook Mountain. They included the following:

Charles Sherwood Carnright
Eno Compton Jr.
Charles Diandrea
George De Freese
Paul Lemay
Caleb Milne
John Alexander Peacock
Charles Benjamin Pierpoint
Roger Paul Peyre
Robert Oren Russell
Leonhard Scholl Jr.
William John White

Others, such as Newton Shultis, who had been wounded twice and faced ongoing treatment at Halloran General Hospital, also made their return. Still others bore the emotional scars imposed upon their young lives, though their experiences often remained theirs and theirs alone.

Woodstock, of course, like small and large towns across the nation, celebrated the end of the war and the defeat of Fascism. Townspeople gathered once again at the Village Green. Speeches and prayers were offered, the "Star-Spangled Banner" was played, and "America" rose again from the voices of those gathered. And yet, as villagers wandered home following celebrations over the defeat of Germany and Japan, they no doubt wondered what the days that followed would bring. In all that was sacrificed and lost, a certain unity had been gained. Could a town that had known its own unique form of division move forward in the postwar days and embrace what four years of war had taught them? There was much to consider and much work to do, including, how they would choose to honor and remember the cost of the last four years.

# Chapter 4

# Honor and Dishonor

On September 25, 1947, Town Supervisor Kenneth Wilson stood before a large gathering of townspeople to launch the formation of the Woodstock War Memorial Association. To date, while discussions had come and gone over time regarding a memorial that would mark the ultimate sacrifice of Woodstockers since the founding of the Republic, they had not led to any tangible result. Following World War II, however, several Woodstockers were intent on not letting time pass once more without honoring those who had served and—more specifically—those who never would again enjoy life in the shadow of Overlook.

Wilson opened the meeting with a call to elect the officers who would guide the town's effort toward creating the memorial. In a vote that was unanimous, Wilna Hervey was selected to lead the new organization as its president. Hervey—an artist and former silent film star once cast as the Powerful Katrinka in the Toonerville Trolley series—was a very popular member of the Woodstock community. While her physical stature certainly commanded attention, her parties, hosted with partner Nan Mason, were a must-have invite among many Woodstockers.

During the initial meeting, with particular reference to Woodstock's Village Green, speakers offered varying thoughts on what form the memorial might take. Architect Albert Graeser presented a draft sketch depicting "a park in miniature with trees, gravel walk," and, as he said, a "prickly hedge" that would keep undesirables from walking through it.[1] (Unforeseen at the time, Graeser's reference to "undesirables" proved prophetic a decade and a half later.) In addition, the architect's plans called for two benches of bluestone to be crafted by local sculptors. Upon mention of bluestone benches, Tomas Penning, Woodstock's foremost stone sculptor, rose to strongly insist that any benches erected be made of native stone. Referring to the town's local bluestone history and the many quarries that once produced extensive quantities of bluestone for urban areas, Penning suggested, "It will look better in Woodstock than anywhere else. There is an old adage that goes back to the Middle Ages, namely, a stone should never be moved more than a mile."[2]

Although consensus was forming around the idea of a memorial on the Village Green, others in attendance that evening suggested different possibilities. By far, the one suggestion that received the most vocal attention was what became known as a "living memorial": an athletic field and playground. While this suggestion found support among many as the planning for a memorial moved forward over the next months, Supervisor Wilson made clear where he stood on the additional suggestions, stating "that these were things the community needed and would have—but to dedicate them to the service men was not his idea of the proper thing to do." Rather, referring to the original idea of a memorial on the Village Green, Wilson offered, "As I see it, what we do for the boys should be something extra and that is why I believe in the type of memorial we have proposed. It can always be added to."[3]

As 1947 began to move toward fall, Supervisor Wilson stressed to those gathered that time was of the essence if the memorial was to be completed by Memorial Day, 1948. "In order to accomplish this goal," said Wilson, "no time can be lost." As a result, a deadline of October 23 was announced for those wishing to submit suggestions for the memorial's design. Although the deadline was a tight one, Eugene Ludins made clear that submissions could be made by anyone in town and that the process was by no means open only to architects or those with a design background.[4] Town clerk Grant Elwyn was asked to take on the task of compiling a record that listed all Woodstock servicemen who had given their lives in battle from the Revolution forward. Reverend Todd, as treasurer, was given the authority to make deposits of all funds donated to the project. As Woodstock was still a town without a bank of its own, Todd had to travel to Kingston to deposit contributions made toward the memorial.

At the time, it was anticipated that some two thousand dollars would be required to complete the memorial, depending on the final design. To that end, it was also announced that funds were already being contributed, including from the Woodstock Riding Club, twenty-five dollars; Margaret Kenyon, one hundred dollars; the Women's Society of the Wittenberg

Methodist Church, twenty-five dollars; and Manuel Komroff, twenty-five dollars.[5] Underscoring the fact that contributions were needed no matter the amount, Wilna Hervey mentioned being approached by Archie Lee, who at the time served as an employee of Dr. William Hitzig. Handing over two dollars, Lee, referring to the memorial plan that would list those Woodstockers killed in action over the years, said, "I just want to give you these two dollars because my name won't be on it. I fought overseas and I know what it means."[6]

On the evening of October 23, Albert Graeser, chair of the design committee, announced that a design had been chosen. While competing designs had been presented, the committee determined that a design submitted by the artist Marianne Appel "had the most appeal" resulting from its "extreme simplicity."[7]

Marianne Appel had arrived in Woodstock in 1934 and married artist Austin Mecklem in 1936. A year later, both artists were on their way to Alaska, having received WPA commissions. There, according to her daughters, "they backpacked and made their way from town to mountain glacier with their artist companions, painting landscapes and villages under the auspices of the New Deal Easel Painting Project." Back in Woodstock, the couple settled in a two-room cabin in Hervey White's Maverick Colony as they completed

Figure 18. Marianne Appel, Woodstock artist whose design formed the basis for the War Memorial originally constructed on the Village Green. *Source:* Courtesy of the Mecklem Family.

murals for the WPA post office project.[8] Appel further integrated herself into the Woodstock Colony through various associations and activities, including joining the cooperative gallery known as the Sawkill Group and the Woodstock Artists Association. During the war she joined her husband at Stonecrop as a plane spotter and later worked to establish the Woodstock Parents Teachers Association at the Woodstock Elementary School.[9]

While times and circumstances have changed over the years, Appel's original concept for a visual memorial on the Village Green remains as a public reminder of her work and commitment to Woodstock. Under Appel's plan, the bluestone memorial was to be incorporated into the base of the flagpole that stood on the Village Green with a "bluestone path running through [the] plot in line with the church" (the Reformed Church that stands behind the Village Green). Affixed to the flagpole, the names of Woodstock's war dead were to be etched on a bronze plaque. While the number of benches to be included in the plan would be determined later, the committee turned to Graeser to assist Appel in finalizing details for the memorial.[10]

Figure 19. Woodstock War Memorial on the Village Green as conceptualized by architect Albert Graeser. *Source:* Historical Society of Woodstock Archives/Town Center Collection.

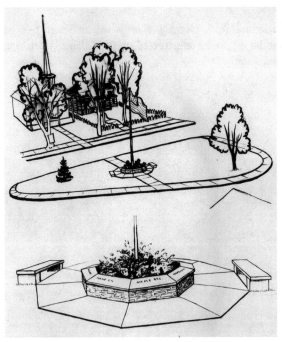

In just over a month, Woodstock had come together in ways reflective of the unity seen during the war years. Not only were key community leaders involved in pushing the idea of the memorial toward completion, but the variety of local organizations that worked to contribute and support the plan was as close to universal as Woodstock could ever get. Included within that support were such diverse groups as the Woodstock Artists Association, the Woodstock Lutheran Church, the Woodstock Riding Club, the Red Cross, the Zena Country Club, St. Joan of Arc Chapel, the Woodstock Library, the Woodstock Guild of Craftsmen, the Wittenberg Sportsmen's Club, the Wittenberg Methodist Church, the Woodstock Boy Scouts, the Woodstock Cemetery Association, the American Legion Auxiliary, the Rebekah Lodge, and the Odd Fellows.[11] With unity in evidence, planning for the war memorial proceeded; planning that seemed to be on its way to fruition without opposition—or even the occasional Woodstock grumbling.

Well, almost.

As the town moved forward with Appel's plan for what became known as a "visual memorial," the idea of creating a "living memorial" through the donation of the athletic field to the town continued to surface. The transfer of the field, owned by the Fish and Game Club, to the town of Woodstock was the subject of a meeting in December between members of the club, representatives of the War Memorial organization, and the American Legion. At that December meeting it was proposed that the club hire architect Albert Graeser for the purpose of "laying out plans for a regulation baseball diamond and space for playground equipment for younger children as a living memorial." With the passage of the resolution and the creation of a committee by the club to work with the Woodstock Memorial Association, all seemed to be moving in a positive direction. General agreement was reached, for example, to allow the American Legion to use the field for the two baseball teams it was planning to field the following year.[12]

Later in the meeting, however, as Wilna Hervey finished outlining the progress the War Memorial Association was making, Joe Friedberg of Woodstock's American Legion post rose to speak. Friedberg noted that at a previous meeting of the American Legion, "members went on record with a majority vote against the visual memorial which is to be erected on the Village Green." Continuing, Friedberg offered that "in his opinion, the visual memorial was not desired by the residents . . . that such a memorial would mean nothing but sadness for the families who had lost their sons in the wars."[13]

Reverend Todd, who was attending the meeting as a representative of the Memorial Association, was quick to counter Friedberg's assertions. Claiming that "Mr. Friedberg was entirely misinformed since within the past two days, three such families had made contributions amounting to $175 for the visual memorial," Todd concluded, "We will have a visual as well as a living memorial and I am very sorry for these few people who do not agree with us, because I feel they will regret their present actions."[14]

Rising to speak, Benjamin Buley, commander of the Woodstock American Legion, attempted to clarify its position and actions the local post had taken. Buley noted that at the meeting Friedberg referred to, only twenty members of the post—which counted ninety-eight as its full membership—were in attendance. Of the twenty in attendance, "three voted in favor of the memorial, eight against it and nine did not vote either way." As a result, Buley suggested, "I do not see how that can be regarded as the general opinion of the American Legion." Buley, who favored the visual memorial as well as the living memorial, told those gathered that the Legion would meet again that week to fully discuss the question.[15]

True to his word, Buley assembled the membership of the Woodstock American Legion on a Friday evening to take up the proposed visual memorial on the Village Green. Following a report by post member George Hard—described by the *Kingston Daily Freeman* as a "clear and factual description of the proceedings of the Woodstock Memorial Association from its inception to the present time"—Joe Friedberg presented a "detailed report . . . in opposition to the association." During the discussion that followed, the *Freeman* reported, those members that had previously voted against the memorial on the Village Green said that they had done so "due to the fact that they didn't fully understand what was being done."[16] Ultimately, with the clarification provided, opposition to a visual memorial melted away as members voted to support the plan and to contribute to the memorial.

The Memorial Association moved on as the calendar turned to 1948 with both the construction committee and fund-raising committee shifting into high gear in anticipation of meeting the Memorial Day deadline. Late in March, however, Wilna Hervey, due to ill health, was forced to step down as its president. In turn, Supervisor Wilson was elevated from his role as vice president to fill out the remainder of Hervey's term while Grant Elwyn, who also served as Woodstock town clerk, was appointed vice president. In recognition of "her fine leadership and untiring efforts to raise sufficient funds for the erection of living and visual memorials in the Town of Woodstock," the Association voted unanimously at its March meeting to bestow the title "honorary president of the War Memorial Association" on Hervey.[17]

On Memorial Day, 1948, Commander Benjamin Buley approached the newly installed memorial on the Village Green. Placing a wreath at its base, Buley stated, "In the name of the citizens of Woodstock and the American Legion Post 1026, I now dedicate this Memorial to the memory of those who died in the service of our country." As Buley stepped back from the natural bluestone memorial, a young Paul Van Wagenen raised the flag to the upmost height of the flagpole firmly planted at the center of the monument. As he did, according to the *Kingston Daily Freeman*, "Hundreds of residents and visitors lining the streets stood at attention."[18]

The solemn words the speakers offered during the dedication of the war memorial had barely faded when the purpose of the memorial was brought into stark reality. On June 7, 1948, a train pulled into the West Hurley station bearing the body of First Lieutenant Roger Peyre. The son of Gabriel Peyre, who played viola for the Metropolitan Opera for fifty years, Roger Peyre had been killed by a sniper's bullet four years earlier in the Marianas. Finally home, Peyre's body was met by a contingent from the Woodstock American Legion and escorted to St. John's Church in Stony Hollow. Following the funeral service at St. John's, burial took place in the Artists Cemetery. As a last salute was fired, Roger Cashdollar sounded taps.[19]

Despite all that had been accomplished, the work of the Woodstock Memorial Association was not complete. While a meeting of the Association following the Memorial Day celebration began with thanks from Supervisor Wilson to all who lent their efforts in making the visual memorial possible—with specific appreciation going to Wilna Hervey and Tomas Penning—the set of bronze tablets that were to be affixed to the memorial had not been completed. The tablets, which included the names of all Woodstockers who had given their life in defense of the nation throughout the town's history, were to be the final addition to the work that had begun almost a year earlier.

It was another year before Woodstockers gathered again on the Village Green to observe the unveiling of the promised bronze plaques. And, while the Memorial Association continued its work throughout the remainder of the year, 1948 saw others in town begin to turn in a different direction as factions began forming in support of progressive ideals dramatically at odds with the town's conservative ways. As a result, Woodstock joined the rest of the nation as suspicions and charges began to break through a curtain of silence—suspicions and charges directed at neighbors believed to be leaning a little too far left for comfort.

The year 1948 was a presidential election year. And, while there was little doubt Republican candidate Thomas Dewey received the vast majority of votes when Woodstockers made their way to the polls in November, history recorded Harry Truman's election day victory as one of the greatest political upsets in American election history. That said, there was yet another presidential candidate that year who a number of Woodstockers rallied around: Henry Wallace.

Woodstock's flirtation with the former vice president had begun as early as the first month of 1948. Meeting at the Woodstock Artists Association, members of the Ulster County Chapter of the Progressive Citizens of America debated the national question of merging with a third party—likely the American Labor Party—in support of Wallace. With Woodstocker Richard Burlinghame presiding, the local chapter voted not to support such a merger but, keeping an open mind on the question, agreed to send representatives to the next convention.[20]

Additional fuel to the burgeoning support for Wallace was added in March with the appearance before a Woodstock discussion group by Reverend Lee Ball from Mahopac, New York. Blasting President Harry Truman's handling of the Cold War and urging support for Wallace, Ball claimed that the United States was selling "out our honor" and that "the nation was coming to a judgement day." He continued, "We are sowing the wind when we sell our human dignity and decency for the sake of stinking Arab oil to fight the Russians." Declaring that, "the people want peace," Ball urged Woodstockers to "build a third party" and claimed, "Henry Wallace is the only American statesman talking common sense."[21]

By summer, additional backing for a Wallace campaign began to emerge in Woodstock. At an early August meeting of the Woodstock for Wallace Club held at the Town House restaurant, Howard Bird presided over a meeting of approximately one hundred eager supporters. Leading off the meeting, Woodstock's Dr. John Kingsbury charged that the press had engaged in lying about Wallace and his accomplishments while also saying, "My friends thought I was crazy for supporting Wallace as I had formerly supported Franklin D. Roosevelt. I don't care, since I am glad to be associated with the young virile Wallace organization."[22]

Following Kingsbury, Reverend L. A. Weaver of Kingston similarly stressed the importance of a campaign that was gaining support among the young. Providing his reflection on his experience at Wallace's national convention, Weaver stated that he "was impressed by the youth of the delegates and their obvious enthusiasm." Weaver, a Black minister, also noted that when he left the national convention, he did so with the "desire to do what he could with his own people as well as those of the 'white race' to further Wallace's interest." Continuing to reflect on the issue of race—an issue rarely discussed in Woodstock's public realm—Weaver, pointing to the difference between the progressives and the two major parties, told the audience that, while "Negroes are denied their vote" in the South, the Wallace convention carried out its work with "37 Negroes on his slate."[23]

Following the words of Kingsbury and Weaver, a young man named Pete Seeger provided some music. The founder, along with Alan Lomax and Leo Hays, of the organization Peoples Songs for the purpose of disseminating "songs for political action to Labor and other progressive organizations,"[24] Seeger had thrown his personal and organizational support behind the candidacy of Wallace. Following his performance that evening, he commented on the importance of folk songs to the movement, noting, according to the *Kingston Daily Freeman*, "Children between the ages of five and twelve should be taught special songs which they would enjoy singing and which would also carry the message for the Progressive Party." Quick to follow up on Seeger's comments, Dr. Kingsbury added, "Singing will count in spite of the scoffing press."[25]

Not long after performing for the Wallace Club at the Town House, Seeger and Kingsbury joined together again in support of Wallace for what Alf Evers described as a "swimming hootenanny" at Kingsbury's home in the hamlet of Shady. As historian Alf Evers and others have noted, rising concern over leftist thought in the earlier years of the Cold War was giving way to the Red Scare; Woodstock was not immune to this trend, as longtime Woodstockers began to look at such activity by neighbors such as Dr. Kingsbury through a suspicious lens.[26]

Kingsbury—who had had an impressive career on many levels, including administrative consultant to Harry Hopkins and the Works Progress Administration, commissioner of Public Charities for New York City, general director of the New York Association for the Improvement of the Poor, and executive director of the Milbank Memorial Fund—was a strong supporter of socialized medicine, including "some health phases of the Soviet system."[27] Over time, such support and his chairmanship of the National Council of American–Soviet Friendship, an organization that was listed as subversive by the attorney general in 1947, led, as Alf

Evers wrote, to the *New York Daily News* labeling him the "Red Doctor of Shady."[28]

And yet, Kingsbury's reputation in Woodstock's history tells a somewhat different story. While he served in varying capacities during his time in Woodstock with his wife Mabel—including as a trustee to the Woodstock Library and the town's Historical Society—Kingsbury is better remembered for the role he played in establishing the Woodstock Memorial Society, more commonly known as the Artists Cemetery. Following the tragic death of his son in an automobile accident in 1934, Kingsbury sought out a fitting site for his burial. Wandering past the tombstones that constitute what is known as the Evergreen Cemetery off Rock City Road, Kingsbury came to the top of the hill where the Evergreen ended. There he looked out across a gentle slope of land that led to a clear view of Overlook Mountain. Although he originally purchased only an eighty × one hundred foot plot of land for this son's final resting place, once viewed by his friends, including James Shotwell, Carl Lindin, James Stagg, and Bruno Zimm, it was agreed that the entire plot of land should be purchased; in November 1934, the group officially incorporated the site as a cemetery.

Figure 20. John Kingsbury. *Source:* Historical Society of Woodstock Archives/ People Collection.

As the town moved into the summer months of 1948, a summer highlighted by the appearance of famed actress Lillian Gish at the Woodstock Playhouse, political suspicions and deliberations heightened. That August, the Woodstock Forum hosted a debate on the national security of the United States and its faltering relationship with the Soviet Union. Held at the town hall, it was, according to the *Kingston Daily Freeman*, the largest turnout the forum had ever seen, as "it was necessary for over a hundred to stand in the side aisles, the back of the hall and at various exits." Moderated by *Reader's Digest* editor and author Henry Morton Robinson, the speakers for the evening included former war correspondent and author Ira Wolfert, economist and former member of the Communist Party Nathaniel Weyl, and historian Frank Meyer.[29]

For all practical purposes, the evening's discussion pitted Wolfert against Meyer and Weyl. While Weyl, according to the *Freeman*, blamed "Russia for the present state of affairs" and Meyer, also a former member of the Communist Party, "had denounced Communism several years before," Wolfert put forth that it was the US "bi-partisan foreign policy [that] was responsible for the situation."[30] Labeled by the *Freeman* reporter in attendance as "one of the most stimulating discussions held in the Town Hall this year," it was noted that those in attendance were decidedly split into the two camps represented by the speakers. As the speakers debated back and forth through the evening, time seemed to become irrelevant. At one point late in the evening, chairman of the forum, Walter Van Wagenen, reminded Robinson that the agreed end time of 10:30 had since passed. Robinson, according to the published report on the evening, "took exception and stated that it was an open forum and everybody present should have the opportunity to speak their minds and that it was up to the audience as to when the meeting should be concluded."[31] So it was, and the meeting continued.

While the forum illustrated the decided differences among neighbors when it came to the concerns of the day, it was as reported a civil debate, conducted on a high level. What was about to occur—and had been occurring—outside the confines of the town hall was far less than civil. Toward the end of that August, another Wallace meeting took place at the home of Howard Bird, president of the Woodstock Wallace Club. The meeting had been specifically set aside for attendance by young people, particularly students from the Art Students League. Yet, the main news of the evening centered on a cross-burning incident less than a football field away from the Bird home.

Figure 21. Cross burning headline as it appeared in the *Kingston Daily Freeman*, August 31, 1948. *Source:* Author's collection.

## TWO

# Woodstock Agog Over Burning of Cross Near Bird's

## Progressive Youth Group Will Petition Dewey to Put an End to 'Form of Violence'

The cross, made of pipe and appearing to be covered with burlap soaked in kerosene, spurred indignation throughout town. More central to the evening, the young people in attendance wrote a petition to be sent to then Governor Dewey in which they declared, "We the undersigned wish to protest the burning of a cross at an open democratic youth party sponsored by the Progressive Youth of Woodstock. The group feels that some definite action should be taken by authorities in order to prevent future similar demonstrations. We welcome opposition which is presented in the normal channels consistent with American tradition."[32]

Sadly, in 1948, the cross burning was not the first such incident believed to have been directed at the Wallace movement in town. On March 19, an initial cross burning had taken place in a field along Route 212 heading toward Bearsville. Only days later, on March 27, the threat had moved to the center of town, where a hand-forged hammer and sickle was set ablaze. The second blaze, coincidently, occurred as the Woodstock Town

Board was in special session to discuss planned activities for a community playground. The meeting took a different turn when it was interrupted by the appearance of a deputy sheriff sent to investigate the blaze.

Following the burning of the cross in August and the obvious targeting of the Wallace meeting held at the Bird residence, many in the town had had enough. Rising to speak at a Town Board meeting on September 15, part-time resident Isadore Halpern presented a petition signed by more than six hundred Woodstockers demanding an end to such hateful protests. Threatening to gather enough votes in the next election to oust the current Town Board unless action was taken, Halpern, referencing Woodstock's nonenrolled summer residents, specifically stated, "We have enough voters who are not now voting in this community but if they enrolled here and they organized, their voice would be felt."[33] In concluding his lengthy plea to the board—in which he noted that he, and many like him, had come to Woodstock "because we believed we could really live in the most tolerant American community"—Halpern further warned, "Another cross burning must not happen in this town again, because I assure you outside agencies with plenty of funds will come into this town and will get some action."[34]

For his part, in accepting the petition, Supervisor Wilson stated, as he had previously, that he was "opposed to violence in any form in the town" but that the "Town Board had no authority to take action in a matter of this sort." Instead, Wilson noted that the matter had been referred to the Ulster County District Attorney's office for investigation. Asked to comment on the matter by the *Kingston Daily Freeman*, the district attorney's office stated only that an investigation was underway by the State Police, that "he had not received a report yet, and that when he did it probably would be of a confidential nature for a time."[35]

As the public record indicates, however, no action ever resulted in identifying or apprehending the parties responsible for any of these incidents. That those supporting the Wallace campaign and his progressive polices found themselves the target of such threats should, perhaps, not have been unexpected. Over the many years of Woodstock's political history, diversity of opinion had not been a strong suit. The consistent adherence to a monolithic political structure grounded in conservative ideology led, as had been repeatedly demonstrated, to the repeated dismissal and outright disregard of minority views and beliefs.

On election day in 1948, little seemed to have changed despite the efforts of the progressives in town. Of the 1,402 votes cast in Woodstock's two election districts, Wallace tallied only 110 votes. Truman, though the eventual national winner, managed to poll only 193 votes along combined Democratic and liberal lines.[36] And yet, while the Republican stronghold on Woodstock politics remained intact for the time being, a seed had been planted by the efforts of the Wallace progressives. It represented a faint indication that something new might, once again, be on the horizon for a town where challenges continued to confront the status quo.

# Chapter 5

# Here Come the Fifties

Almost three decades prior to the end of World War II, a young aspiring artist by the name of Marion Bullard arrived in Woodstock on a horse-drawn coach after disembarking at the West Hurley train station. As the coach came to a halt in front of Beekman's store near Woodstock's Village Green, her first encounter with her new home was to witness three men exiting Beekman's with their hair cut in various patterns. One had plaids, one polka dots, and the third appeared to have a face neatly shaved into the back of his head. While she would later come to know the three as fellow artists Allen Cochran, Henry Lee McFee, and Walter Goltz, the newly arrived, conventional city girl—after taking in the scene before her—could not have imagined where life in Woodstock was about to take her. Nor could those who went about their business near Beekman's store that day have imagined the change that the coach's singular passenger would eventually bring to their town.

She arrived in Woodstock with the intent of making a go as an artist, but over the years Woodstock would come to know Marion Bullard in many different capacities. There was the remarkable artist who would see her paintings exhibited at the Pennsylvania Academy, the National Association of Women Painters and Sculptors, the National Academy, and the Architectural League. She presented a one-woman show in 1923 at New York's Ferargil Gallery and, in 1928, joined other Woodstock artists at the R. H. Macy Galleries, of which, noted the *New York American*, "The work of Marion Bullard is the chief attraction."[1]

Later, Bullard began to turn her imagination to the writing and illustration of children's books, many with a decidedly Woodstock connection.

In addition to staying close to home, her stories were populated by an imaginative collection of animals. In the *Sad Garden Toad*, the plot unfolds in a garden alongside her beloved Woodstock home. *The Travels of Sammy the Turtle* sees the book's hero traveling to New York City and returning to the nearby Ashokan Reservoir, while the action in *The Hog Goes Downstream* centers on a Woodstock flood in the 1930s.

Beginning in the prewar years, however, Bullard's focus began to shift from her art to a larger community purpose and to efforts that would confront a town that was not used to being challenged. Hired to write a newspaper column about Woodstock for the *Ulster County News*, titled, appropriately enough, "Sparks," Bullard saw the column as a platform through which she would call out the inertia of the status quo. She wrote, "We could do with a Jeremiah to stir us out of our indifference in this town, the Republicans feel so sure of reelection that they don't lift a finger, and the Democrats, knowing they have a small chance of getting in do less. Democracy is hard work and demands of each one something more than a shrug of helplessness."[2]

Figure 22. Marion Bullard, artist, children's author, and Woodstock reformer. *Source:* Historical Society of Woodstock Archives/People Collection.

And "stir" she would. Through both her writing and, later, a radio program over Kingston radio station WKNY, Bullard championed causes during both the pre- and postwar years that would eventually move Woodstock into the 1950s and beyond. From proposing a new elementary school, to advocating a town water system, decrying billboards that marred the landscape, changing the names of the town's main roads, fostering humane care for animals, and opening town board meetings to the public, Marion Bullard was unabashed when it came to voicing her opinion. And, along the way, when hypocrisy was right in front of her, she was not hesitant in calling it out, as she did when she saw Woodstockers claiming support for the First Amendment but threatening "to tar and feather any person daring to bring up the subjects of Socialism and Communism."[3] As her sister would later write in a brief biography of her life for the Historical Society of Woodstock, "No parent of a gifted child could have done more to develop and spread its fame than she did for her beloved Woodstock. Marion's was the brain and the heart that led every forward step the town took. She crusaded, she cajoled and exposed until she won for the town what she thought was necessary for its welfare and growth."[4]

As Woodstockers began to move away from the hardships of the Depression and the war years that followed, several townspeople—with prosperity beginning to rise and newcomers arriving in town—joined Bullard in looking forward and advocating a future that would bring change. An important ingredient of that future arrived on August 15, 1950, when Woodstock employee George Albert Riseley turned a valve and water spouted from the sink in Blanche Hoodes's kitchen. As it did, Hoodes's son, Michael, according to the *Kingston Daily Freeman*, "blasted loudly, if not melodiously, on a horn" in celebration. The Hoodes' home, in the village proper, was the first to benefit from Woodstock's newly constructed municipal water system—one of the improvements Marion Bullard had pushed for.[5]

Fearing disease and even epidemics from polluted wells, Bullard had undertaken a campaign for the construction of a proper water system in Woodstock since the end of the war. Underscoring her tenacity was Bullard's tireless work for four years before the economically conservative Republican Town Board could no longer avoid the reality of Bullard's campaign and voted to construct such a system. In 1949, with local elections on the horizon, Republican candidates, with little credit extended to Bullard, cited the water system project as their own accomplishment.

Touting that construction of a system for the village was underway, while acknowledging that the water drawn from village wells could prove "polluted or unpalatable," campaign literature dispensed by Republican candidates claimed credit for the advancement by offering:

> Your current administration determined that the need for a municipal water system was so acute, that the project could no longer be postponed. Accordingly, it met the problem head-on and a new water supply system is now under construction. When completed, the system will afford an abundant supply of pure and wholesome water to the densely populated village area at a reasonable cost. It will provide, too, an effective protection against the hazard of fire and its installation will result in a substantial reduction in insurance rates. . . . The building of this water system marks another milestone of progress for Woodstock.[6]

On September 14, Florence Peper succinctly summed up what the new water system meant to those in the village who no longer had to rely on drawing water from a well. Recording in her diary at the end of the day, she wrote, "We have water in house and it is nice."[7]

In many respects, 1950 was the year in which Woodstock began the slow turn away from the war years and toward the future. While Woodstock life never ceased to carry on during the war and the immediate years that followed, a review of events held in town in 1950—from the arts to sports—offers a vision of what a small town in the Catskills might be about as a new decade dawned.

As the year began, youth basketball drew the attention of many locals, beginning with the organization of a Woodstock girls basketball club. With the aid of the Masonic Square Club and a dance to raise funds, team uniforms were purchased and, under the leadership and coaching skills of Winnie Davis and Ginny Hastie, the varsity team jumped off to an impressive start by defeating High Falls on two occasions: 33-21 and 43-20.[8] Meanwhile, the boys' varsity team, with Walter Van Wagenen at the helm as coach, began the 1949–1950 season with an impressive 19-4 record behind the play of Don West, Eugene Snyder, Barry Neher, Paul Van Wagenen, Joe Holdridge, Andre Neher, William Kleine, Art Sohmers, Ken Harder, Sam Wilson, William Waterous, and Grant Gavin.[9]

Summer, as summers always seem to do in Woodstock, saw the town come alive with social and cultural activities, including the announcement that Margaret Webster, cofounder of the American Repertory Theater, would present ten weeks of summer theater at the Woodstock Playhouse. Webster, who first came to Woodstock in 1949, was joined by the actress Eva Le Gallienne while also introducing Woodstock to several young actors who were part of her theater school. Woodstockers quickly got to know the young theater students by the 1931 Buick that transported them to the Playhouse each day, a vehicle, according to the *Kingston Daily Freeman*, that "they paid $7.00 for . . . and invested $5.00 for an enormous cow bell which hangs from the side of the car." Among this young group of actors was the son of *South Pacific* star Mary Martin, Larry Hagman.[10]

In June, the Woodstock Riding Club, off Ohayo Mountain Road, attracted more than five hundred spectators to their annual horse show. The show, licensed by the American Horse Show Association, was described by the *Freeman* as one of the "most colorful and eventful ever to be presented in Woodstock."[11]

For many Woodstockers of the day, however, summer would not be summer without Woodstock's annual Library Fair. Held on Thursday, July 27 with Priscella Kennaday as chair, the fair, as has been its way over the years, included multiple tables of items to be perused—and hopefully purchased—by visitors in support of the library. As they had for several years, the many tables set out in 1950 included aprons, artists' supplies, books, china and glass, clothes and accessories, flowers and vegetables, jewelry, linen, and food. (Supervisor Wilson was placed in charge of hot dogs.) Always a major part of library fairs over the years was the particular attention given to children, including the provision of balloons, a carousel, a toy table, pony rides, and, on this occasion, the Herrick Puppets. The Woodstock School Band provided musical entertainment along with the intrepid music makers often found at such events: John Huffine, John Pike, Bill Moore, and, with her accordion, Clementine Nessel.[12]

In August, the Woodstock Playhouse made more news—but not in a way they might have wanted. As Joe McCarthy was starting to grab headlines in Washington, suspicions surrounding purported leftist activity continued to seep into all corners of the land, including Woodstock. As August neared its end, rumors that "some big Communist from New York was coming to read some poems" began to swirl about town. The alleged Communist turned out to be poet Langston Hughes, a primary

Figure 23. The Woodstock Library Fair, long the highlight of a Woodstock summer. *Source:* Historical Society of Woodstock Archives/Woodstock Library Collection.

force behind the Harlem Renaissance and a man who did not shy away from his support of leftist causes. Problem was, he was not coming to Woodstock. In fact, even the rumors were unclear as to why he might even be coming to perform at the Playhouse. Was it to read poems? To present a concert? Or for a performance of his opera *The Barrier*? No one was quite sure, but the rumors persisted, causing what the *Kingston Daily Freeman* called "a storm of controversy" throughout town.[13]

Hoping to avoid what had taken place in Peekskill, New York, where only a year earlier a white mob had attacked attendees at a civil rights concert featuring Paul Robeson, Supervisor Wilson moved quickly. Upon his inquiry at the Playhouse, Wilson learned that a September appearance by Hughes had simply been canceled due to a scheduling conflict with the opening of his opera in New York. Rumors being rumors, however, it was believed by some that the cancellation of Hughes's performance was due to pressure from within the community being brought to bear against him and his political beliefs. That rumor, too, was dispelled by a spokesperson for Margaret Webster as Supervisor Wilson summed up his reaction to the entire controversy by stating, "It seems to me like witch-hunting to start tracking down the authors of plays."[14]

As fall came to Woodstock, some good news greeted several Woodstock artists. A new exhibition—titled *American Painting Today–1950*—was about to open at the Metropolitan Museum of Art in New York. Among the 307 works chosen from over six thousand entries, twenty-nine were the creation of Woodstock artists, many of whom had become quite familiar to their Woodstock neighbors, including Arnold Blanch, John Carroll, Edward Chavez, Marion Greenwood, Wendell Jones, Yasuo Kuniyoshi, Doris Lee, Eugene Ludins, Ethel Magafan, Fletcher Martin, Henry Mattson, Anton Refregier, Andree Ruellan, Eugene Speicher, Lucille Blanch, and Henry Lee McFee.[15]

As 1950 ended, Woodstock unwrapped one last, belated Christmas present. On Friday, December 29, a new elementary school was unveiled for public inspection. As members of the community moved through the building following its dedication by state associate commissioner of education Harry Gibson, Chairman Adolph Heckeroth, and trustees Lorenz Stowell and Clark Neher, the facilities they viewed were far beyond the one-room schoolhouses most had known growing up. The new building included six classrooms, a library, a kindergarten "segregated from the rest of the building," and a combined auditorium and gymnasium.[16]

Throughout its history, Woodstock's educational structure had relied on the existence of one- or two-room schoolhouses located in each of the town hamlets. Evelyn Stone, who taught grades one through eight in the Bearsville school until 1950, recalled, "In that one-room schoolhouse in Bearsville, I was everything. There was no phone. We had two outhouses and we heated with wood in spring and fall and coal in winter. I tried to get in every subject in every class, every day."[17] In the village proper, academic facilities consisted of two small one-story frame buildings and a rented structure a short distance away. As a result, Woodstockers had discussed for some time the need to improve its educational services. Having, in 1942, already purchased property across from the Woodstock Golf Club as a projected site for a school that would incorporate students from kindergarten to eighth grade, the town, following the war, was determined to move forward with the construction of a modernized facility.

In September 1949, the question of constructing a new school and the authorization of a bond set at 225,000 dollars was put to town voters. In a vote that clearly reflected the community's strong desire for a new facility, the bond was overwhelmingly approved, 369-54. Construction on the new school began on April 1, 1950, and in less than a year students were seated in their new classrooms following the 1950 holidays.[18]

Figure 24. Construction begins on new elementary school along Route 375, 1950. *Source:* Historical Society of Woodstock Archives/Woodstock Schools Collection.

Among those who had favored and pushed for a new school in Woodstock, Marion Bullard was, once again, advocating from the front line. It was a crusade she had undertaken six years earlier during the height of World War II, when she wrote, "Five years from now the babies of 1943 will be ready to attend school. We should have ready for them a school built on the foundations their fathers are now even making sacrifices for, freedom and peace. A new school for Woodstock should be a memorial honoring all those in the township who have fought for freedom. This building could stand with a sculptured façade with freedom as its theme, facing Overlook Mountain."[19] While the new school would not be dedicated as the memorial she had envisioned, Bullard could only rejoice when voters approved its construction. Unfortunately, Woodstock's voice of change was not among those who toured the new school following its dedication. Only eleven days earlier, Marion Bullard had been found dead in her home. On Monday evening, December 18, upon noticing Bullard's

Sunday papers were still on her porch, Louise Lindin summoned friends and neighbors Fred Mower, Kathryn Mower, and Charles Rapp to help investigate. Upon entering Bullard's home, they found a shocking scene. In a report later issued by the State Police, Marion Bullard's body was found, fully clothed, partially submerged in 12 inches of bath water. According to police, and as reported in the pages of the *Kingston Daily Freeman*, there was "no evidence of foul play," and it appeared Bullard "had drawn a tub of hot water preparatory to a bath when she fell into the tub after being seized with an attack of some kind."[20]

While she had arrived in Woodstock as a young woman determined to make something of her life as an artist, Bullard found, along the way, that she could apply that same resolve to bettering the town she cared so deeply for. And, while she never held elected office, her "cajoling" and her "scolding" moved Woodstock forward in ways that demonstrated the power of one woman's voice. While art had originally given purpose to her life, Woodstock itself, ultimately, became the focus that drove that life.

As the decade of the fifties began in Woodstock, it became apparent that growth and change was on the horizon. It arrived in different forms, forms that impacted the town's economy as well as Woodstock's relationship with the outside world. But growth was a fickle thing for some. On one hand, it was welcomed as a simple component of life in the second half of the twentieth century. On the other hand, there were those who resisted, pointing to the belief that something was being lost.

One thing most Woodstockers could agree on, however, was they were tired of having to travel to Kingston to conduct a simple basic bank transaction. That inconvenience ended in 1952, when the Bank of Orange and Ulster opened on Rock City Road. A cause for celebration, the opening even received notice in Florence Peper's diary. Writing on May 17, 1952, Peper observed, again succinctly, "Our bank opened today. Everyone got a red rose for calling."[21] In 1955, Elbert Varney arrived as manager of the bank. Mr. Varney, as he was respectfully known, became a mainstay in Woodstock affairs and central to its future growth. In addition to being the key person when it came to seeking a mortgage or loan, Varney served as a member of the Woodstock Rotary Club, treasurer of the Library Fair, and, later, a member of the committee that eventually constructed a new Methodist church in Bearsville.[22]

Beyond a village water system, a new bank, and a new elementary school, however, forces beyond Woodstock's boundaries were engaged in actions that eventually bore directly on the future direction of the town.

On October 26, 1954, Governor Thomas Dewey arrived just outside of Kingston to officially open the newest New York State Thruway interchange. The over four hundred in attendance were greeted by Ken Wilson, who had moved on from Woodstock supervisor to state assemblyman. The governor, while acknowledging that additional construction was still needed, told the crowd that the Thruway "has already brought to the state more jobs, more industries, more construction than any other single enterprise in 100 years." Likening the construction of the Thruway to that of the Erie Canal, Assemblyman Wilson said, "That canal opened up all of New England, New York became the Empire State and hasn't surrendered that supremacy in 130 years." The governor thought Wilson's comparison was a "fantastic parallel."[23]

With the completion of the Thruway and the Tappan Zee Bridge, Woodstock now lay within two hours of New York City and the visitors it could send north. Tourists and second homeowners, although they had to forego stopping at the popular Red Apple Rest diner on Route 17 along the way, would not miss the lengthy car ride over the two-lane roads they had to endure prior to the construction of the Thruway.

Almost simultaneously, IBM announced a major investment in a new plant outside of Kingston in the town of Ulster, bringing further growth to the region. In the same year that the governor was touting the benefits to upstate of the construction of the Thruway, IBM began transforming what was once farmland into a new facility that, in 1955, saw the transfer of its typewriter assembly operation to the Kingston site, bringing with it nineteen hundred employees that would need housing and quality schools for their children. By the end of the decade, more than five thousand employees were onsite at the Kingston operation as the company forged ahead into the brave new world of computers.[24]

Already anticipating the need for additional housing, it was announced early in 1954 that a large tract of land had been purchased in the Bearsville area by developers. Locally known as the Bearsville Flats, initial plans for construction called for thirty-six, four- and five-room homes, requiring a down payment as low as five hundred dollars and a monthly mortgage of $39.50.[25] In addition to the anticipated development in Bearsville, developers had their sights on undeveloped tracts in Zena.

IBM, however, was not the first manufacturing operation to impact Woodstock. Following World War II, J. Constant van Rijn, an engineer and refugee from Holland, had chosen Woodstock as his new home. Recognizing the need for small, reliable fans that would be integral to the burgeoning electronic and defense industries, van Rijn established the Rotron Manufacturing Company in Woodstock, providing a major source of employment for the area.

In 1959, van Rijn hired a young engineer named John Ebbs. While van Rijn's new employee went on to leave his own mark on Woodstock, heading at one time the Woodstock Library and the Maverick Concerts, Ebbs, upon his retirement, wrote fondly of his memories of van Rijn and his early Rotron experiences. Noting the conditions at the time of his arrival, Ebbs later recalled, "Engineering was all performed in a red barn, and my office was a converted chicken coop attached to the front end of the barn with a beautiful country surrounding." With hopes of improvement, he continued, "I knew of Jack's [van Rijn] frugality at that point and hoped that business would allow an improvement in facilities." Ebbs got his wish when, in 1961, the construction of a new engineering building housing the company's labs and offices was completed.[26] Ebbs also credited van Rijn's "aesthetic sense" and his understanding of the community he called home, noting, "The new building contained a number of art works created by Woodstock artists commissioned by Jack and, appearing in the lobby, was a metal casting of a Buddha statue. A quote

Figure 25. J. Constant van Rijn, community leader and founder of the Rotron Manufacturing Company. *Source:* Historical Society of Woodstock Archives/ People Collection.

from Krishnamurti appeared in a prominent location as follows, 'Peace is a state of mind. It is the absence of all desire to be secure.' "[27]

While van Rijn, according to Ebbs, "reveled in the entrepreneurial game," he was, for the period, the rare boss who was sensitive to the needs and plight of his employees, several of whom were integral to the town's art community. He encouraged employees to take time to engage in "community activities," and early on, according to Ebbs, he "introduced profit sharing" for employees and for his production group "would personally hand out $10 bills every month they had a record high shipping month."[28]

Not only did Rotron become a central part of the local economy and the Woodstock community, but van Rijn himself went on to follow his own advice and engage in critical activities surrounding his adopted community, often taking a leadership role. A founder of the town's tree trust, van Rijn was an early member of the Woodstock Association for Conservation and Development, an alliance that ultimately led to the town's first zoning laws and the establishment of the Woodstock Planning Board.[29] Ebbs concluded that van Rijn was "a man of great entrepreneurial skill who used the proceeds of his financial success generously to the benefit of his employees and the Woodstock community, not to mention the many Woodstockers whose immigration from Europe he sponsored. His personal efforts toward improving the quality of life in Woodstock will not, I'm sure, be forgotten."[30]

With the promise of easier access from New York City, the attraction and availability of employment on a professional level, affordable family homes, and a new elementary school, growth was indeed a part of both Woodstock's present and future. And as an increasing number of tourists and new homeowners undertook that migration north, new shops would be in place to welcome them. Woodstock was becoming a busy town and differences were surfacing on what that would mean for the community.

In 1953, the newly published *Woodstock Townsman* debated the question of growth, suggesting, on one hand, that while it was not their intent "to take a stand one way or the other on the issue," the paper believed, "that those industries already established here have proved a boon to the town; they have taken up the employment slack caused by the short summer seasons hereabouts. They have swelled purchasing power and made the merchants happy."[31] In addition to its opinion on local "industries" as Woodstock headed into the summer of 1954, the *Townsman* believed that "it's time for the voice of the tourist to be heard in our town." Citing new businesses that were opening—including a new motel and steak house operated by Joe Holdridge off Orchard Lane, the Town House restaurant and bar directly across Route 212 from the Woodstock golf course, and the Robert John Shop operated by Warren Hutty, featuring handmade furniture and leather goods—the paper also noted that the Irvington Inn (later the Woodstock Pub) would soon "roll down the awning and start serving meals on its outdoor terrace—the coolest of all cool places when the humidity hits in July and August."[32]

One Woodstocker who took exception to the *Townsman*'s pronouncements and railed against the influx of newcomers, tourists, and the businesses that catered to them was Holley Cantine. Cantine was one of Woodstock's more interesting citizens, and if some in Woodstock were looking for someone who professed leftist leanings, Holley Cantine was there in plain sight. Cantine, along with Dachine Rainer in the late forties and early fifties, was the editor of *Retort*, an anarchist quarterly. The pair also edited *Prison Etiquette: The Convict's Compendium of Useful Information*, which featured accounts by those who were imprisoned during World War II for declaring themselves conscientious objectors. However, it was Cantine's publishing efforts in Woodstock that, in the 1950s, earned his place in town lore. He called his new newspaper *The Wasp*—so named because of its purported sting. On July 10, 1954, *The Wasp* featured the headline "Tourists Go Home." Troubled by the changes he was seeing and disconsolate over the fading spirit of small-town life and the art colony within, Cantine wrote:

> Since *The Wasp* last appeared, there have been a great many changes in Woodstock, most of them for the worse. The process of conversion from a country town whose principal occupation was farming, and which also happened to be the site of one of the major art colonies in the country, into a semi-industrial, highly commercialized tourist resort seems to be moving at an accelerated tempo. In the past two years, more of the few remaining spaces between buildings in the village have been filled, and the last cow-pasture fronting the road between Woodstock and Bearsville has yielded progress in the form of a curious pink hardware store. There are more motels, and several new shops. An increasing proportion of the population—including a number of artists or former artists—is made up of industrial workers in the growing local factories, or in out-of-town plants. A depressing looking low-cost housing development is under construction on the Bearsville Flats.[33]

Figure 26. Masthead of Holley Cantine's *The Wasp*, July 10, 1954. *Source:* Historical Society of Woodstock Archives/Holley Cantine Collection.

Asserting that "the [art] colony, at 52, is helplessly senile, and nothing can be done to rejuvenate it," Cantine called for a "group consciousness among the artists, [and] a strong sense of unity of creative purpose regardless of school or medium of expression, that they could feel free, once again, to laugh, publicly and unrestrainedly, at the pitiful spectacle of the commercial vision of Woodstock's destiny."[34]

Needless to say, several in the community, especially the town's business leaders, were none too pleased with Cantine's assertions. And, when he continued his attack on the unfavorable changes he viewed in Woodstock with the July 31 headline "Tourists! Are You Still Here?" *The Wasp* was not welcomed for sale at several establishments. Responding to the efforts of those local businesses seeking to dismiss his complaints, Cantine charged, "The Woodstock Businessmen's Association, for the past several years, has been carrying on an extensive campaign to attract more tourists to town, and they have succeeded in convincing a number of local residents who should know better that this campaign is for the benefit of the entire town."[35]

While professing no "personal dislike for tourists" (whom he called "trudgers" because they tended to block and slow down movement along town sidewalks), Cantine, nonetheless, continued to forward the belief that "there are too many of them, and we believe most Woodstockers feel the same way. The handful of merchants, real estate brokers et al, who want the tourists to increase and multiply don't speak for the town, but only for themselves. Their alleged friendliness toward tourists has a ring resembling that of a cash register."[36] In his arguments against the commercialism of a small town, Cantine's rhetoric has remained a stream of debate over the years. The balance of commercial growth and its benefits to small-town life as opposed to the degree of change those benefits bring to that life—including congestion, higher rents and prices, and general inconvenience—has been an argument heard ever since *The Wasp* was first published. It has been a debate that has carried well into the twenty-first century and one that Cantine would most assuredly recognize—even today.

Beyond Cantine's protestations and the influx of "trudging" tourists, several newly arrived families had made their way to Woodstock following war's end to embark on new beginnings. Many, in their own way, left their mark—civically, culturally, and sometimes, quietly—on their adopted home.

No doubt, neighbors along Tinker Street, as they peered out from their windows on Thanksgiving Day 1951, must have wondered why a Voice of America truck was parked at the home of Joe Holdridge. Inside the Holdridge home, the announcer Sonny Fox had arrived in search "of the typical American family in a typical American town" and, according to the *Kingston Daily Freeman*, to "present to the world an account of what might occur in an American home on this, one of the country's most American holidays."[37]

Joe Holdridge had arrived in Woodstock shortly after World War II and in his interview with Fox was not shy in singing the praises of his adopted hometown. Pictured in the *Freeman* with his wife Nora, son Joe Holdridge Jr., and daughter-in-law of fourteen months Virginia, the senior Holdridge said that the Woodstock he had come to know "is the nicest town I have ever been in. In Woodstock you can find a mind to match your own, whether you are a writer, artist, deep thinker, or anything else. To me Woodstock has been the most wonderful place in the world."[38] Offering a tour of her kitchen to the reporter as Thanksgiving dinner was being prepared, Nora Holdridge related "that she does all her own housework but still finds time for outside activities." She spoke of her work with Home Bureau projects, the church, and the Eastern Star. Meanwhile, her daughter-in-law remarked, "I always think how thankful we are to be together, to enjoy the meal together and pray that things will be the same next year."[39]

Underscoring his family's sentiments—while also noting his preference for bowling and fishing—Joe Sr. added similar thoughts when describing his own, simple desire to lead "a good and decent life" and to "support myself and my family." "I don't want to get rich," he said, "and I don't want to be poor. I only ask the ability to work."[40] Joe and his son did just that, operating a painting business as well as establishing the motel just off Tinker Street that Holley Cantine wasn't too happy about. More importantly, as an integral part of Woodstock's longest-standing tradition, Joe Jr. served as Woodstock's Christmas Eve Santa Claus for several years, appearing, often by surprise, to hand out stockings to a long line of wide-eyed Woodstock children.

At about the same time the Holdridges were settling into their Woodstock home, yet another family was undertaking a similar journey of their own. Theirs, however, was a story that began across the Atlantic and one that took years before the full scope of their remarkable efforts during World War II were revealed to their Woodstock neighbors. It was a story that spoke to defiance against the dark shadow Nazi Germany had cast over Europe.

Married in 1942, Johtje and Aart Vos lived as a family—Johtje had two children from a previous marriage—in the Dutch town of Laren, southeast of Amsterdam. By this time in the war, the Netherlands had already fallen under the control of the Nazis, who brought with them their determination to eliminate the Jewish population. One evening a Jewish couple appeared at the Vos's door asking to be hidden for the night as they were fleeing from the Germans. Following that fateful evening, Johtje and Aart Vos provided refuge to thirty-six more Jews over the course of the war, with, according to the *New York Times*, "as many as 14 hiding in their home at any one time."[41] For the most part, those being sheltered would not leave the house unless the Vos telephone "rang twice, then twice again." With that signal, Mr. Vos "would lead them to a shed attached to the back of the house, down through a camouflaged trapdoor under a coal bin and into a 150-foot tunnel through which they would crawl before slipping into the woods." When the Gestapo arrived, Johtje later explained, "I would take questions from them and lie and lie and lie."[42]

During Johtje's first marriage to the artist Heinrich Molenaar, in the years prior to war, the couple "were part of a Bohemian community in Paris." There, Johtje "would introduce future Woodstockers Louise and Brock Brokenshaw." Following the war, the Brokenshaws immigrated to the United States, where they took up residence in Woodstock to pursue their artistic careers. With their decision to settle in Woodstock, the Brokenshaws had, unknowingly, set in motion the eventual connection between the Vos family and their future home, a home very distant from the memories of the previous years.[43]

Arriving in the United States, the Vos family—which now, in addition to their two daughters, included two sons born after the war, a son of Aart's from a previous marriage and an adopted nephew—made their way to Woodstock in 1952. Originally, they settled at Byrdcliffe, eventually taking over a French Camp for children run by Fernande Angiel. There for a period they undertook operating an international summer camp until they moved to what became known as Peter Pan Farm, an eighty-acre property on the border between Woodstock and Saugerties. (Today it is the site of the Woodstock Day School.) Once settled, the Vos family did what they knew how to do as they began creating a home for children from families under stress. As Sarah Mecklem later wrote, "As one of the children welcomed to the Vos family at 8 years old, I have memories of 18 or more people around the dining table and marvelous storytelling by Mr. and Mrs. Vos, surrounded by an endless parade of animals, indoors and out."[44]

It was not until the 1980s that the Voses began to speak publicly of their experiences during the war. And while numerous awards and, indeed, recognition finally came their way—including, in 1983, a medal in commemoration of the fortieth anniversary of the Warsaw Ghetto Uprising, the Act of Courage Award in 1989 from the Rockland Center for Holocaust Studies, the Courage to Care Award presented by the Anti-Defamation League/Jewish Foundation for Christian Rescuers, and, in 1992, recognition as "righteous people," by the Rabbi Meed at the Israeli Consulate in New York—the Voses insisted that they were not heroes but simple people just doing what people needed to do.[45]

Johtje continued her good work in the community as one of the initial founders of Woodstock's Meals on Wheels program while also working in support of migrant workers. Aart died in 1990, and Johtje in her own words brought their story to the written page with the publishing of *The End of the Tunnel* in 1999. And as with many things in a small community, the property that hosted the home they created for children and more than a few animals, in time, came to host a new generation of Woodstockers in a way no one, at least during the Eisenhower years, could have imagined. Something called a Sound-Out was on the distant horizon.

Chapter 6

# Small-Town Life

As Woodstock entered the latter part of the 1950s, signs of change and transition continued to make an appearance. In the summer of 1955, the town learned of the death of Jane Byrd Whitehead. Recalled by historian Alf Evers as a "striking" woman who was very much "interested in the arts" and a "very important part of Byrdcliffe," Jane Byrd Whitehead was instrumental in working alongside her husband Ralph Whitehead in establishing the art colony in Woodstock and, at the outset of the twentieth century, altering the future course of Woodstock.[1] And yet, as the memory of those early days along the base of Overlook Mountain began to fade, new forces and institutions—many involving artists who followed in Byrdcliffe's wake and took up residence in Woodstock—were already emerging within the community.

In 1955, St. Gregory's Episcopal Church broke ground on a new facility along Route 212. For some time, a growing congregation had been meeting in a converted corncrib on property owned by Frederica Milne. The unique design of the proposed church brought a new look to Woodstock architecture and, no doubt, to Woodstock's established vision of what a house of worship should look like. In announcing plans for the new church a year earlier, its designer, Willian Van Benschoten, remarked on the important connection that had formed between the Church and Woodstock's art community. He noted that "St. Gregory was the patron Saint of the arts" and that, following a meeting at the home of Doris Lee, a number of artists "have offered to contribute their time and talents to enhance the church"—a list that included, beyond Lee, Arnold Blanch, Edward Chavez, Konrad Cramer, and John Pike.[2]

Interestingly, as Alf Evers wrote regarding past relationships between artists and the more traditional houses of worship in Woodstock, "The local people found the artists' ways irritating. They were especially annoyed at the artists' refusal to join their churches. When Roman Catholics built St. Joan of Arc's Chapel on Rock City Road in 1923 and some art-colony people aided in organizing a Christian Science Church, members of the town's earlier churches were not warm in their welcome."[3] The "town's earlier churches" included the Reformed Church, the Methodist Church, and the Christ Lutheran Church, each, in the 1950s, located within the village proper. Long before anyone with an easel and a paintbrush arrived in town, all three Churches were at the core of Woodstock's religious community throughout much of the town's history.

The current Woodstock Reformed Church on the Village Green has its origins with the arrival of the early Dutch settlers in the late 1700s and early 1800s. After petitioning for an organized Church in 1805, parishioners purchased the property now known as the Village Green and constructed their first church on the site. In 1844, that church was dismantled, and the current church rose at its present location. Unknown to many Woodstockers, even today the Church still maintains ownership over most of the Village Green and oversees its use in conjunction with the town of Woodstock.

The Christ Lutheran Church on Mill Hill Road was founded in 1806 by Palatine descendants. While the current church was constructed in 1894, the congregation's first home was known as the "church on the rocks" and was located along Route 212 near Plochmann Lane. The structure later became the home of the artist Carl Lindin. Many of its founders were among the families that formed the foundation of early Woodstock, including the Reisleys, Bonesteels, Shultis, and Rick families.[4] In 1956, the same year St. Gregory's Episcopal Church held its first service in their new home on Route 212, the Christ Lutheran Church celebrated its 150th anniversary with the Reverend Olney Cook, the Church's twenty-second minister, presiding.[5]

And the Methodists? By the mid-twentieth century, according to a 1941 pamphlet offering an overview of Woodstock, the Methodists seemed to be everywhere, with congregations in Woodstock village, Wittenberg, Shady, and Willow. (Though a break in the Willow congregation resulted in the formation of the Willow Wesleyan Church, which stands today along Route 212.) Originally established in the 1830s, the Woodstock and

Wittenberg Methodist congregations eventually merged while the Shady Methodist church, built in 1880, continues as of this writing. Through the 1950s and into the 1960s, the Woodstock Methodist Church held forth on Tinker Street in the building that later became home to the Tinker Street Cinema. In 1967, with the number of parishioners growing, the Church left its Tinker Street home and undertook a major construction project along Route 212 in Bearsville, where it operates today as the Overlook Methodist Church.

Early on, arriving artists seeking something beyond the offerings of Woodstock's three primary congregations, found welcome in other, newly formed religious establishments. Founded in 1909, the Christian Science Church first held its services in family homes and then on Mill Hill Road. The congregation eventually moved to its current location on Tinker Street, originally constructed to house the Art Students League. In addition to several older Woodstock families such as the Cashdollars, several of its earlier members included "artists attracted to both the creative atmosphere of Woodstock and the radical spiritual concepts of Christian Science."[6] At the fore of those artists who became members of the Christian Science congregation was the lithographer Clarence Bolton. As Bolton once wrote regarding the connection he felt between art and Christian Science practices, "The student of Christian Science who is also an artist has a sacred task to perform. His work, if inspired by divine Principle, will be of a high standard and will take its proper place in the world, thus presenting a measure of true expression and harmony to mankind."[7]

In addition to his prominence as a lithographer, Bolton was etched into the pages of Woodstock history in multiple ways. Arriving in Woodstock as the proverbial struggling artist, he first took up quarters over "Wash" Elwyn's garage, paying four dollars a month in rent. In 1922, following his marriage to Mary (Louise) Cashdollar, the couple opened an ice cream parlor. Their venture was known as the Nook and was housed in a former tannery barn that later became home to one of Woodstock's more legendary establishments, the Cafe Espresso. In later years, Clarence published *The Clatter*, offering news and thoughts about life in Woodstock, while Louise partnered with Winnie Haile in operating the Red Barn antique shop. Louise also claimed another credit in Woodstock history when she became the first woman taxi driver in town.[8]

The Roman Catholic Church arrived in Woodstock in the 1920s, although its origins, for several Woodstock families, dated back to the

Figure 27. Clarence and Louise Bolton outside the Nook, forerunner of the Cafe Espresso. *Source:* Historical Society of Woodstock Archives/Jean White Collection.

post-Civil War era. As bluestone quarrying became an increasingly important industry in the area over the course of the nineteenth century, Irish immigrants, possessing the necessary stonecutting skills, began to settle in and around Woodstock and West Hurley. To meet their religious needs—and the needs of those in surrounding communities—St. John's Catholic Church was established in the area of Bristol Hill and Stony Hollow in 1869. By 1890, it is estimated that St. John's was home to more than seven hundred parishioners, drawing from Woodstock, West Shokan, and West Hurley. In the early 1900s, with the establishment of the art colony and the increasing number of visitors to Woodstock's mountain and boardinghouses, further demand was placed on the Church to serve worshippers in Woodstock proper. To meet that demand, services were initially held during the summer months in the Woodstock Hotel on the corner of Mill Hill and Rock City roads.[9]

By 1921, recognizing the need for a more permanent presence in Woodstock, St. John's, under the pastorate of Father Peter Spellman, began construction of the St. Joan of Arc Chapel on Rock City Road. The first mass at St. Joan's was held the following year on June 25, 1922, with seventy-five worshippers in attendance. During its early years, the simply constructed church was used only during the summer. As membership grew, however, the building was enlarged, and, with heat and electricity added, St Joan's opened its doors year-round to parishioners. St. Joan's continued to serve as a mission of St. John's until 1975, when the parish made the choice to centralize under one roof and construct a new church off Route 375 in West Hurley. Shortly thereafter, the Woodstock Town Board purchased the vacated church and, following renovations, opened the building as a community center named in honor of Mescal Hornbeck, who, as a member of the Town Board was instrumental in urging the building's purchase and who worked tirelessly on behalf of numerous causes, including the Ulster County Office of the Aging, health care, and the environment.

While the midpoint of the 1950s saw the passing of Jane Whitehead and reflection on all she and her husband had brought to Woodstock, she is also remembered in a religious context as the person who brought Father Francis to town, the founder of the liberal Church on the Mount. William Henry Francis Brothers was born in England in 1885 and, at age twelve, arrived with his family in the United States. As a child, he counted among his friends Clarence Darrow and Carl Sandburg. A part of the Old Catholic Church movement, which separated itself from the Roman Catholic Church over such policies as papal infallibility, he was consecrated a bishop in 1916 and as archbishop in 1917. Father Francis was a man intent on following his convictions. He was, for example, an early advocate of the right to vote for women, he campaigned with Margaret Sanger in support of birth control, and, at one time, he served as a theological adviser to his childhood friend Clarence Darrow in support of the theory of evolution.[10]

Whitehead had met Father Francis while she was on vacation in California in the 1930s and, in 1936, with concern over the spiritual direction of her son Peter, urged Francis to come to Woodstock and serve as her son's spiritual guide. She also expressed the desire for him to take up ministry in the former chapel on Overlook that once served visitors to the Meads and Overlook Mountain houses. When the Episcopal diocese, owners of the property at the time, objected to a prominent member of the Old Catholic Church practicing on Episcopal property, Jane White-head purchased the property and Father Francis set about rebuilding the structure that became known to Woodstockers during this era as the Church on the Mount.[11]

Few could have foreseen, upon the arrival of Father Francis in Wood-stock, the lasting impact he would have on the town—both in connection to the arts and on those who arrived years later as the 1960s descended upon Woodstock. Known in terms of both praise and derision as the "hippie priest," it was Father Francis—despite Woodstock's unwelcoming attitude toward the newly arrived young people in the sixties—who opened the doors of his small chapel on the mountain to those who, much like himself, questioned the powers that be and their establishment lifestyles.

While it is more difficult to trace the early years of the current Jewish congregation in Woodstock, suffice it to say that those of the Jewish faith have long been a part of the Woodstock community. Much of the difficulty in tracing that history lies in the anti-Semitism directed at Jews over the course of Woodstock's earlier history, from prohibitions imposed by some of the local boardinghouses to the appearance of the Ku Klux Klan and burning crosses in town. Still, as Alf Evers wrote on

Figure 28. The Church on the Mount in earlier years. Now the Church of Holy Transfiguration, the structure was placed on the National Register of Historic Places in 2005. *Source:* Author's collection.

the importance of Jewish artists to the early art colony, "Jews arrived in ever increasing numbers . . . many were gifted people with interests and skills in the arts. They merged into the colony, kept its traditions alive and gave it strength without which it might have foundered."[12]

While several of the local religious institutions provided programs for young people in their congregations, in the 1950s the town of Woodstock also began to turn its attention to recreational activities beyond basketball for the younger members of the community. While Girl Scouts, Boy Scouts, Cub Scouts, and Brownie troops were in full swing, the town's Recreation Committee, following its formation in 1948, began focusing on improving and upgrading the recreation field on Rock City Road. In 1951, Supervisor Wilson announced the construction of a swimming and wading pool at the field, and, through additional community donations and matching grants from New York State, the town began to undertake further improvements at the field. Bathrooms were constructed, buildings enlarged, and the baseball field improved just in time for discussions to begin over the inauguration of Little League Baseball in Woodstock.

Baseball in Woodstock has had a considerable history over the years as Woodstock fielded adult teams both before and after World War II. "Washy" Wilber was one of those young Woodstock men who loved baseball—so much so that his mother once suggested he might be better off moving his bed down to the recreation field because he spent most of his time there. Wilber played infield and pitched for the Woodstock team over several years and, with eyes smiling during an interview conducted by the Historical Society of Woodstock, recalled that a few of his pitches ended up clearing the fence in right field, a fence that separated the field from the town cemetery.[13] Wilber was but one of the many young men who wore the Woodstock uniform, men with longstanding Woodstock names like Harder and Peper, Wilber and Lapo, Van Wagenen and Longyear—and more. Some also wore another uniform, when World War II interrupted those summer days when Woodstock teams ventured forth, usually on a Sunday afternoon, to take on teams from nearby towns.

Woodstock artists, too, were not without their love for America's pastime. In fact, noted artist George Bellows at one time might have forsaken a future that included a well-worked canvas for that of a Louisville Slugger. Born in Columbus, Ohio, Bellows excelled at baseball during his high school years and received an offer to play semipro baseball from a team in Indianapolis—an offer he declined. But, like many during the golden years of baseball, love of the game did not leave him. Throughout his time in Woodstock, Bellows—whose Woodstock home is now listed as a designated state and national historic site—could often be found at the recreation field observing the Woodstock team in action or joining in when the opportunity presented itself. According to artist and neighbor Charles Rosen, "Bellows was greatly loved by all the boys on the baseball team on which he played and was also an important factor in organizing. This friendship was on a man-to-man basis and in no sense did the fact that he was a great artist affect the relationship. As far as they were concerned, he was just a grand guy and they liked him—while his feeling for all of them was just as warm and generous."[14]

Although many years of baseball had been played on the field along Rock City Road, a Woodstock tragedy in 1956 altered the name of the field for future generations. Andy Lee was the type of teenager who would make any town proud. An excellent student, Lee also participated in a wide variety of extracurricular activities while attending Kingston High School (as Woodstock high school students did during the 1950s). He served as vice president of the student council, a member of the Key Club, and treasurer of the junior class. Lee also excelled at football, joining Kingston's varsity team as a sophomore. Well loved by his fellow students, Andy Lee was elected as both the best athlete and the most popular boy in his junior class.[15] Lee's young life came to an end in January 1956 as the result of a hunting accident. While hunting with two friends, one member of the group slipped as he was about to fire upon partridges that had just taken flight. Lee was struck in the chest by a round from a twelve-gauge shotgun and died almost instantly. Five days later, responding to a petition submitted by many of Woodstock's young people, the Woodstock Town Board voted to rename the recreation field in Lee's honor.[16]

In many ways, as 1957 turned to spring, it seemed only fitting that many of Woodstock's youth took to the field named after Andy Lee for the inaugural season of the Woodstock Little League. The League, with Maurice Hamilton elected as its first president, fielded four teams that first season: Yankees, Dodgers, Giants, and Indians. By season's end the Indians were atop the standings, and at its first annual dinner, held at the Odd Fellows Hall in Bearsville, a "beautiful gold trophy" was presented to Allen Carlson, the Indians' manager.[17]

While 1957 brought baseball to summer evenings in Woodstock, an active cultural scene was also flourishing. Through July, the Woodstock Playhouse offered George Axelrod's farce "Will Success Spoil Rock Hunter," to be followed by Graham Greene's "The Potting Shed." The work of numerous Woodstock craftsmen was on display at the Woodstock Guild of Craftsmen, while next door the Woodstock Artists Association offered a juried show of paintings and sculptures.[18]

As Woodstock moved through the year, however, a storm began to brew over the question of whether Woodstock's multiple school districts should consolidate by joining either the Onteora or Kingston districts. With the town still divided into distinct districts based on which hamlet one resided in—most of Woodstock village, for example, was within Woodstock District 2, Zena in District 7, Bearsville in District 3—debate over which direction to take had been building over the years. That debate proved to be, at times, a bitter fight when it came, specifically, over the future of Woodstock District 2. While the Bearsville District had opted as early as 1954 to align itself with Onteora, a final decision on the future of the Woodstock District continued over multiple turns of the calendar.

Only three years after the new elementary school had opened, discussions were underway on a proposal to add three additional classrooms to accommodate both seventh and eighth graders in Woodstock. At the same time, there were those within the community voicing an alternative plan that would consolidate Woodstock with the Onteora School District. Paralleling those voices, however, was growing support favoring a different option: consolidation with the Kingston District. While the arguments underpinning each choice bounced back and forth over the months that followed, it was finally decided to go to the voters and put the choice between Kingston and Onteora on the ballot.

On April 13, 1957, more than eight hundred votes were cast to decide the question. At evening's end, it appeared that the Onteora forces had won, 417-391. But, at least in this instance, appearance wasn't necessarily reality, as the issue of what constituted a legal voter in Woodstock cast a shadow over the election's outcome. As noted by the *Kingston Daily Freeman* in their coverage of the questions raised by the vote, "Woodstock is an art colony where many prominent persons maintain summer homes. Many of these also live in New York City and vote in political elections there."[19]

Opponents of the Onteora move were quick to pounce on the possibility that several of the votes cast in the April referendum were, in fact, cast by voters not qualified to vote in Woodstock. As a result, sixty-nine questionable ballots were submitted for review to the state. In his review of the ballots submitted, the state education commissioner James Allen Jr. ruled that "upon the basis of the record before me it is clear that at least 26 persons [who] cast their ballots were not, in fact, qualified voters of the

Figure 29. Counting the votes as Woodstockers decide between joining the Onteora or Kingston school district, 1957. *Source:* Historical Society of Woodstock Archives/Schools Collection.

common school district," and as a result he had no alternative but to set the vote aside. Allen added that he did so "without prejudice, however, to the filing of further petitions seeking to call upon another special meeting to vote upon such questions."[20] By disqualifying only twenty-six of the sixty-nine ballots questioned, Allen's decision rendered the April vote a tie. Only in Woodstock. With new life on one side of the question and frustration on the other, a new election was called for August.

As the town moved toward a second vote that summer, two competing full-page advertisements representing the schism between those who favored consolidation with Kingston and those favoring Onteora appeared in the pages of the *Kingston Daily Freeman*. On August 16, the Committee of 500 for Centralization with Onteora, under the heading "Machine versus Child," offered, in part, the following in support of the Onteora move:

Because in 1957 we found ourselves saddled with a big debt and with hopelessly inadequate school facilities for our children and nothing definite was being done to correct that situation, this Committee of parents and friends was formed. We investigated the two solutions—consolidation with Kingston or centralization with Onteora. We found both schools and their teaching staffs to be exceptionally good but, for a variety of reasons—chiefly the smaller size of Onteora with a resulting emphasis on individual attention to its students, its modern plant and equipment and its pleasant county setting—our findings heavily favored Onteora. Also, our neighboring communities like Bearsville, where our children had many friends, had already chosen Onteora. We saw no good reason why we should be the only one left out of a system that satisfied all our neighbors and their children. Moreover, under centralization we would retain a voice in our school affairs and in the use of our present plant, whereas consolidation with Kingston would divest us of ALL control. A final consideration was the substantially lower tax rate estimated by Onteora in comparison with the Kingston estimate.[21]

The full advertisement was signed by David Carlson, Committee Chair.

Two days later in an equally lengthy advertisement, the group named Mothers against Onteora offered their counter to the assertions made by the Committee of 500:

Mr. Carlson describes what he and his committee did to investigate the comparative merits of Kingston versus Onteora. They found, according to Carlson, that "both schools and their teaching staff" were good but favored Onteora "chiefly" because of the "smaller size" and "pleasant country setting." We have no quarrel with Mr. Carlson, or any of his friends, in the reasons they assign for the school of their choice. Everyone has a right to his opinion.

But for us, the primary consideration is which is the best school. On that score no one can gainsay the superiority of Kingston. We would not select a school merely because of its pleasant country setting unless the alternative school was located in such an undesirable area that it would be harmful to our children. To us, Kingston is just as pleasant a place for a High School as Boiceville. Our High School pupils have done very well there.

As for size, we concede that Onteora is a much smaller, though overcrowded school. But its "smallness" is what is responsible for its educational deficiencies. A school as small cannot offer a diversified and well-rounded educational program. True, they do the best they can with their limited teaching staff and facilities, but in the last analysis, why should we be content with an inferior High School educational program for our children? Unfortunately, Onteora graduates have a difficult time when they get to college.[22]

As the polls closed on August 20, results showed that, once again, voters had favored association with Onteora. Still, the vote was close enough—415 in favor, 359 opposed—to result in yet another challenge by the opposition on the basis, again, that unqualified voters had cast ballots. So it was that Woodstock waited for yet another ruling from the state commissioner. It was a long wait.[23]

Meanwhile, the Zena District was determined to move forward on its own. Joining the nearby town of Hurley and their neighbors in Lake Katrine, Zena voters, in March 1958, diverged from the apparent sentiments of their fellow townspeople and voted to cast their lot with Kingston.

For Woodstock District 2, it was not until May 2, 1958, that Commissioner Allen finally held a hearing on the appeal made by opponents—almost eight months following its submission. Two months later, the acting commissioner of education Ewald Nyquist dashed the hopes of those in opposition to the Onteora merger by sustaining the vote for consolidation held the previous August. And yet, the saga did not end—even though by this point Woodstockers were receiving tax bills from both the Woodstock District and the Onteora District.

Following Ewald Nyquist's decision, an appeal by the Kingston group now moved to the courts. That effort also failed in October 1958 when Supreme Court Justice William Deckelman refused to vacate the state's decision, writing that the court "should not substitute its judgement for that of the acting commissioner, acting under statutory direction."[24]

While threats of pursuing further legal action were announced in the press, effectively the battle was finally over. It had been a bitter fight, a fight that, in some cases, left friends and neighbors no longer speaking to each other. In many respects, lost in the fog of battle, the confusion over two elections, and decisions handed down from Albany and the courts were the students themselves. Due to the lateness of the decision in 1958, with the school year already underway, Woodstock students did not begin the academic year at Onteora until September 1959.

Change was also on the horizon as local elections approached in 1957 and Tobie Geertsema announced her candidacy for the Woodstock Town Board. Pledging to "bring new life into town government," not only had Geertsema become a powerful woman's voice in Woodstock affairs—she was a strong advocate of the Woodstock school district joining Onteora—she was also the rare Woodstocker who possessed the ability to cross party lines. A registered Republican who also managed to obtain the endorsement of the local Democratic Party, Geertsema ultimately ran on her own line as an Independent. And, echoing a cause once brought to the fore by Marion Bullard, she pledged regarding Town Board meetings to "open the doors" to town government so that the Town Board no longer "goes through its cut and dried motions with almost no public knowledge or participation."[25]

On November 5, 1957, Geertsema won her race by more than one hundred votes, becoming the first woman ever elected to the Woodstock Town Board. In the years that followed, she became a strong influence in community affairs not only as a councilperson but also later as a journalist for the *Ulster County Townsman* and the *Kingston Daily Freeman*. Much like Bullard, she took her voice to radio, where she hosted with local radio personality Bill Skilling *Coffee Break* on Kingston's WGHQ.[26]

While the decade of the 1950s is often referred to as the quiet decade, enough had transpired in Woodstock over recent years to leave several Woodstockers content with simply getting back to what small towns were supposed to do. Important challenges were on the horizon, and with the battle over school consolidation behind them, the townspeople seemed to readily accept a return to some degree of normalcy while also addressing changes necessitated by a growing population.

Efforts were fully underway in the 1950s to expand Woodstock's volunteer fire department. While the town had been protected for almost fifty years by one company, expansion of the department had already begun in 1951, when Wittenberg Company No. 2 was formed and incorporated in 1954. With Everett Cashdollar serving as president—and the one truck that was integral to their service housed in the garage of Gus Shultis—construction began on the Wittenberg station on Wittenberg Road in 1955.

Wittenberg was followed in 1954 by the formation of Company No. 3 in Lake Hill; its incorporation followed in 1957 along with the election of Merlin Wilson as president. In the fall of 1956, Lake Hill began construction of their own new home on Route 212. Of all Woodstock's hamlets in the 1950s, Zena, due in part to the arrival of IBM, had seen proportionately the greatest increase in new housing. Accordingly, Company No. 4 was added in 1956 with John Casey serving as its first president. In 1957, with the donation of land by Fred Thaisz Sr., Company No. 4 volunteers, also intent on construction of a new station to service their needs, soon broke ground at the intersection of Zena and Sawkill roads and submitted their petition for incorporation to the department's fire commissioners.[27]

The medium of television also became a point of discussion in the 1950s. Since the technology's introduction, Woodstockers had long suffered with snowy images relayed from a rooftop or backyard antenna. Poor reception was also caused by the town's location at the edge of over-the-air broadcasts from Albany, New York, and Connecticut, while signal strength was further diminished by the surrounding mountains. In 1958, Elliot Clark of Clark's Sound and Television Service of Kingston appeared before the Woodstock Town Board with a proposal for "community television." In essence, offering an early form of cable television, Clark was seeking a site on Meads Mountain on which he could construct a large "community" antenna. From there, lines would extend to nearby homes with the assertion from Clark that "we can reasonably guarantee snow-free pictures on at least six channels." While promising to serve "more than five hundred television sets," Clark's proposal was tabled on the basis that more information was needed by the town before any further discussion could continue. Though it is unclear if Clark ever returned to the Town Board, what is clear—or maybe not so clear for those relying on their backyard antennas—is that the snowy pictures their televisions displayed did not appreciably improve until Kingston Cablevision came to town in the 1960s.[28]

Meanwhile, despite the fury that had surrounded their academic futures, Woodstock students were presented with a rare gift in the spring of 1958 as more than one hundred participated in a musical pageant titled "From Sophocles to Rogers and Hammerstein," written and directed by noted pianist and composer Hans Schimmerling. Having arrived in Woodstock in the 1950s, Schimmerling, who had served in Prague as conductor of the German Opera and was "accompanist for Michael Bohnen, the leading Metropolitan bass," went on to teach music in local elementary schools while developing unique and "widely acclaimed" music programs for them.[29] In a review of the spring concert given by Woodstock students under Schimmerling's direction, Lisa Tiano, a correspondent for the *Kingston Daily Freeman*, wrote, "Even the most hardened musical critic would have found joy and delight in the two-hour performance that revealed a caliber of musical achievement rarely found in elementary school pupils." School principal, Walter Van Wagenen, according to Tiano, closed out the evening's performance offering similar praise, telling the audience that "the show was further evidence that Prof. Schimmerling was without peer in his field," a "sentiment," Tiano added, "that was enthusiastically shared" by the audience.[30]

In many respects, the high level of Woodstock's cultural landscape, as represented by Schimmerling and several of Woodstock's artists, provided opportunities for Woodstock's young people over the years not found in most communities. In return, it also offered occasions for artists to give back to the community in ways other than serving on a committee, as a coach. or even as a volunteer fireman. Over the years, it was a partnership that benefited numerous students, artists, and the community alike.

The arts were on the minds of many Woodstockers in May 1958 as rumors fueled speculation that the town might be without the Art Students League's summer session. That rumor was dispelled when the League announced it would return in June. Having served as a premiere center for instruction in Woodstock since 1906, the Art Students League also brought to Woodstock the energy and youthful exuberance of its many students. And, while that exuberance may have at times been of concern to the more conservative inhabitants of the town, by the 1950s, Woodstock very much counted on the influx of new students each summer. While the 1957 session had attracted 140 students, it was estimated that in 1958 the number of students preparing to receive instruction from Arnold Blanch, Frank Reilly, and Zygmunt Menkes would surpass the previous year.[31]

One institution that left Woodstock in 1958 was the Reverend Harvey Todd. Todd had served as pastor at the Reformed Church in the center of town for thirty-four years. In addition to his duties as a Church leader, Todd had been central in supporting numerous activities and groups in Woodstock throughout his many years. A recipient of the first Citizen of the Year Award in 1956, he was actively involved in supporting Woodstock's home defense efforts during World War II. That support led to his participation in moving the Woodstock War Memorial to reality. Additionally, Todd was involved with the Boy Scouts, the Historical Society of Woodstock, the Christmas Eve celebration, and numerous other civic groups and events in a town that relied on volunteers.

As if reflecting on his years of commitment to Woodstock, Todd chose for his final day occupying the pulpit to present a unique service by bringing back those couples he had married over his thirty-four years. In a service broadcast over WKNY Radio out of Kingston, seventeen "couples renewed their vows before a battery of cameras which included photographers from national periodicals."[32] On June 7, 1958, Wayne C. Olsen was ordained as Todd's replacement.

At the last Town Board meeting of 1958, Tobie Geertsema brought the voice she had promised to the table and laid down an early marker in support of a planning board for Woodstock. Growth was a major issue facing the town, and the councilwoman believed it was time to take it on, offering, "I feel such Town Planning is urgently needed because the town is growing and will continue to grow to the extent that we will need a plan for projects . . . long-term projects for future improvement, expansion, beautification and problem solving."[33] While legal counsel for the town Abram (Abe) Molyneaux argued that further study would be needed "before a concrete proposal could be presented to the taxpayers at a public hearing," others in attendance declared the belief that the time had indeed come for Woodstock to take such a major step. Artist and councilman John Pike thought Geertsema's proposal merited "serious consideration." J. C. van Rijn, Rotron founder and an early advocate of town planning, rose from the floor to state how glad he was that "the subject has been brought forward." But regarding what type of board the town should create, he cautioned, "I am compelled to think that nothing would be worse than a planning board that was weak or badly conceived." Although Geertsema's call for the creation of a planning board was deferred at that last meeting in 1958, it remained a major point of discussion in the community, one that shadowed the town for the foreseeable future.

As 1958 folded into 1959, good news arrived for a select group of Woodstock artists when the National Academy of Design announced that works by Marion Greenwood, Sidney Laufman, Henry Mattson, Ethel Magafan, and Zygmunt (Sigmund) Menkes had been selected for the Academy's 134th annual exhibition. The five Woodstock artists were selected through a juried process that reviewed 919 submissions from nonmembers of the Academy.[34]

Meanwhile, another Woodstock artist and member of the Woodstock Town Board, John Pike, was at work preparing a unique addition for the

1959 Library Fair. A noted watercolorist who also possessed excellent mechanical and design skills, Pike engaged with builder Willie Mellin in the crafting and construction of a replica of Henry Hudson's ship the *Half Moon*. According to the *Woodstock Press*, the completed ship was pulled through town on the day of the fair "with Gale Brownlee, beautiful New York model and daughter of Mr. and Mrs. Jack Feeley of Woodstock, as hostess."[35]

Woodstockers took on yet another creative challenge in 1959 when the Woodstock Artists Association announced that it would hold its annual Hat Party. Woodstock was seldom without a good reason to hold a party, and the debate over high and low culture could always be put off for another day. Woodstock "crowds mobbed" the event held by the Association on the property of the Art Students League on Tinker Street. With entertainment provided by members of the Turnau Opera Company performing selections from *Die Fledermaus* and folk music provided by Billy Faier, Bernard Steffen and folklorist Sam Eskin, the party moved on into the Woodstock night. The highlight of the event was, naturally enough, the selections by the judges for "outstanding head pieces." The award for Most Beautiful went to Gail Rainsford. Rainsford's creation consisted of a globe atop her head with flags of all nations represented. The Most Original award went to Frances Halsband for her hat featuring "a jug of wine, a loaf of bread and the words—'And Thou.'" Finally, the award for Funniest hat appears to have been an easy selection by the judges. Worn by Mitzi Rogers and titled "Some Like It Hot," the hat featured "frankfurters, pickles and peppers."[36]

While hat parties may not have been the norm for all Woodstock cultural events, fundraising often was. One of the more unique organizations at the time dedicated to supporting local artists was the Woodstock Foundation. Annually, it raised funds that would, in turn, be distributed in the form of financial grants to Woodstock artists in support of their work.

The Foundation's 1959 fundraising effort saw Virginia Hubbell and Fritzi Striebel come together to write, produce, and stage *Bettina's Promise* at the Woodstock Playhouse in September. Advertised as an original melodrama, *Bettina's Promise* offered the added benefit of featuring a cast of local names familiar to most Woodstockers. Woodstock thespians occupying the main roles in the production included Jules Viglielmo, Billy Faier, Barbara McGrath, and Paul Hamilton. Truly a community production, it brought together not only a larger cast of locals in support of the principles but also a host of additional Woodstockers lending their talents to everything from sets, lighting, stage managing, publicity, box office, auctioneers, local bartenders to serve at intermission, and even the "pretzel children" who, presumably, offered edibles commensurate with their name.[37] In all respects, the Woodstock Foundation's production of *Bettina's Promise* and their previous efforts on behalf of local artists exemplified the unique ability of Woodstockers to come together in support of their fellow townspeople. Local arguments—political or otherwise—come and go; community does not.

And yet, politics returned in the fall of 1959 as differences between Town Board members began to heat up. Less than a month after the good will generated by *Bettina's Promise*, sparks flew at a Town Board meeting over the perennial issue of transparency and the preparation of the town's 1960 preliminary budget. As Supervisor Fitzsimmons presented the budget, two councilpersons, Tobie Geertsema and the town justice Dixon McGrath,

Figure 30. *Bettina's Promise* artwork by Bruce Gregory, 1959. *Source:* Historical Society of Woodstock Art Collection/Robert Angeloch Collection.

objected to not having input into the figures the supervisor had placed on the documents before them. Said Geertsema—as if guided by the spirit of Marion Bullard in her earlier calls for transparency in town government—"I have absolutely no intention of giving my approval to a budget on which I was not consulted beforehand, and, in whose preparation, I had no part." Similarly, Justice McGrath voiced his objection by stating, "I couldn't vote on something I haven't seen." (McGrath, a Democrat, had put yet another dent in the hold Republicans held over Woodstock government by successfully winning an election for town justice in 1958. At the time, town justices were voting members of the Town Board.)[38] Responding to the objections made by Geertsema and McGrath, Supervisor Fitzsimmons claimed, "Anytime I sign a paper carrying figures above my name, the figures will be mine. I feel that I am capable of making out the budget, according to law, and when I'm not, someone else will be called upon to do it."[39]

When the vote was called, the preliminary budget passed, 3-2, with Geertsema and McGrath voting no. With the vote taken, both Geertsema and McGrath rose and walked out of the meeting just as attorney Maurice Goldberg asked permission to speak in defense of the supervisor and to the fact that what was on the table was only a preliminary budget. As Geertsema exited down the "center aisle," according to the *Woodstock Press*, she remarked in reference to Goldberg, "I have no intention of listening to another of his lengthy tirades. He is out of order as usual."[40]

It was election season in Woodstock and tensions were running high. Supervisor Fitzsimmons had decided not to run for another term and was replaced at the head of the Republican ticket by town attorney Abe Molyneaux. Local Democrats had chosen Charlie Tiano to oppose Molyneaux. Tiano was a well-known figure in Woodstock, having worked as a reporter and sports editor for the *Kingston Daily Freeman* for several years as well as serving as director of numerous area golf tournaments. Democrats hoped that his visibility in the community might finally counter the solid majority Republicans always brought to the polls.

Woodstock Republicans, however, were not about to grow complacent. Only a few weeks before tensions had boiled over at the Town Board meeting, local adherents to the Grand Old Party staged a campaign event rather unique for Woodstock. On a Friday evening, the party faithful gathered in front of the Woodstock Playhouse to embark upon a torchlight parade up Mill Hill Road and down Tinker Street. As part of the parade—although the connection is somewhat unclear—a float carrying several Republican women "garbed in the fashions of the gay nineties" moved along with the torchbearers.[41]

Not to be outdone, Democrats decided that they too would hold a rally, although theirs would be indoors. Held at the Holiday Country Inn between Woodstock and Saugerties, Democrats offered up two of Woodstock's most popular folk musicians, Sonia Malkine and Billy Faier, in addition to their own list of political speakers.

On election day, Democratic hopes of finally breaking through and taking control of the Town Board were, once again, dashed as Republicans emerged victorious. In fact, with the defeat of the justice of the peace, Dixon McGrath, by Rudi Baumgarten, Republicans now held a 4-1 majority on the Town Board as Tobie Geertsema remained the lone councilperson with Democratic backing. In the race for supervisor, Molyneaux easily swept past Charlie Tiano by a margin of 408 votes, 1,156-748.[42]

As Woodstockers prepared to leave behind the decade of the 1950s, they did so with a contrasting picture of Woodstock's young people that, in some respects, put the town on notice that the approaching decade would call for greater attention to be paid in that direction. The year 1959 saw the unwelcomed phrase *juvenile delinquency* first applied to the actions of a select group of Woodstock's youth as a nighttime spree of vandalism impacting Woodstock's business district on Tinker Street and Mill Hill Road drew the predictable ire of several adults.

Beginning on the upper end of Tinker Street, signs were torn down at the Woodstock Motel and the Block Print Studio. Garbage was tossed at the entrance of the News Shop across from the Village Green. On Mill Hill Road, banners were torn down at the Gulf gas station. Across the street, garbage and broken glass littered the Grand Union parking lot, while more signs were removed and the front entrance to the supermarket was blocked. From there, heading toward Route 375, an antique carriage at the Louis Lewis Junke Shoppe was hauled to the other side of the Sawk- ill Creek, making the vintage carriage inoperable. Even the office of the *Woodstock Press* received the attention of the vandals as various posters on its outdoor bulletin board were ripped down.[43]

While Woodstock constable Clarence (Clancy) Snyder was familiar with coping with the usual pranks that might be found on Halloween night, this was a different matter. And within the brief span of a few days, he reported that through cooperation with the State Police three Woodstock young people were identified, arrested, placed on probation, and fined. The vandalism, however, became a focal point for several Woodstock adults, including the editor of the *Woodstock Press*. In an editorial, noting letters he had received regarding the incident, the paper launched into an attack not only on the young people involved but on their parents as well:

> It's about time parents woke up! In light of the current comments on juvenile delinquency, it is most evident that something should be done, not said. Our young adults should realize by this time that they cannot get away with it. Witness the fact of our competent local constables and State Troopers who have brought in the culprits of recent and past incidents. Yet, the incidents still occur! The seat of all the difficulty in delinquency has long been pointed out by those who cared to take the trouble, and that is—in the home.[44]

While some would point to the belief that such acts by teenagers in any town were not that uncommon, the reaction in Woodstock to such vandalism only highlighted, as the town moved into the sixties, the question of what more could be done for the youth of Woodstock while also coping with the influences the next decade would bring to bear on those coming of age.

For those in Woodstock who were quick to comment on stories involving vandalism and young people with the declaration "not my child," an announcement at the end of the year neatly fit their perceptions (and, perhaps, prayers) that the kids were going to be just fine. As Christmas approached, Woodstock's chapter of the Jaycees service club announced that the chapter's youth group—the Woodstock Jay-Teens—would be raising funds for the organization by volunteering and braving the cold to sell Christmas trees at a lot next to Deanie's Restaurant on Mill Hill Road. In addition, the Jay-Teens announced that they would be hosting their annual Snowflake Ball, a semiformal affair for local young people to be held at the Woodstock Town Hall prior to New Year's Eve.[45]

As Woodstockers came to learn as they entered the sixties, however, nothing regarding their teenagers—or the town itself—could be framed in black-and-white. Unknowingly, change was barreling in their direction.

Chapter 7

# The Sixties Arrive

When we look at history, we invariably tie ourselves to time. We mark events by the year in which they happen, allowing it to fix itself within a context that is somehow more relatable. We also celebrate the passing of time. We herald the arrival of each new year when the clocks strike midnight. We seem to celebrate even more when a new decade arrives as if we've just finished a long chapter in a book in which we were the main characters. Before us, a new chapter lies. As Woodstock began the transformation from the 1950s to the 1960s, it did so by exploring where this new chapter in the pages of its story might take its citizens. Early on, an integral part of that exploration fell, once again, to the arts as attention began to focus on the rise of folk music in town and on where a new path in music might lead.

In 1959, the first annual Catskill Mountain Folk Festival was held at the Colony Arts Center on Rock City Road, to be followed by additional performances in the years to come. In 1960, Sam Eskin headlined the festival along with Sonia Malkine, Bernard Steffen, Edward Chavez, and, in one of her earliest appearances in Woodstock, Betty McDonald. Not long after, many of the same performers gathered at the home of Sam Eskin to form the Ulster County Folklore Society. Early members included Sonia Malkine, Barbara Moncure, Billy Faier, Opus Forty creator Harvey Fite, Sy and Estelle Kattleson, and Aaron Van de Bogart. Eskin, who served as president of the newly formed group, was without peer in the exploration of folk music, folk culture, and native customs. At the time, it was believed that his home on Overlook offered one of Woodstock's earliest recording studios and one of the nation's most complete collections of folk songs and folklore. Much of his work and the product of his explorations and recordings would eventually find their way to the Smithsonian.

In line with Eskin's work exploring the multifaceted aspects of folk culture, the newly formed Ulster County Folklore Society began, in the early sixties, plans to stage a folk festival that offered the public more than just folk music as a spectator sport. Within the announced plans for a festival to be held at the Woodstock Estates in the fall of 1962, the Society promised "song swapping, folk dancing, seminars and discussions with prominent folklorists and collectors."[1]

Such reflection on folk culture and music was also to be found at Camp Woodland, located in the nearby town of Phoenicia. Operating under the guidance of its founder, Norman Studer, from 1939 to 1962, Camp Woodland offered its young campers a focus on gathering folk stories, folk songs, and Catskill crafts and presenting an annual Catskill Folk Festival over the years, which drew throngs of folk enthusiasts from the region. Among its early campers, Camp Woodland included future Woodstocker John Herald, who went on to be the lead singer and guitarist in the Greenbriar Boys. Early campers also included longtime Woodstocker and Grammy winner for "Dueling Banjos," Eric Weissberg. As Brian Hollander later recalled in an article for *Hudson Valley One*, though Weissberg is probably best remembered for the music behind the film *Deliverance*, "the guy was a Julliard trained classical upright bassist and could play virtually any stringed instrument at a moment's notice—guitar, mandolin, fiddle, dobro. . . . He played the steel guitar on John Denver's *Country Roads*, without having played the complicated instrument before. That's a pretty good guy to have in any band."[2]

In a similar vein, Camp Camelot, located on Boggs Hill in Woodstock, offered a celebration of folk music featuring Barbara Moncure in the early sixties. Camp Camelot, which opened in 1959 under the ownership of Henry and Jean Miller, served children from four to thirteen years of age and, in addition to music, offered many of the traditional camping experiences, including arts and crafts, swimming, dance, dramatics, and horseback riding.

Barbra Moncure, along with Sam Eskin, Sonia Malkine, Billy Faier, and others, became central to Woodstock's early folk community over the years. Moncure, the stepdaughter of Woodstock artist Rolph Scarlet, teamed with folk artist Harry Siemsen in 1963 to release an album titled *Folksongs of the Catskills*. In addition to her own music and her popularity as a performer, Moncure was instrumental in organizing "an interracial teenage steel band," which, according to local historian Alf Evers, "had arisen as an offshoot of a Brooklyn settlement house program." As Evers later related to poet and historian Ed Sanders, he would invite members of the band over the course of several summers to camp on his property and "many of the teenagers in the band had never been in the country before and were very responsive to my attempts to teach them a little about woodcraft and the plants and animals of the Catskills." The group, under Moncure's leadership, performed at numerous functions in Woodstock over the years, including the Library Fair.[3]

As folk music flourished, Evers went to work organizing a series of performances under the title of the Huckleberry Festival. According to Sanders, the first Huckleberry Festival was held at "the Colony Center, the next year at the Parnassus Square Barn, and the third year it was at the Maverick Concert Hall." Over the course of the series, featured performers included Barbara Moncure, Harry Siemsen, Holley Cantine's Woodchuck Hollow Band, and the Wiltwyck Steel Drummers. As Evers described the festivals, "They were local people who sang or had something to say about folk matters—mostly singing and I told folk stories in between." The local performers who also made appearances included banjo picker Art Sutton and his Blue Grass Cut Ups, Robin Wetterau's jug band, Van Winkle's Rippers, Sam Eskin, Eddie Rivers, and Carmen Goode.[4]

Woodstockers, however, could be forgiven if on a winter's night in 1963 they did not recognize a young folk singer by the name of Happy Traum disembarking from the New York City bus in front of the News Shop. Traum, who with his brother Artie was at the center of Woodstock music for years to come, had arrived in Woodstock for the first time to play at the Cafe Espresso and described his initial encounter with Woodstock and the Espresso in an essay later published by the Historical Society of Woodstock:

> I took the bus from New York City and was picked up by the proprietor, Bernard Paturel, French and suave with his brushed mustaches and vaguely Gallic accent. He took me to his apartment above the club to meet Marylou and their small children, and then down to the cafe, which was warm and cozy after the long, snowy bus ride. The room was already crowded with local folk who had come to see a young unknown folksinger

Figure 31. Broadside advertising the "original" Huckleberry Festival. *Source:* Author's collection.

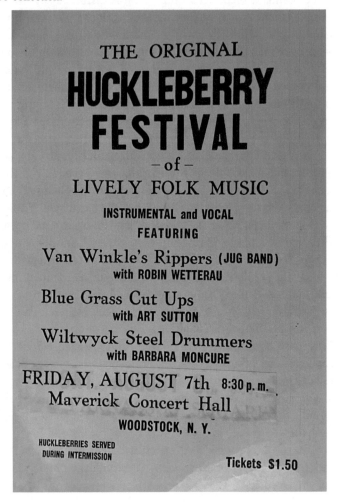

THE ORIGINAL

# HUCKLEBERRY FESTIVAL
– of –
LIVELY FOLK MUSIC

INSTRUMENTAL and VOCAL
FEATURING

Van Winkle's Rippers (JUG BAND)
with ROBIN WETTERAU

Blue Grass Cut Ups
with ART SUTTON

Wiltwyck Steel Drummers
with BARBARA MONCURE

FRIDAY, AUGUST 7th 8:30 p.m.
Maverick Concert Hall
WOODSTOCK, N. Y.

HUCKLEBERRIES SERVED
DURING INTERMISSION

Tickets $1.50

from the city, but everyone was as welcoming as the room itself. That summer, I was invited back to perform at a much larger venue, the first of many appearances I made over the years at the Woodstock Playhouse. As before, many Woodstockers showed a keen interest in the folk music that I loved and I began meeting more of the colorful citizens of the art colony.[5]

In 1964, Edgar Rosenblum, who had assumed ownership of the Woodstock Playhouse in 1960, had the foresight to recognize the increased popularity and demand for folk music in the area. The result became a series of weekly folk concerts at the Playhouse. While simply advertised in the 1964 edition of the *Woodstock Festival* booklet as "Folk Music," the concerts went on to include, in addition to Happy and Artie Traum, folk luminaries such as Tom Paxton, Peter Yarrow, Tim Hardin, Jack Elliot, and Pete Seeger.

As Woodstockers undertook their personal connections to folk music and the artists who engaged them, they also began to give increasing thought to the direction their hometown was heading. In February 1960, the Woodstock Association for the Conservation and Improvement of the Township published the results of a survey it had conducted focusing on how Woodstockers envisioned the future and the actions required to attain that future. While the results were not overly surprising, they offered a baseline that underscored the need for regulation as a growing town attempted to maintain not only environmental control over the land but Woodstock's traditional, small-town character as well. By degree of importance, Woodstockers showed the most concern over the following issues:

Counter steam pollution: 93%
Favor residential and artistic development: 86.2%
Regulate minimum size of building lots: 71.5%
Conserve Woodstock's looks: 67.5%
Regulate appearance of residential buildings in certain area: 66.3%
Favor moderate increase in population: 65.0%
Favor year-round residents: 63.8%
Shopping facilities are adequate 63%[6]

Beyond the primary sentiments polled, however, the Association went deeper into the responses received by adding to their report comments returned as part of the survey. While acknowledging that moderate expansion was inevitable, growth beyond moderate was dismissed in several comments. "Woodstock does not need to be enlarged, it needs to be saved," said one. "The charm of Woodstock has always been its simplicity and way of living. There was peace for creative workers and natural beauty surrounding it," remarked another. Most comments averse to greater growth were summed up by one simple comment: "What is so great about growth?"[7]

The survey's respondents also showed disfavor toward housing developments, in obvious reference to what had occurred in the 1950s: "Pre-fab individual houses should not be permitted within the sight of public roads." "I like all of Woodstock except the housing developments." "There should be a ban or strict regulations on housing developments." "Insure that careless or unscrupulous developments do not add to our town burden." "Real Estate agents and profit-seeking builders should be checked by town planning from indiscriminate building."[8]

Other areas receiving attention on the survey included sidewalks (need more), trees (protect the maple-lined roads), lack of parking, signage (prohibit the garish ones), and traffic (reroute traffic in center of town and move the bus stop from the center of town). For many in Woodstock today, such complaints ring familiar. As Mark Twain is said to have observed, "History doesn't repeat itself, but it often rhymes."

In response to past and present pressures relating to growth in Woodstock and advocacy from such groups as the Woodstock Association as well as recommendations by a study group appointed the previous year, the Woodstock Town Board took a major step in local regulation by creating the Woodstock Planning Board as the new decade began. Finally adopting a resolution previously offered by Tobie Geertsema, the Town Board called upon Rotron's J. C. van Rijn to move the new effort forward. Rising to speak following his appointment, van Rijn was clear—and prophetic—that the new creation "would face no easy task and might become controversial from time to time." To that end, he also said, "Members of the board would approach their task without any atmosphere of coercion or pressure."[9]

What the Planning Board was expected to oversee in the early sixties was, for the most part, a self-sustaining town. And, while a drive to Kingston for certain services might be occasionally required, local needs were for the most part met locally. From supermarkets to banks, everyday clothing to insurance, and car repairs to health needs Woodstock worked hard to take care of itself, mostly through family-run businesses.

While Woodstock's main street architecture has changed little over the years, certainly the businesses that have moved in and out of the central business area have morphed in accordance with the times. And yet, for Woodstockers of longstanding, the storefronts they pass today still echo past services, the wares they once dispensed, and the faces of those who unlocked their doors each morning.

So, what was Woodstock like in the years before the town lent its name to a generation? What might Mill Hill Road, for example, have presented to the casual passerby before much of the world "found" Woodstock in the years prior to a certain festival?

As one enters Woodstock today, the Woodstock Golf Club—once a carding mill and farmland—has since 1929 served as sentry to the turn onto Mill Hill Road. Directly across from the course, the former Riseley boardinghouse has over the years hosted multiple Woodstock restaurants. The late fifties/early sixties would have presented the Townhouse to visitors entering town, although its name was later whispered quietly by a community not yet eager to deal with questions of sexual identity and a growing gay community.

Next door, the original Woodstock Playhouse rose to complete the vision of Robert Elwyn in 1938, serving as an integral link in Woodstock's cultural DNA throughout the postwar era and beyond. Taken by a suspicious fire in 1988, it has risen again to welcome residents and visitors alike. Directly across from the Playhouse stands a series of connected shops that once included the domain of Louis Lewis and his Ye Olde Junke Shoppe (aka Lewis Art Gallery). The same Louis Lewis who, at one time, once held sway over Woodstock's Democratic Party was also known for the fact that he once played football alongside Lou Gehrig at Commerce High in New York. Immediately next door, overlooking the Sawkill, breakfast, lunch, and dinner could be ordered up at Miss Mary's. An advertisement from the period proudly proclaims, "Sea food, clams and cocktails by Eddie Logan," one of Woodstock's long line of noted bartenders over the years.[10] Continuing along the same row of storefronts Warren Hutty, yet another Woodstock force, operated multiple businesses in his day, including the Robert John Shop (antiques and imports) and Hutty Real Estate.

As we cross the street to where Woodstock's shopping plaza now sits, the reader should imagine a field devoid of structure and envision a setting once occupied by artists and art classes as the open field delivered one of the more impressive, unobstructed views of Overlook Mountain.

Heading up Mill Hill to where a gas station and convenience store operates today, we come to a site that has been radically repurposed. In its earlier days, Sarah Cashdollar operated the Homestead there, a boardinghouse that catered to visiting artists and theater folk in town for performances at the Playhouse. At some point the home was demolished, and in its place a service station rose.

Figure 32. The Homestead, operated by Sarah Cashdollar, was later replaced by a gas station. *Source:* Historical Society of Woodstock Archives/Jean White Collection.

Stopping here for a moment, it should be noted that Mill Hill Road at one time was home to four gas stations, leading Alf Evers to once describe the road as "Gasoline Alley." In addition to the station where the Homestead operated, the site of Catskill Mountain Pizza once housed Charlie Kullman's Garage. Later the site dispensed repairs and gas under the ownership of Ken and Dodie Reynolds. Anyone with a Volkswagen or foreign car in need of repair in those days will clearly remember the good-natured abuse dispensed by Ken and his preference for products made by the American automotive industry. Directly across Mill Hill, where a restaurant now operates, there was a Mobil gas station that later became a Stewart's ice cream shop. To the far right of the complex (before it was all connected), locals moved daily in and out of Dot's—later Duey's—where the Duey burger and a bucket of chicken could be had. Returning across Mill Hill, one would once find Lou Wilson's Woodstock Garage offering gas and service and being the one place in town where one could purchase a new car: Fords only.

Finally, we come to Peper's Garage. Begun as a blacksmith shop by Henry Peper, the operation expanded over the years to include the construction of the front brick building that currently houses business offering various wares to visitors and locals alike. It is said that in the rear building where Maria's Cafe once operated, the first meeting of Woodstock's American Legion was held. As one faces the building, the house to the right was the home of the Pepers, where the aforementioned Miss Florence Peper, Henry's daughter, lived, gardened, and kept her diary; across the street is the Lutheran Church, where she attended church well into the 1990s.

Back out on Mill Hill and down the road a bit where a chain pharmacy now operates is the site that once housed Woodstock's two-room schoolhouse. The schoolhouse was later moved behind the current building to make room for Woodstock's Grand Union supermarket in 1956. Before becoming a private residence, the schoolhouse lived on as Harrison Muller's School of Dance and, later, as the first home to Woodstock's Youth Center.

Traveling a bit further up the same side of the street to the corner of Mill Hill Road and Deming Street, we come to a building that now houses yet another restaurant. For any Woodstocker of longstanding residence, it is remembered as the iconic home of the music venue Joyous Lake. Prior to the Lake, however, the building's housed Elwyn's grocery store, a restaurant, and, as recalled fondly by many who grew up in Woodstock, Charlie's Ice Cream Parlor, owned and operated by Mr. and Mrs. Charles Goodrich.

Stepping outside the door of Charlie's (later named Rick's), one would only have to wander a few paces across Deming Street to enter Woodstock's most fondly remembered restaurant, Deanie's ("Known from Coast to Coast"). Built and operated by Deanie Elwyn, Deanie's, perhaps more than any other establishment, symbolized the Woodstock that was the fifties and sixties. First operating out of a trolley (it is claimed the trolley remains buried beneath its original location on Mill Hill Road), Elwyn later constructed his restaurant on the corner of Deming Street following his return from Navy service during World War II. In 1948 a bar was added, and in 1950 a second floor was constructed. As time moved forward, Deanie's became the central gathering place for Woodstockers from all walks of life. On any given evening one could find the local plumber, an artist, an off-duty constable, a craftsman, a musician, and, more than likely, a few politicos huddled together over one last drink before Flo O'Dell's piano played them home. And while Deanie's remained central to Woodstock nightlife into the 1980s (it later moved to the former Riseley boardinghouse following a fire in 1974), O'Dell became a Woodstock institution in her own right. As one passed her small home on Orchard Lane, Broadway showtunes could often be heard spilling out onto the street as she practiced. Self-taught and never making use of sheet music, O'Dell could play most anything upon request. In her many years as a mainstay at Deanie's, one story remains in Woodstock lore centering on the night George Harrison walked into the restaurant. Harrison, the former Beatle, had arrived in town following his Concert for Bangladesh while still embroiled in the battle with Paul McCartney over the dissolution of the Beatles. Upon being told that Harrison was in the building, Flo immediately launched into "Michelle," a Paul McCartney song. When told it wasn't probably the best choice of music for Harrison at the time, O'Dell quickly switched back to showtunes.

Moving up Mill Hill and crossing the street, we find where Donald and Elise Twine operated Twine's Catskill Bookshop. Twines was a cozy bookstore that also sold artist supplies. It was a store, according to

Figure 33. Iconic napkin from Deanie's Restaurant. *Source:* Author's collection.

their daughter, Olivia, "which always smelled like paint, linseed oil and turpentine," and in which, "dogs were welcomed and offered biscuits." In an upstairs apartment, Agnes Ridgeway, scriptwriter for the *Dr. Kildare* television show, resided.[11]

During its stay on Mill Hill Road, Twine's was also noted for its book-signing parties, which feted such authors as Howard Koch (*The Panic Broadcast*), Alf Evers (*Woodstock: History of an American Town* and *The Catskills: From Wilderness to Woodstock*), and Heywood Hale Broun (*Whose Little Boy are You?*). But perhaps the most memorable evening is best described by Olivia (Tinker) Twine herself, who wrote:

> *Faustus's Keyhole* author, Jean Arnoldi (Attractive wife of artist Fletcher Martin, former wife of musician Frank Mele and mother of Andre Mele) set the stage for one of Twine's most successful parties in 1970. I remember it even though I only heard about it second-hand. Donald was awed to have witnessed a spontaneous pugilistic encounter between Fletcher Martin and abstract painter Bud Plate, both macho he-men. The fight was over a woman; though it wasn't clear which woman. No one was hurt. Not much, anyway. The scene was reminiscent of Martin's artwork. One of his signature themes was the prizefight.[12]

Crossing Maple Lane to where Candlestock is today, you would be greeted, should you have chosen to knock on the door, by Woodstock's Reverend Harvey Todd. The building once served as the parsonage for the Reformed Church on the Village Green. Next door (Pegasus today), the first floor presented one of Woodstock's few clothing stores, Bonnie's, where its owner, Bonnie McManis, offered the latest in lingerie. Upstairs, Irving Kalish later worked the local real estate market as locals and tourists alike passed beneath his business sign. The building that is now, once again, the Pub, has long existed as a home for libation and food. While at one time it operated under the ownership of Bill and Janet Dixon as the Irvington, most remember it today as always being the Woodstock Pub under the ownership of Chris Lynch and later the Scales family.

Finally, at the corner of Rock City Road, we arrive at a series of stores housed in what is known as the Longyear Building. While the Longyear Building itself dates back to 1933, in the late 1950s/early 1960s it was home to Allen Electric, Victor Basil—Hairdresser, and Peggie's

Gift Shop (operated by Peg Barryann). On the corner of the building a visitor returning over time would have found a store changed more by its ownership than by what was dispensed (newspapers, candy, a soda fountain, etc.). Originally known as Stowell's (owned by Stowey Stowell), the business later operated under the name of Luden's and then Schneider's when it was owned by Walt and Emily Schneider.

Crossing the street one last time, we arrive at H. Houst and Sons. Houst's and the Woodstock Lumber Yard (owned by the Neher family further down Mill Hill Road) are the two operations that have seen the passing parade that is Woodstock the longest. They remain, in many ways, the anchors to Mill Hill; family operations that have met Woodstock's needs throughout the decades while also serving as exemplars of how to give back to the community.

As the visitor turns onto Tinker Street, the name itself bears an explanation. More than likely, the actual explanation for the origin of the street's name is based on fact, although fiction might also play a role. There once was an actual tinker shop on what is now Tinker Street. Located on the corner where today one turns onto Comeau Drive, John Brandow held forth as the town tinker. While Brandow's skills as a tinker were without dispute, his character, it seems, would have easily failed any customer service test offered today. Described in his day as a "necessary evil" due to a gruff and sharp manner, Brandow's large black beard led to a comment by one contemporary that "he had some whiskers, but they didn't look as if they liked him."[13]

The mythical part of the street's name comes from a man named Jim Twaddell, known in earlier years as Woodstock's "teller of tall tales." According to Twaddell, a traveling tinker passing through Woodstock one day encountered the deep springtime mud that was Woodstock's main road. Slowly the horse, the wagon, and the tinker himself began to sink. With his cries for help unanswered, the tinker was lost beneath the very road we now travel. Twaddell further claimed that, when conditions were right, you could still hear the jingling of tinware echoing from below.

Whichever origin of the street's name you wish to choose, Tinker Street has long been central to much of Woodstock's history. And at the heart of life on Tinker Street through the years, the Village Green has been its nexus. The Village Green was actually green at one time. Constant foot traffic across the grass each summer rendered the center of town more brown than green by August. The most important event that unfolds each year on the Green takes place on the evening of December

24. Since 1932, Woodstockers have gathered to celebrate Christmas Eve and await the arrival of Santa Claus, an arrival that is cloaked in secrecy as each year he arrives in a different, often magical way.

The Green, by virtue of its location at the center of town, has also been home to numerous celebrations over time. From speeches at war's end to the countless parades that have marched by, Woodstock's Village Green is simply the place where Woodstockers and visitors gather. Gathering on the Village Green, however, will eventually take on new meaning as the sixties moved on—a meaning not appreciated by Woodstock's conservative hierarchy—as young people arriving in town began to assume residency alongside Woodstock's War Memorial.

While we are still standing on the Green, if we turn right to face Old Forge Road, we see the building that presently houses the Garden Cafe, originally known as the Krack House. (Not because of any nineteenth-century illicit drug activity but because it was built as an inn by Colonel Krack in 1875.) The store on the Rock City Road corner of the building was home to Kirshbaum's Woodstock Bakery (also owned at one time by the Leonard Scholls and later the DiNapolis). Farther down the row of storefronts, Ross (Pagliaro) the shoemaker held forth in the space that eventually housed Magic Markie's head shop—later the Pinball Palace. While the opening of a head shop in the center of town dedicated to selling pipes and roach clips sent a shudder through Woodstock's conservative majority, for many Woodstock youth of the day it became a second home.

Crossing the road from the Green, we head to the corner (more like a curve) of Tinker Street. Woodstockers of longstanding residence will recall, first, Anne's Delicatessen. Originally owned by the Dordicks, ownership later passed to Pan Copeland. The upstairs of the building once housed the office of the *Ulster County Townsman*, published by Marian Umhey as she, Kiki Minervini, and Sharon Cherven ran the entire operation. Later, Ted Sclaris took up proprietorship of the deli and operated under the sign the Corner Cupboard.

Going back in years a little further, to the right of where the Corner Cupboard was located, the Woodstock Post Office once operated. Later, when the post office moved farther up the road, the Roger Jones Shop occupied the vacated space. Offering both clothing and unique gifts, Jones later took to the classroom as a teacher at Onteora. Today, a reminder of what once could be found on the second floor is the original teardrop window that continues to look out over Tinker Street. Next door was once home to Cousins Home Appliance Store operated by Karl Cousins.

Like many Woodstock business owners of his day, Cousins was deeply involved in community affairs through twenty-five years of service to the fire department, as a board member of the Woodstock Cemetery, and as a member and director of the Reformed Church.

Equally involved in his community was Fred Strassberg. In 1960, he purchased the News Shop from Sydney Greenberg and Paul Fenster. The News Shop (now a part of Jean Turmo's) had been at the center of Tinker Street life since 1924. Featuring a luncheonette and, as the site still is, home to the town's bus stop, the News Shop, much like Dot's and Duey's, was a part of a daily routine for many Woodstockers. During his tenure at the News Shop, Strassberg was known to befriend and serve as a mentor to several of Woodstock's young people who passed their time in the center of town.

Crossing the alleyway to where Oriole9 is today, we recall another town institution, Mower's Market. Mower's began when Fred Mower and his twin brother Bill took over operations of the store following the death

Figure 34. Along Tinker Street. *Source:* Historical Society of Woodstock Archives/ Town Center Collection.

of F. B. Happy in 1931. Mower's, for many, was Woodstock's local supermarket on a mom-and-pop scale. And, even as the A&P and Grand Union supermarkets arrived along Mill Hill Road, longtime customers remained faithful as ownership passed from Fred Mower to Louis Feinberg around 1960 and to Ann and Perk Gentilin in 1972.

Immediately next door, yet another Woodstock legend could be found under the sign of Carey's Delicatessen. The store's original namesake, Leon Carey, like Cousins, was a Woodstock businessman whose name is well documented in town annals. Carey served as town postmaster for fifteen years, town clerk during World War II, president of the PTA, member of the Woodstock Library's Board of Trustees, and charter member of the Woodstock Fire Department. Ownership of the delicatessen eventually passed to Zane Zimmerman. Not only were the roast beef sandwiches at Zane's larger than life, but Zane himself, as well as his red Cadillac convertible, still lives large in Woodstock memory.

Directly across the street and recently designated for inclusion on the National Register of Historic Places is the Woodstock Artists Association and Museum. Founded by artists John F. Carlson, Frank Swift Chase, Andrew Dasburg, Carl Lindin, and Henry Lee McFee, the Association rose on the site that was once home to Rose's General Merchandise store. In its day, Rose's (later Beekman's) was at the center of Woodstock life, serving as the post office, the place to go to for town news, and the site where a coach, having picked up visitors from New York at the train station in West Hurley, deposited the town's first wave of tourists.

To the left of the Artists Association is the Woodstock Byrdcliffe Guild. The structure at one time was home to the very wealthy Orson Vandervoort, owner of the tannery that operated in the middle of town. (Vandervoort is said to have paid more taxes during the Civil War era than any other Woodstocker.) In 1939, the Woodstock Guild of Craftsman began operations at the site, offering through the years local crafts for sale and a variety of arts and crafts classes. In 1976 Peter Whitehead, son of Byrdcliffe founder Ralph Whitehead, bequeathed Byrdcliffe to the Guild, and today the Woodstock Byrdcliffe Guild continues its mission as a center for excellence in the arts and crafts.

Crossing back across the street, we come to a series of stores running toward Tannery Brook Road. Included within the businesses that once occupied storefronts along this stretch were the Little Shop (women's clothing), Dr. Vlock's dentist office, Joe the Barber (Joe Relia), Horner's jewelry store, a liquor store, and a toy and gift shop. Remembered by most Woodstockers of longstanding, however, is Joe Forno's Colonial Pharmacy (where the Golden Notebook is today). Joe Forno represented the type of pharmacist many yearn for today. When a child took ill in the middle of the night, the light went on in the pharmacy a short while later as a prescription was readied. Even while operating his pharmacy, which also included a much-beloved soda fountain, Forno also involved himself heavily in the community. In addition to serving two terms as town justice, he served on the town's Recreation Committee, was president of the Woodstock Little League, received the PTA's Jenkins Award, and, equally important, sponsored, along with wife Barbara, Woodstock's annual Easter egg hunt from 1947 to 1994.

Wandering down to the building at the corner of Tinker Street and Tannery Brook Road, several establishments have offered visitors and locals alike a variety of eating experiences, including (as best as can be determined) Fischer's Restaurant, Galina's, the Eatery, Little New England, and, residing the longest, Joshua's Cafe, through which owner Joshua

Figure 35. Hanging out at the Colonial Pharmacy soda fountain. *Source:* Historical Society of Woodstock Archives/Town Center Collection.

Schachter convinced most Woodstockers early on that they loved Middle Eastern food. Crossing Tannery Brook Road, we pass the small shop that once housed Larry Elwyn's barbershop. Businessman Schuyler Shultz later offered insurance to Woodstockers who passed through his door.

Making the way over the bridge and the Tannery Brook, we come to yet another Woodstock building steeped in history. The building, which recently housed the Center for Photography at Woodstock, began life as a barn until Clarence Bolton and Louise Cashdollar came along. Artists in their own right, the two with little more than an idea converted the barn to open the Nook, a cafe and soda fountain of sorts that became a popular spot for local artists to socialize. That popularity continued when Frank Drake, in 1959, took over the building and renamed it the Cafe Espresso. Lasting fame would be cast upon the building under the ownership of Bernard and Mary Lou Paturel when an upstairs' room was occupied by a young musician named Bob Dylan. Later recalling those early days and first encountering Dylan, Maty Lou Paturel noted that before live music was ever heard at the Espresso, she and her husband played classical records most of the day, offering that Bernard was no fan of rock and roll. To underscore that fact, Paturel later recalled: "Bob Dylan had gone to Kingston and bought some rock and roll records, and he was all excited about hearing them and he comes into the Espresso and he goes over to Bernard and he says, 'Can I play these records?' And Bernard says, 'Well what are they?' And he [Dylan] says, 'rock and roll,' and Bernard says, 'No.'" Laughing, Mary Lou concludes, "I mean I never heard anybody say no to Bob Dylan. Why would you want to say no to Bob Dylan? But, no, you could not play rock and roll at the Espresso because Bernard does not like rock and roll."[14]

Though the attachment of Dylan's name to the Espresso remains the cafe's most noted connection with the past, he was not the only musician whose music—including rock and roll—found a home at the Espresso. Whether operated by the Paturels or, later, Victor and Dagmar Balsamo or Marty Cohen, the Espresso was a place from which remarkable music rang out over the years (performed by Tom Paxton, Dave Van Ronk, Jerry Moore, Happy and Artie Traum, Tim Hardin, Jack Elliot, Sonia Malkine, Joan Baez, Billy Faier—who also booked acts—and so many more), much as it did from the Joyous Lake, the Sled Hill Cafe, the Elephant, and other venues around town. Indeed, even through its final incarnation as the Tinker St. Cafe, there was no better place to watch the parade that was Woodstock go by than to be seated on its front patio.

As the sixties arrived, Woodstock had one foot in the past decade and the other dipping its toe cautiously into the new. As forces were slowly gathering that would test a small town's resolve, Woodstock remained, in many ways, content to burnish its conservative resume through its traditions. Over the years, rituals such as the town's Christmas Eve celebration had obtained long-lasting stature within the community, while others, such as the selection of Miss Woodstock fell victim to changing times.

According to press reports, it appears that the first Miss Woodstock was 1959's Carol Bishop. Bishop, a student at New Paltz's Teachers College (as it was called at the time), went on to represent Woodstock in the Miss Ulster County pageant later that year. In 1960, Sandra June Andrade was selected to wear the crown of Miss Woodstock and eventually appeared at the Miss New York State pageant held in Kingston before an audience of fifteen hundred. Andrade made her way to the pageant in rather dramatic fashion. According to the *Kingston Daily Free*man, "The honey blonde Miss Woodstock will come to Kingston on horseback accompanied by 20 of her friends from Mink Hollow Ranch for registration at the Governor Clinton Hotel." Not to be outdone, the paper noted that Miss Schenectady would arrive at the Island Dock Marina in Kingston via a Navy destroyer.[15]

While Andrade did not go on to be crowned Miss New York State, she did receive two awards. An aspiring ballerina who, according to the *Freeman*, planned to "continue her studies at the American School of Ballet, Drama and Arts at Juilliard School of Music," Andrade won the "preliminary talent competition and a $150 scholarship as the most Talented Non-Finalist" for her selection from *Swan Lake*. Two of the officiating judges for the evening included Woodstock artist John Pike and Jane Wilson (wife of Abe Molyneaux). They were joined by Barrytown resident, author, and playwright Gore Vidal.[16]

While the Miss Woodstock idea appears to have met its demise in the early sixties, other endeavors filled with aspiration were launched as the new decade began moving forward. Woodstock artist, craftsman, and local politician John Pike announced in August 1960 the opening of his watercolor school at the end of Pike Lane off Orchard Lane. Held in an informal setting with Pike demonstrating before students seated bleacher style, Pike told the *Kingston Daily Freeman*, "The purpose of the school is to teach water-color techniques, controls and value relationships. This can be achieved through demonstrations and constant personal supervision."[17]

As folk music was echoing throughout town in the early sixties, local attention was also turning to questions focusing on the youth of the community—both educationally and socially. With the new decade one year old, the Onteora PTA took up a debate over the use of corporal punishment within the district. The ensuing debate centered on a motion submitted by Abraham Kramer at a PTA meeting that would "bar the use of physical force in any degree or manner on Onteora Central District pupils." While recognizing school official's right "to restrain or correct by force, when it is necessary as an emergency measure," Kramer's proposed resolution stated that "nowhere and in no wise, does the present state law give any school official the legal right to sanction the application of physical violence in any degree upon a school child as deliberate punishment procedure." Concluding, the resolution offered the belief that "we do not accept the thesis that corporal punishment is wise or effective as a school disciplinary measure. We feel it has no place in modern education."[18]

Not surprisingly, Kramer's resolution received immediate pushback from school officials and the president of the Onteora PTA, Ginger Anderson. Noting that a PTA committee had done extensive research and held multiple meetings with school officials, Anderson stated that the Onteora Board of Education had put "in writing a definite policy on discipline," an important step also noted by Ronald Vanni, director of elementary education. Vanni reaffirmed "the board's right to administer corporal punishment but insisted that it was used only after every other possible method had been exhausted trying to correct an unruly student." Vanni ended his rebuttal by appealing to "the PTA members to have faith in the good sense and fair play of the teachers and administrators."[19] While the resolution against the use of corporal punishment might, today, be seen as a harbinger of changing attitudes regarding the relationship between students, school officials, and teachers, it was a change whose time—at least within the Onteora School District—had not yet arrived. The resolution suggested by Abraham Kramer was soundly defeated, 68-4.

A year later, the long, evolving saga of a Woodstock Youth Center continued to unfold. Stemming from a workshop held by a subgroup of the League of Women Voters where several local teenagers and town leaders urged the town to commit to the establishment of a youth center, Supervisor Abe Molyneaux agreed to seek a temporary location for the operation. At the end of January 1962, during a special meeting of the Woodstock Town Board, Molyneaux and board members approved a resolution to spend twenty-five dollars a month to rent the former schoolhouse located behind the Grand Union.

Three months later as the temporary arrangement neared its end, Sara Mulligan, who had been appointed acting director of the Youth Center and remained a driving force behind its continuation, reported to the Board on the Center's early operation. Stressing that the trial period set aside by the Town Board had proven that that the Youth Center was "vitally needed," Mulligan reported, "Over 100 teenagers used the Center at least once a week," with a total of 250 attendees over the course of the three-month period. As the town had only allotted twenty-five dollars per month for rent, Mulligan further stressed that the teenagers using the Youth Center had, through dances held at the Woodstock School, "been financially responsible for the heat, electricity, supplies, equipment, maintenance and clean-up of the building and toilets."[20] She urged the Town Board to pledge to making the Center an ongoing commitment. In doing so, she cited the need for a professional director and a budget of twenty-five hundred dollars a year, a portion of which could continue to be provided through activities organized by the town's young people.[21]

In a final plea to the Board for continued support, Mulligan made clear what she believed was at stake: "These are our future citizens and leaders. They have all the energy and talent to become useful teenage citizens working for and with the community. And they will be able to do so under the proper guidance. Otherwise, we have done nothing but provide them with a place to go to get off the streets and this idea will pall, and we will be faced with failure. They won't have failed. . . . We have failed."[22] Sara Mulligan's report to the Board seemed to have an impact. Shortly thereafter, the Woodstock League of Women Voters urged the continuation of town support for the Center. In a statement released by the League reflecting Mulligan's report, they stated, "Now is the time for continued action by the community in support of the splendid work already accomplished and that is planned for the future of these young people."[23] Two weeks later, the Center's future received a further boost as the town's Recreation Committee voted to "formally accept all responsibility for the Woodstock Youth Center." Following pressure brought by Mulligan and others, the Committee reasoned that it was "morally committed to embrace this teenage group and to help it function in the best possible manner."[24]

Still, for the Center to operate throughout the remainder of 1962, the issue of funding remained problematic. While the Town Board seemed willing to commit to including a budget line for the Center in 1963, the 1962 budget had already been set. As a result, discussions centered on how to raise the funding required for the remainder of 1962. Councilman

William West, who later went on to serve as town supervisor, advanced the idea that "a foundation-type organization be formed to finance and operate the center." On a more immediate level, noting the successful efforts at fundraising conducted by the teenagers earlier, the Recreation Committee announced that it would work "with a committee of young people from the Youth Center to set up and conduct a finance campaign."[25]

With practical solutions finally moving in the direction of offering permanence to the Woodstock Youth Center, it is doubtful that such progress would have been possible without the efforts and persistence of Sara Mulligan. And while the operation of a youth center moving forward would have continued ups and downs (the original site of the Youth Center was sold and operations moved to the Woodstock Town Hall), Mulligan persisted in her drive to engage support for the Center. In 1964 and 1965, she organized various raffles of artwork donated by local artists, which brought some six thousand dollars for the Center's operation.

Like others of her generation in Woodstock, Mulligan centered her life on community. An actress who over the years appeared in numerous productions at the Woodstock Playhouse, with Kingston's Coach House Players, and in other local Woodstock productions, Mulligan was honored by the Woodstock PTA with the Jenkins Award for her contributions to Woodstock youth and received the Alf Evers Award for her many years volunteering on behalf of the town.

In November 1963, Woodstockers began to turn their attention to the holidays. Thanksgiving was just around the corner, following which the town began to come alive with holiday decorations and anticipation of yet another visit by Santa Claus to Woodstock's Village Green on Christmas Eve. Those preparations and plans came to a screeching halt on November 22 as the news broke from Dallas that President Kennedy had been assassinated. Like most Americans, Woodstockers heard the news in their classrooms, at work, in their cars, and in their homes. While Woodstock was a decidedly Republican town in 1963, the shock and suddenness of the news hit with an impact that overcame local partisan barriers. And while that may be a concept not readily understood by those only familiar with the political landscape of today, the fact was Kennedy was America's president, and with his death the nation's knees buckled. Stunned and tear-stained faces seemed to ask for answers.

For former Woodstock supervisor Jeremy Wilber, much of the entire event played out over radio. At home on that Friday, admittedly faking a "bellyache to stay home from eighth grade classes," Wilber was reading in his bedroom when his mother "burst into" his room with the report that "the president has been shot." Without access to a television, Wilber recalls, "We hurried to our 1955 Chevy station wagon to listen to updates on the radio. We did not know the president's wounds were fatal. In moments the president's death was reported. My mother wept. Soon after school buses brought kids home early. I met my friends. We were all numb with shock and disbelief. I think it was a sunny day."[26]

As the reality of the news from Dallas began to take hold, schools began to dismiss students. Stores, offices, and restaurants began shutting down. The early morning commute and school bus ride, which had begun only hours before, were reversed as Woodstockers of all ages headed home. As they did, what had begun as a tragedy first delivered by radio soon gave way to the pull of the single black-and-white television set found in most homes. As he watched, Bill West wondered "what was happening to the country?" A member of the Woodstock Town Board at the time, West learned of the assassination while having lunch at Deanie's Restaurant with his wife Mary. "General shock," was his reply when asked to characterize the reaction of Woodstockers during that long weekend. West underscored the notion that the assassination fell heavily on all, Republicans and Democrats. Whether you "agreed with his philosophy or not," recalled the life-long Republican and former Woodstock supervisor, "he was a pretty unique person—young and vital. He had charisma, style, and grace."[27]

Like many Woodstockers, West also recalls watching events unfold through the sometimes snowy images of broadcast television in the days before cable television. At the time, if you were one of the lucky ones in Woodstock, you could possibly view three channels, depending on the size of your antenna and the direction it was pointed. (Ironically, in the week prior to the assassination, the Woodstock Town Board approved leasing property at California Quarry to Kingston Cablevision as the first step toward bringing better reception to Woodstock.) Whatever the quality of the picture, however, few ventured far from the screen. Not only was a national tragedy unfolding before their eyes, but the medium of television was forging its place as a dominant force in American lives.

"We sat with trays in front of the TV so we wouldn't miss a minute of it," recalled Lynn Sehwerert. "My parents and sister and I were glued to the TV." Echoing the same thought, Sara Mulligan also remembered being "glued" to the television in her house, "waiting for the next thing. No one spoke, no one called anyone."[28] Eschewing her television set for a brief time, Florence Peper returned to her diary, writing simply as she always did on Sunday, November 24, "We watched on TV all afternoon the changing of the casket of President Kennedy from the White House to the Capitol & the man held for shooting Pres. Kennedy was shot this afternoon & he is dead—Lee Oswald."[29]

On that same Sunday, a telegram addressed to Woodstock town supervisor Abe Molyneaux arrived from Governor Nelson Rockefeller announcing a day of mourning on Monday, November 25. As a result, businesses along Mill Hill Road and Tinker Street closed, and the flag on the Village Green continued to fly at half-staff. Woodstock and the rest of the nation had a funeral to attend.

Eventually, businesses and schools reopened as Americans struggled to move through the holiday season and into a new year. As the calendar changed, so too did the mood of the country. The young saw a partial

Figure 36. Telegram addressed to Woodstock town supervisor Abraham Molyneaux from Governor Nelson Rockefeller declaring the day of President Kennedy's funeral a legal holiday. *Source:* Historical Society of Woodstock Archives/Town Government Collection.

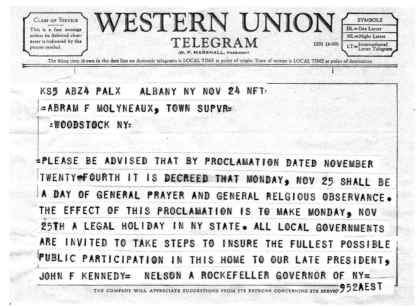

return on their investment in innocence as, a few months later, the same black-and-white television sets that had brought so much tragedy gave them the Beatles. In Washington, Lyndon Johnson pushed landmark civil rights legislation through Congress. In Woodstock, Albert Grossman, along with a young talent by the name of Bob Dylan, had arrived. Seeds were being planted; they would grow.

# Chapter 8

# Changing Times

No one can really say when the page turns to a new chapter in the history of a small town. For Woodstock, however, that day may have been in July 1964.

Woodstock's Village Green has long been a place where locals and visitors alike have gathered over the years. Its central location in the village offers a natural setting where townspeople have joined together to celebrate the end of wars, Memorial Day parades, and, for many years, the weekend Market Fair. The annual gathering of Woodstockers on Christmas Eve awaiting the arrival of Santa Claus to the Green has been a cherished town tradition since the early days of the Depression. On a July day in 1964 a gathering of a different sort took place on the Green, and the result left many in town with the understanding that something entirely different was in the air.

While Albert Grossman and Bob Dylan had already arrived in Woodstock—an arrival that lent itself to how a lot of the world eventually viewed the town—their impact had not yet fully resonated with most townspeople. Rather, it was a group of young people visiting Woodstock from a nearby summer camp that signaled to Woodstockers that the times were indeed about to change.

In addition to the many gatherings that the Village Green hosted over the years, it remained, at the time, the site of the Woodstock War Memorial. As an editorial in the *Ulster County Townsman* argued regarding its importance to the community, "Let us remember that the original purpose of our Village Green is to serve as a war memorial. It is a place of peace and repose in the midst of a busy village."[1] Such was not the case on July 12, 1964, however, when the words "police brutality" first filtered down from the national ether to land squarely on Woodstock. The cause? Folk singing.

On that Sunday in July, some thirty visiting young people found themselves on the Village Green having arrived as part of a visit from their summer camp. Upon disembarking from a truck in the center of town, it was decided to offer up some Sunday afternoon music. With benches in short supply on the Green, the grass and the bluestone wall at the base of the War Memorial offered an opportunity to sit as guitars were removed from their cases. Likely unknown to the young visitors at the time was the fact that the town of Woodstock's regulations regarding the Green provided that "it should be occupied only on the benches."[2]

By the time local constables arrived at the Green to enforce the regulation, it was estimated that between forty to seventy-five people had now gathered. In part, the larger crowd accounted for some of the confusion that followed once the arriving officers began ordering those gathered to disperse. Many of those assembled, however, simply did not hear the commands directed at the crowd by law enforcement. Additionally, some of the constables who approached did so in civilian clothes. Without the benefit of uniform, it was unclear to many of the young people exactly who was demanding their dispersal. As a result, several of the young people on the Green that day simply did not move—or did not move quickly enough. Some demanded to know why such orders were being issued and proceeded to hold their ground.

With that, out came the billy clubs. Wading into the group, constables began an attempt to disperse those who hadn't moved quickly enough. Legs were treated to the force of the clubs, and as resistance continued arrests were made. It was the arrest of two of the individuals involved in the fracas that further escalated claims of police brutality. Escorted to the police station and individually taken to an upstairs bathroom, it was later alleged that each of the young people was beaten by the arresting constable. No witnesses were present. One of the youths stated that he had been struck by the officer, while the other reported that while trying to protect himself he was kicked in the face by the same constable. Whatever the actual sequence of events was, it is known, as they later came before a local judge, that both the constable and one of those arrested showed "some sign of a scuffle having taken place."[3]

Almost immediately, petitions and letters to the editor of the local paper appeared protesting the actions of the local constables. Taking the lead in presenting a petition calling for an immediate hearing by the Town Board and an investigation into the actions of the constables—signed by more than one hundred individuals—was noted science fiction author and Woodstock resident Ted Sturgeon. Little did Sturgeon and those calling for an investigation realize that the process had a long way to go.[4]

Support for the local constabulary was also voiced—as well as resentment of outsiders harbored by several Woodstockers—as evidenced by a letter to the *Kingston Daily Freeman* a month following the incident:

> Who are those strangers who come to this peaceful and artistic colony to start discord and cause incidents to happen?
>
> As an eyewitness to the July 12 fracas on the Village Green, I was surprised to see a truck drive up to discharge total strangers who immediately took over this town by throwing themselves all over the Green in their scanty attire, drinking beer and sitting on the monument dedicated to our war heroes, and crushing the beautiful flowers so lovingly cared for by our Woodstockers. Others were singing and strumming their guitars to the annoyance of many people.
>
> When the Town Police interfered to restore order they were met by a great deal of abuse, and also by some of our citizens who intervened in behalf of those troublemakers. Why?[5]

Concluding her letter, Sonia Rice of the hamlet of Shady offered, "As to my version of this incident, the Police did a good job in dispersing them. My only regret is that the Police were too lenient with them, and not tough enough."[6]

Following the incident and press reports that accompanied the event, several town citizens, headed by Sturgeon, continued to press the Town Board for a public hearing on the incident. While Supervisor Molyneaux offered a promise that such a hearing would be held, the Town Board first announced that it would begin a "formal inquiry into alleged police brutality" behind closed doors on August 27 with no press allowed.[7]

Six weeks after the initial incident, the Woodstock Town Board finally met to hear from witnesses to the event. Twenty-four witnesses were heard over the course of one day. According to press reports, the Board interrogated each constable that was on duty on the day of the incident. In addition to Supervisor Molyneaux, a full Town Board was present for the testimony, including Councilmen William West, Gottlob Wagner,

Figure 37. August 26, 1964, *Kingston Daily Freeman* headline announcing Town
Board inquiry into allegations of police brutality. *Source:* Author's collection.

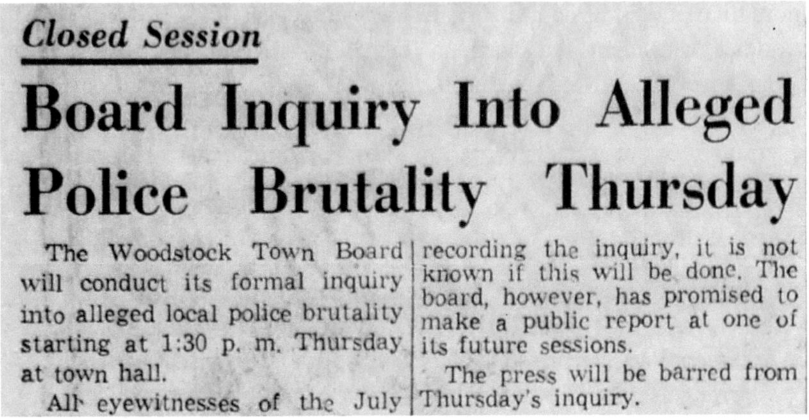

## Closed Session

# Board Inquiry Into Alleged Police Brutality Thursday

The Woodstock Town Board will conduct its formal inquiry into alleged local police brutality starting at 1:30 p. m. Thursday at town hall.

All eyewitnesses of the July recording the inquiry, it is not known if this will be done. The board, however, has promised to make a public report at one of its future sessions.

The press will be barred from Thursday's inquiry.

and justices of the peace Charles Farley and Rudi Baumgarten. Attorney Gerald Wapner was also part of the day's proceedings, representing the two young people who had been arrested. Following a day of questioning, Supervisor Molyneaux announced that "a full report on the board's findings would be made public in the near future."[8] However, September and October passed without a word from town officials.

Finally, on November 5, 1964, Supervisor Molyneaux issued what the *Kingston Daily Freeman* described as a "preliminary oral report" on the July incident. In his report delivered at a Town Board meeting, Molyneaux announced that the inquiry "failed to produce any evidence of police brutality based on the testimony of 24 eyewitnesses."[9] According to Molyneaux, the incident stemmed in part from a "lack of communication between the constables at the Village Green," as the evidence indicated that "some people heard the officers' orders, and some did not." The supervisor also cited the problem of identification as an elemental cause of the fracas because "two of the constables called to the scene when efforts were being made to clear the Green, arrived in civilian clothes and this added to the confusion."[10]

As a result of the investigation, Supervisor Molyneaux announced that new regulations were to be put in place, including the requirement that all constables "carry their badges and hats at all times." In addition, citing the need to protect both police officers from false charges and the arrested individuals from "harm," it would now be required that "two constables or a constable and another police officer" be present when an individual is in custody.[11]

Theodore Sturgeon was not satisfied. Rising to speak, he requested that he be permitted to submit additional written testimony. His request was denied. Expressing "tremendous regret" regarding the amount of time the Town Board had taken in issuing a "public statement" on the August incident, Sturgeon offered that the "failure of the board to act more promptly left hanging the question of 'whitewash' in some quarters and also delaying vindication of the police involved if they were innocent."[12]

As with many things in Woodstock through the years, the November report by the supervisor was not the final act in the drama that had come to surround the charges of police brutality. A final, written report was still due, and according to Sturgeon more testimony was needed, as the Town Board had never really addressed what happened in the bathroom above the police station.

It was not until February 1965 that the Woodstock Town Board issued its written—and final—report on the matter. Signed off by Supervisor Molyneaux and the remainder of the Town Board, it was determined that

> Our conclusion with the making of the arrest on the Village Green is that the officers making the arrest were performing their duty according to the orders given them by their superior and that they used only that force which was necessary under the circumstances to make said arrest. We do find, however, that the constables were partly at fault by not requesting the young people involved to move off the Village Green entirely, except for those parties seated on the benches provided. The rules of the Village Green provide that it should be occupied only on the benches. It would seem that some force was necessary to effect the arrest because of the failure of the young people involved to respond to the order of the constables. They instead chose to question the authority of the constables in ordering them from the Green.[13]

The written report noted the preliminary report's mention that many on the Green that day simply did not hear the orders to disperse. To prevent such a failure in the future, the report notes that a bullhorn had been purchased by the town.

In addressing the alleged incident that occurred later at the police station, the report, citing that the primary defendant had not later appeared before the Board to provide testimony, noted that the Board had heard only "hearsay evidence" regarding what had occurred in the upstairs bathroom. In addition, the defendant, though showing "signs of having been crying and a redness in the face" during his earlier appearance before Justice Baumgarten, had not raised the issue of the alleged beating to the judge. Rather, Molyneaux and the Board seemed to rely on testimony provided by the constable that he had struck the suspect "only to prevent what he thought was an attempt to escape" and that the injury to the constable had occurred on the Village Green during the attempted arrest and not in the upstairs bathroom.[14]

While the final report left many unsatisfied, the community moved on. A lesson suitable for the future had been delivered, however. Only time would tell if the powers that be had listened.

Only a year later, the town's constabulary found itself under the spotlight once again when Woodstock historian Alf Evers was falsely arrested on suspicion of petty larceny. For Evers, it was a case of being in the wrong place at the wrong time, finding himself in the Bearsville laundromat at about the same time as the wife of one of Woodstock's constables. Shortly after that chance meeting, the wife of Constable John Melia reported that her wallet had been stolen. By coincidence, Evers once again encountered the woman, in Lake Hill at the general store known as the Trading Post. Accompanied by her husband at the time, "Mrs. Melia is alleged to have claimed that a man resembling Evers was in the laundromat at the time" her wallet went missing.[15]

Although not in uniform, Officer Melia proceeded to confront Evers in front of the store and place him under arrest. As Evers later described his ordeal to the *Kingston Daily Freeman*, "Melia ordered me into his car. . . . I naturally resisted at first. The man, unknown to me was not wearing a police uniform or badge. After some discussion during which I insisted he show me some identification, Melia produced a badge. He then took me by the arm and propelled me firmly into his car and started to town hall."[16] At the police station, following a search of Evers, the constable told Evers that "I'm no grand jury and I don't have enough evidence. My wife won't press charges."[17] With that, the Melias drove the town historian back to Lake Hill.

A short time later, Mrs. Melia's wallet was found on the top of one of the machines in the laundromat with what money it contained still there.

In yet another effort to deal with the questionable actions of one of its law enforcement officers, the Woodstock Town Board met in executive session to hear testimony from both Evers and Melia. Following that meeting Supervisor Molyneaux, citing the rules of conduct established following the incident that had occurred on the Village Green requiring that two constables be present when questioning a suspect—a regulation Melia had not followed—announced the suspension of Constable Melia for ninety days.

It was now time for apologies. Following the announcement of the suspension, members of the Town Board took time out from their meeting to shake hands with Evers and offer their apology. Evers also noted that Melia had contacted him by telephone to offer his apology. Said Evers, "I told Melia that I accepted his apology on a personal basis . . . however, [it] in no way closes the matter and I have not completely abandoned the idea of a suit against the township for false arrest."[18]

While Evers did "file a notice of claim for $25,000 in damages," it is unclear that the lawsuit ever went forward.[19] Evers, however, suspected for some time that the incident may have been in response to his opposition to plans for the development of a commercial plaza at Bradley Meadows on Mill Hill Road—a development that allowed "the beautiful Bradley Meadows with its supernal view of Overlook Mountain to be blocked by a mall."[20]

Long a favorite site for artists to set up their easels before an unobstructed view of Overlook Mountain, Bradley Meadows had been slated for the construction of a series of commercial establishments. Although Evers had charged that the Woodstock planners, in approving plans for the plaza, had ignored an earlier study—the Brown and Anthony Plan—recommending the property be considered as "open space for public use," construction of the plaza went forward. As Evers argued before the Commission, "What Brown and Anthony sought to avoid by making the meadow [a] park or recreational land, and what the preamble of the present ordinance seeks to avoid, is now a reality because of the commission's actions."[21]

Despite the opposition, the opening of the Bradley Meadows Plaza—complete with ribbon cutting ceremony—began at 9:00 a.m. on February 9, 1966. With numerous dignitaries in attendance, the plaza opened with parking space for 130 automobiles, a new A&P supermarket, a new branch of the Rondout National Bank, and plans for three additional stores, including Joe Forno's Colonial Pharmacy. According to the *Kingston*

*Daily Freeman*, not everyone had been in opposition to the project as, "hundreds upon hundreds pushed their way through the doors of the newly opened A&P supermarket and Rondout National Bank." Claiming the opening had been "a gigantic success," the gathered dignitaries moved on to a "gala cocktail party at the Woodstock Lounge" at day's end.[22]

In addition to the Bradley Meadows property, other land use changes were underway in the mid-1960s. As fall settled in toward the end of 1965, Woodstock's Town Board was busy on two different fronts: the extension of Ricks Road and a lease for a town dump. At the time, Ricks Road was a dead end as it extended off Route 212 in Bearsville. Under the plan proposed by retiring highway superintendent (and former supervisor) Albert Cashdollar, the town could extend Ricks Road and connect it directly with Glasco Turnpike. While the extension would pass through "sparsely settled" property, said property included "a private junk yard owned by Cashdollar." The authorization to proceed with the project passed with one "no" vote cast by then councilman Bill West.

The town was not done working deals with Cashdollar, however. At the same time negotiations for the Ricks Road project were underway, Supervisor Molyneaux was authorized by the Board to negotiate a lease involving property owned by Cashdollar along West Saugerties Road for

Figure 38. Bradley Meadows Plaza at its inception. *Source:* Historical Society of Woodstock Archives/Town Center Collection.

the purpose of establishing a town dump. Under an agreement that went into effect at the beginning of 1966, the town paid Cashdollar twenty-five hundred dollars a year for the use of his land.[23]

Small towns, by the very fact that everyone knows everyone, can over time often border on the incestuous when it comes to local politics. Such were the suspicions surrounding transactions involving the town's dealings with Albert Cashdollar. Granted, Cashdollar had been a force for many years both on the town and county level, having served as Woodstock town supervisor for six consecutive terms, town highway superintendent, Ulster County treasurer, head of the Ulster County Defense Council during World War II, and as a member of a variety community service organizations. And yet, it was that record alone that seemed to allow Cashdollar to move in and out of various lucrative arrangements with the town. Concerns had been expressed even before the Rick's Road and local dump issues came to the fore as Cashdollar, serving as highway superintendent, urged the town to purchase property contiguous to the town highway garage—property for which Cashdollar, following the death of the property's owner, served as the estate's executor.

Attention later was drawn to Cashdollar's affairs when concerns were expressed over repeated fires at the dump he had leased to Woodstock while the town was under a no-burning ban. Despite the ban, not only had fires been allowed to burn at the privately owned dump, but adjacent homeowners also pointed to the fact that no summons was ever served and that town "firefighting apparatus and equipment" and other taxpayer resources were called upon to respond "every time a fire breaks out." As one local firefighter put it regarding the repeated violations at the dump, "he was sick and.tired after two years of chasing to the Cashdollar dump."[24]

While clouds of suspicion lingered over interactions between Cashdollar and the town, little save complaints to the state's Conservation Department ever came to merit legal action. In fact, one further transaction underscored the closeness of those engaged in the town's political hierarchy, as Woodstock eventually purchased the Cashdollar dump property for twenty-nine thousand dollars.

As Woodstock began to make the turn to the second half of the sixties, however, attention moved to far more ominous charges than the proper use of the town's firefighting equipment. Drug abuse—a growing national problem—began to move to the fore, beginning in 1965 with reports of a horrific incident involving "sadistic torture" at the abandoned Reynolds House on Mead's Mountain Road. The victim was allegedly "tied to a wheelchair at the point of a knife and tortured."[25] Beyond the shock that such a brutal incident had occurred in their small town, Woodstockers were forced to confront additional—and unsettling—reports that arose from the incident. Following initial news of the attack, connections were drawn between the incident and rampant drug use in Woodstock, as the victim alleged in a radio interview that drugs were readily available in Woodstock "and that there was more than 200 narcotic users in the community."[26]

With such damaging allegations now front-page news, both the incident and the drug question moved front and center. At the county level, the district attorney's office announced that the "sadistic torture case of a Woodstock man and alleged narcotics activity in that township" would be part of a grand jury investigation into the Reynolds House incident.[27] Locally, Supervisor Molyneaux, via a telegram to state officials, called for legislation that would "provide funds to increase staffs and facilities" to oversee local efforts at stemming drug addiction. Even the Business and Professional Women's Club of Ulster County chimed in by demanding "positive and decisive action in Woodstock."[28]

Others, however, saw the spotlight now aimed at Woodstock and the implication that the town was the center of a rising drug problem as a disingenuous and unfair attack. Although pledging, "as citizens, parents and local residents," to offer "full cooperation to any proper effort" to investigate the Reynolds House incident, the Woodstock Chamber of Commerce also stated, "We regret, however, the uncalled-for attempt to present this as a purely Woodstock problem and to use it to besmirch the reputation of many fine individuals as well as that of a famous community, which attracts many visitors from all over the world to the area." Noting recent drug-related arrests in other local communities such as Kingston and Ellenville, the Chamber concluded, "To attempt to point an accusing finger in self-righteous anger at one town is rendering a disservice not only to that community but to the county and state as a whole."[29]

In part, the controversy that was now swirling around Woodstock, its political leaders, and the community itself had begun a year earlier when an investigative article published by the *Kingston Daily Freeman* began, "Woodstock is stinging with rumors about possible narcotic operations" and further inquired, "In [the] wake of recent and persistent rumors about the use and distribution of various forms of 'dope' ranging from the barbiturate 'goofball' to the deadly marijuana—the Big 'M'—which have run rampant on the subject, the *Freeman* sought answers to the question: Is there any evidence of a narcotics problem in Woodstock?"[30] In response to this question, John J. Bellizzi, the state's director of the Narcotic Control Bureau, explained to the paper that suspicions surrounding Woodstock centered on two main points:

> Woodstock was reputed as a community which had a minority segment—an "offbeat" group. This group, more in evidence in the summer months, he said, was comprised of certain "non-conforming" characters who by their very nature and makeup would be characteristically suspect of using or dealing in narcotics and its trade. Secondly, there was a large concentration of summer tourist trade involving circulation of both large sums of money as well as [a] wide variety of tourists. "Professionals," then, he said, would have a function in narcotics traffic, [and] would be particularly difficult to detect. For instance, an "operator" who was unfamiliar to local, full-time residents, could make "drops"—delivery of drugs to a pusher or even an addict, on a regular basis through the summer—and leave town at season's end without leaving a trace of suspicion.[31]

Suspicion and questions surrounding local drug use at the time eventually expanded beyond Woodstock to engulf Onteora High School as well, due to the fact that many of its students were from Woodstock. For the most part, these questions centered, as they often do, on rumors. The rumors surrounding Onteora stemmed from a case involving six students and the possible use of the drug Doroden, a sedative. From that incident, suspicions expanded, including a report that one student had passed out and that another had been seen with a hypodermic needle. Responding to the *Freeman*'s inquiry into drug use at the high school, school superintendent Dr. George Sullivan noted that the student who had "passed out" had simply fallen asleep and that no evidence had ever been produced that a girl had been seen with a hypodermic needle in a school lavatory. Echoing Dr. Sullivan, Onteora Board president, Philip Gorden, told the *Freeman*, "We have not been able to pinpoint any evidence . . . of the use or distribution of narcotics."[32]

Despite drug arrests elsewhere in the county and not a great deal of evidence pointing to widespread drug use within the town, Woodstock continued to find itself at the center of attention. That attention was further amplified by the increasing number of transient youth and unknown individuals who had begun to find their way to town. It was a concern that had been building and only a year earlier had been the center of a discussion sponsored by the Woodstock Democratic Club. There before a crowd of 150 people, doctors, lawyers, and police officials engaged in a heated debate on how best to approach the issue.

Lieutenant Lemuel Howard, representing the Kingston Police Department, suggested that "the peddling of narcotics is a problem among us now and it is on the upswing" and that "dope peddlers who push narcotics on teenagers are guilty of a crime worse than homicide." Urging "stiff prosecution" and "severe court penalties," Howard also placed blame on some members of the public, pointing a finger at " 'do-gooders' who take the 'it can't happen here' attitude."[33]

In reaction to Lieutenant Howard's comments, panel moderator and attorney Frank Gavin was quick to respond that the lieutenant's "methods would set control of the narcotics problem back to the stone age." Following, in a similar vein, Dr. Theodore Drachman, commissioner of the Ulster County Board of Health, though agreeing that "law enforcement is needed" went on to explain that "there is a lot more to the problem than law enforcement." Chiding Howard's black-and-white approach centering on strict enforcement, Drachman noted that the "narcotics laws have been enforced by people who have no medical knowledge" and that the enforcement of narcotics trafficking had been "a complete failure."[34]

Woodstock physician Dr. Norman Burg, who served the community for many years, brought to the panel a more sociological approach, speaking of the generational underpinnings of what was beginning to evolve not only in Woodstock but also across the country. Sharing with the audience his belief that the "increasing use of drugs by children or young adults reflected a general disregard for society, against the 'rules' and the authority set up by parents, police, and school authorities," Burg concluded, "they reject us because we have failed them."[35]

In a town that was no stranger to change over the course of its history, something very different seemed to be descending on Woodstock, a difference fed by outside influences beyond the control of small-town authorities. While the arrival of the early artists had once brought a way of life unfamiliar to the more isolated citizens of Woodstock, the threat to the town—should one want to call it such—was not necessarily one cradled in fear. Rather, while suspicions were raised and misunderstandings were commonplace between longtime residents and the newly arrived artists, there was little that inspired the direct belief that things were spinning totally out of control. Eventually, as the artists settled in, a growing sense

Figure 39. Longtime Woodstock physician and community leader Dr. Norman Burg. *Source:* Historical Society of Woodstock Archives/People Collection.

began to emerge that their creative work was something a community such as Woodstock could point to with pride, while also providing an added attraction that would aid the local economy. Ultimately, despite the changes that had come, Woodstock had moved on, recognizing that their community was still a community and that the neighbor you knew was still just as close as next door. Children—along traditional gender lines—played baseball, attended dance classes, and filled the ranks of the local Boy and Girl Scout troops. Townspeople ensured that the multiple houses of worship were still filled on Sundays, while the Woodstock Jaycees and Rotary service clubs continued their work on behalf of the community.

The changes that the town began to experience as the decade of the sixties progressed, however, seemed well beyond that which had come before. Much of what was occurring in the real world had begun to breech Woodstock's once isolated borders. Civil rights, the burgeoning drug culture, challenges to authority, the early days of an escalating war in Southeast Asia, the distant shadows that now flickered in living rooms thanks to enhanced television technologies, and, of course, the influential role music had begun to take on in the lives of so many—especially the young of Woodstock—were all combining to present new challenges to a small town and seemed to forecast a transformation that eventually catapulted Woodstock to an unanticipated place on the world stage.

# Chapter 9

# Where's the Peace and Love?

On Friday, May 13, 1966, longtime Woodstock resident Maria Longendyke Elwyn wrote in her diary:

> Get up to sunshine, Don Gardner comes and does our windows and mows the lawn, and it cost $12.00. Wow!
>
> Don carrys [sic] up porch furniture and rugs, etc. Somehow I'm glad it's done, but am I tired? Bob goes in eve at 6 to John the barber, I go to Mamie's . . .
>
> Bob comes back without a chance, all I.B.M. men are there, place is full, so at 6:30 we come back home, tuckered out and no haircut.[1]

While husband Bob would go without a haircut for a bit, Woodstock was moving in a direction that would have Woodstockers complaining about more than the cost of a mowed lawn or IBMers hogging the barber chair.

Not far from the Elwyn home, Bob Dylan was ensconced at Byrdcliffe, having moved on from the Espresso and a home on Ohayo Mountain. Dylan, dubbed locally by the *Kingston Daily Freeman* as, "Young America's Answer to Walt Whitman" and the "Crown Prince of Folk Music,"[2] was spending much of 1966 in retreat recovering from his motorcycle accident in July. Despite the bard's absence from the public scene, young people were arriving in Woodstock seeking him out. For Dylan, it would become a problem that would only escalate in the months ahead, with the newly arrived frequently asking locals, "Do you know where Dylan's place is?" As an example, longtime Woodstock resident Laurie Ylvisaker recalled having, as a teenager, just received her driver's license at that time: "I'd pick up hitchhikers going into town, guitar on their shoulders, and they'd say, 'Hey, do you know where Bob Dylan lives?' And I'd say, 'Yeah, but I'm not going to tell you, you know, don't bother him.' "[3] But, bother him they did, eventually reaching the point where Dylan and family would abandon Woodstock. As Dylan explained in his memoir *Chronicles: Volume One*, "Roadmaps to our homestead must have been posted in all fifty states for gangs of dropouts and druggies. Moochers showed up from as far away as California on pilgrimages. Goons were breaking into our place all hours of the night. . . . Woodstock had turned into a nightmare."[4]

Meanwhile, in the Woodstock hamlet of Bearsville, Dylan's manager, Albert Grossman, had no intention of departing Woodstock. In fact, just the opposite.

As one heads west out of Woodstock's village proper, the first of Woodstock's multiple hamlets one encounters is Bearsville. Contrary to popular belief, while bears are not unknown to the hamlet, Bearsville carries the name of Christian Baehr, who immigrated to this country in 1820. By 1839, Baehr was operating a store in what would become Bearsville while also leading the push to establish a post office there. With approval of his efforts, Baehr was named the hamlet's first postmaster.

Baehr, however, was a Democrat in a decidedly Republican town and eventually left Woodstock, first for Saugerties and later to live out the remainder of his life in Malden, New York. Despite his departure from Woodstock, the store and post office he established remained. Later a gas station, operated by Roy Oakley, found its way along Route 212, and the Woodstock Highway Department occupied property nearby. The 1950s saw the construction of a housing development along what was known as the Bearsville Flats, while in 1960 a bowling alley arrived to be joined a bit later by Joe Holdridge's Swim-O-Links, a combination swimming pool, miniature golf course, and snack bar.

For the most part, however, the Bearsville corridor served as a pass-through road leading to Woodstock's outer hamlets of Shady, Lake Hill, and Wittenberg. And, unless one was an avid bowler or in need of a swim, Bearsville, for most, was simply that hamlet most closely connected with the center of town. That began to change with the arrival of Albert Grossman.

Like Ralph Whitehead and Hervey White before him, Albert Grossman fundamentally transformed Woodstock and altered the perception of Woodstock held by the world at large. As manager for Bob Dylan; Janis

Joplin; The Band; Peter, Paul and Mary; Richie Havens; Paul Butterfield; and numerous others, Albert Grossman's arrival in Woodstock not only established a new chapter in Woodstock's creative journey but also lay a foundation that saw the Woodstock name assigned to an entire generation.

Born in Chicago in 1926, Grossman entered the music world in the 1950s. Spurred by the growth in folk music, he opened the Gate of Horn "listening room" in the windy city. Coming east, he eventually teamed with George Wein to launch the Newport Folk Festival. In the early sixties, while in New York and establishing himself as one of the premiere managers in the music industry, Grossman began turning his eye toward acquiring property in Woodstock. Not long after, he purchased a home in Bearsville, where his new wife Sally joined him.

But the "Baron of Bearsville," as he came to be known locally, wasn't content with simply having a home in Woodstock. Albert Grossman's vision extended further than that. Eventually, work began on a recording studio. From there, Bearsville Records was born. Soon, in addition to Dylan, others within Grossman's orbit began arriving. The musical migration to Woodstock was underway.

Purchasing additional land in Bearsville, Grossman sought to reshape his new property through further construction. A devotee of fine food,

Figure 40. Albert Grossman's arrival in Woodstock fundamentally altered the course of Woodstock history. *Source:* Historical Society of Woodstock Archives/ People Collection.

Grossman envisioned and built a complex of restaurants that included the Bear and the Little Bear. Eventually, a theater was also constructed. More important than the physical construction Grossman undertook in Woodstock, however, was the sense of transformation that his activities brought to the town. In Woodstock, where once artists found their way to the foot of Overlook Mountain to share in Whitehead's or White's visions of a creative community, Grossman's own work and presence opened a similar door for musicians to follow.

From the outside, Grossman was not an easy person to know. His imposing figure and deep voice created space. And yet, as his longtime friend and Woodstock resident Milton Glaser (noted graphic designer who created, among other remarkable works, the "I Love New York" logo and Dylan's psychedelic image on *Bob Dylan's Greatest Hits* album) related to the *Woodstock Times*, the Baron of Bearsville's legacy was as much spiritual as anything else: "He made this place attractive for musicians. He amplified a lot of what was already implicit in the town of Woodstock and out of him sprung the Woodstock festival and the whole legacy, as well."[5] In concurrence, Woodstock Festival producer Michael Lang added, "Albert gave Woodstock a new persona. He took us out of our quaintness and really brought us national attention. And that, in turn, is certainly what brought me here."[6]

Michael Lang was not the only one who arrived.

In many respects, the influx of so many young people in the mid-1960s set the stage for the controversies and battles that were on the horizon for Woodstock. A certain element of newcomers, according to the Town Board, was making itself too well known within the community. As a result, local government was about to move in an effort to stem their impact by considering new regulations aimed at eliminating late-night noise and the public consumption of alcohol. The regulations pondered by the Town Board were in direct response to yet another petition from locals bearing some one hundred signatures. In addition to calling for a curfew in town, the petitioners cited several issues that were drawing their ire, including "racing on the public roads; unmuffled mufflers on vehicles; loitering and noisy behavior; car horns blown for other reasons than warning purposes; screaming; public drinking, necking, sunbathing, and playground activities on the Village Green and nearby areas; younger people who insult elderly ladies on the street with slurring remarks; and the inability to easily contact local constables at night either directly or through county or state police."[7]

Along with an ordinance that attempted to clamp down on public drinking, the Town Board explored ways to prohibit the so-called certain element from abusing the use of town-owned or -leased properties and recreational facilities. Under a broad umbrella, a proposed regulation would "prohibit occupancy without special permission of the Town Board during the hours of 11 p.m. to 7 a.m. for the Village Green, Andy Lee Field, the Big Deep swimming hole, and the picnic area at Mallory Grove in Bearsville."[8]

As part of the effort that limited access to the Village Green specifically, the Town Board determined that it would be best to remove several benches on the Green for the remainder of the summer—the very same benches that were at the center of the 1964 fracas on the Green when several young people were forcefully removed from the property. The reason for the removal of the benches, according to those in officialdom, was that they needed repair. And yet, these repairs were, months later, still not complete. As a result, suspicions were aroused. And, again, although from the opposite direction, a petition was launched calling for the restoration of the benches. Emotions were further exercised by the placement of two signs on the Green warning, "Keep Off Grass—Violation of Town Ordinances."

For some in town, the benches and signs became a rallying cry. With the belief that the repair of the benches had simply been put forward as an excuse to limit access to the Green by the "unwanted," petitioners—including a member of the Woodstock Planning Board, a former Town Board member, various business owners, artists, area authors, and members of both political parties—deplored "the fact that the benches were removed from the Green at the height of the summer season, ostensibly for repairs, and feel that sufficient time has elapsed for their restoration and return." Going further, complainants also pointed out that "the prolonged absence of the benches is a continuing hardship to many of our senior citizens and elderly persons who wait for buses in that area."[9]

The *Ulster County Townsman* and its publisher Marian Umhey—who also served as a Republican member of the Shandaken Town Council for twenty years, as Shandaken supervisor, and as a member of the Ulster County Legislature—didn't quite see the issue from the same perspective as the petitioners. Leading with the front-page headline "It's High Time," the *Townsman*, while questioning why petitioners were unwilling "to accept the official explanation that the benches were unsafe," actually seemed to give weight to the suspicions held by many in town regarding the real reason the benches were removed:

Our office windows overlook the Village Green and we have seldom seen bonafide Woodstock residents (or taxpayers, if you will) relaxing on the benches. More often than not this past summer, the "unsavory element" from out-of-town has been weakening the supports with double loads. By that we mean, that 3 or 4 males with a like number of females on their laps have been monopolizing a bench for hours at a time, with one or two others standing with a foot resting on a bench to support their guitars.[10]

Continuing, the *Townsman* delivered a defense that several Wood-stockers clung to in their efforts to push back against the changes that they were seeing:

These conforming "non-conformists" (as we call them) are nothing but modern versions of the "lazy loafers" our parents and grandparents used to complain about. However, the lazy loafers (even the ones who were known as "drunken bums") used to take a bath once in a while or at least washed their

Figure 41. Gathering on the Village Green. *Source:* Historical Society of Woodstock Archives/Town Center Collection.

face and hands and they seldom, if ever, displayed their utter lack of morals in public!

Many permanent residents believe that these pseudo-intellectuals should be run out of town or arrested for vagrancy. Thus, perhaps the supervisor did the village a favor by having the benches removed![11]

For many in Woodstock, the need for greater influence over what was unfolding in their town was beginning to take hold. Not only was that concern expressed in relation to the "certain element" arriving in town, but an uneasiness continued regarding young people who had grown up in Woodstock.

At a Woodstock Town Board meeting held that summer, despite the town's inability to still provide a permanent home for a proposed Youth Center, Supervisor Bill West spoke of the fact that several incidents had occurred in town involving those under the age of sixteen that had taken place between "the late, late hours of from 2 to 4 a.m." Explaining that "local constables have a particularly difficult time with youthful offenders," West appointed a small committee to look into the "pros and cons of adopting a curfew ordinance for Woodstock."[12] Immediately, some in the audience began to raise questions about the proposed curfew. Would such a curfew impact tourism in town, causing parents with children to "take their business elsewhere?" More to the point of local children, however, parents questioned if "such an ordinance would take the disciplining of their children out of their home and place it in the hands of the town?" In short, was town government expanding its role to babysitter as part of its official functions?[13]

While doubtful that a Republican Town Board would be desirous of taking on the role of Big Brother—at least in 1966—consideration of a variety of new town ordinances became the focus of a public hearing held at Town Hall in August. Those gathered were much in favor of asserting more control over what they viewed as the unwelcome changes that had been placed on their doorstep. In reporting on the meeting, the *Ulster County Townsman* stated that, of the large audience in attendance at the public hearing, some 95 percent of comments "centered on dissatisfaction with the present set of conditions in Woodstock," regarding littering, noise, and the "undesirable element and so called 'beatnicks' centered on the Village Green."[14]

Joe Holdridge, once owner of the motel in Woodstock and, at the time of the meeting, proprietor of Swim-O-Links in Bearsville, echoed the consensus of the evening by stating that there had been too "much tolerance with the undesirable element that gives us a 'do as you please' atmosphere. Visitors who in the past would stay for two weeks, view the Village Green and leave town." Presumably, he was referring only to the "good visitors" who enhanced the town's bottom line.[15] While others added their concurrence to Holdridge's statements, they also stressed the need for stronger enforcement. John Bonilla, however, representing Woodstock Democrats, countered with the belief that if "town government had been more sensitive to the needs of the Woodstock youth, this would not have happened."[16] In fact, Bonilla urged opening access to the Green even further by permitting use of the lawn and adding more benches.

Summing up his feelings on the need for the proposed ordinances, longtime Woodstock stalwart and politico Albert Cashdollar concluded that the ordinances "were the best proposed so far, and it puts teeth in enforcement and makes the people responsible."[17] With the vast majority in agreement, the Town Board moved to adopt the proposed ordinances. As they did, one last exchange underscored the fissures that were developing within the community. In response to a statement made by Carol Hinners wishing that Woodstock would return to "just another little, quiet town," Kiki Minervini, co-owner with Marian Umhey of the *Ulster County Townsman*, was quick to respond, "Woodstock was never just another little country town and those who think so, don't belong here."[18]

Concluding the public hearing, the Woodstock Town Board agreed to set a curfew from 11:00 p.m. till 7:00 a.m. In concert with the curfew, alcoholic beverages were banned on town properties, including the Village Green, Mallory Grove in Bearsville, the Big Deep swimming hole, and California Quarry, which was becoming a popular gathering and camping site for newcomers arriving in town. And while the missing benches on the Village Green had received scant mention at the public hearing, the town historian noted in his annual report that the benches still had not been returned by the end of 1966.[19]

Young people in search of something were not the only ones arriving in town, however, a point that might belie assertions that the undesirable element was harming the bottom line of town businesses. In monitoring activity over the course of Memorial Day weekend in Woodstock, the *Kingston Daily Freeman* found that town merchants were excited over the influx of tourists, who were also making their way to Woodstock as the 1966 summer season "opened on a boom note." The paper observed during the long Memorial Day weekend that "a tour of the principal entertainment attractions in town indicated burgeoning weekend business. Parking lots of tourist homes, motels, restaurants, and bars were filled with automobiles bearing license plates from out of the area."[20] In a somewhat ironic twist, reflective of earlier days when visitors, freed by their ability to afford the purchase of an automobile, would motor to Woodstock to simply see the artists, the town wondered, could Woodstock's more recent collection of beatniks—and the publicity given to their presence—now serve as a similar attraction?

It is not clear when the word *hippie* was first uttered to describe the "undesirable" newcomers in Woodstock, but one thing was clear as 1967 moved through the calendar, the hippies were here. Former town supervisor Jeremy Wilber (in his younger days, bartender for some of Woodstock's more notable watering holes) once satirically described the town's reaction to the influx of that certain element and the first hippie to arrive in Woodstock. He called him Link:

> Link wore an earring, which might as well have been a grenade the way we all jumped behind the hedges, gasped and shuddered. He grew his hair down to his shoulders. If he could walk on his hair, we would have been no less fearful. A wispy goatee simmered under his chin and barely sewed his thin lips to his nostrils. We cringed. An odious presence was Link. This Link obviously did not want to build a house. Or renovate a barn into a house. Or have a house with two bathrooms. He wanted to smoke marijuana, drink Yago wine and ravish our daughters. He threw his wishes in our faces by parading himself on our Village Green.[21]

Like most satire, Wilber's description of Woodstock's first hippie sheds light on the collective perspective many in Woodstock were beginning to share regarding the newcomers who had arrived in town. And while town government attended to the business most small towns faced during 1966–1967—an addition to the highway garage, tax reduction for seniors, and construction of additional bays for Fire Company No. 1—Woodstock was set upon a course that inevitably drove it toward additional confrontations over the "hippie problem."

In many respects, sociologists of the day might have agreed with long-time New York Yankee great Yogi Berra that the late sixties in Woodstock was a prime example of "déjà vu all over again." Writing in a 1929 essay for the *New York Times*, R. L. Duffus reflected on Woodstock's reaction to the impact the arriving artists had on a town comfortably set in its ways: "Woodstock fought hard and is still fighting hard against change. 'For here,' says the youthful editor of one of its two weekly journals, 'a group of people with conscious pride have revolted from the categories of American provincialism, setting up their own standards and customs, producing their own art, and enjoying amusements unstamped by the ratification of universality.'"[22] While Woodstock finally moved past the uncertainty the early artists had brought to their community—and, in fact, now took pride in their association—it was hard to see that the Woodstock of the latter 1960s was willing to reach a similar accommodation when it came to its newest wave of immigrants. Unlike their welcoming reaction to the new neighbors IBM had brought to the community, many Woodstockers failed to see any benefit in their newfound residents. In fact, several worried that the presence of that certain element would be to the town's detriment, as the newcomers seemed intent on dismissing the proprieties of an acceptable Woodstock lifestyle. As the editors of the *Ulster County Townsman* bluntly put it:

> Many well-to-do summer people up the line have complained to us. The gist of their gripes goes like this: "We used to love Woodstock and did most of our food, staples and gift-buying there. We also used to take frequent trips in the evenings for the cultural events. However, one trip thru the village was enough for us this season. Instead of seeing artists and gaily-dressed (but CLEAN) colony residents we were confronted with beatniks, lolling all over the benches on the Village Green, cluttering up the streets and actually preventing our entrance to certain shops."[23]

Despite the sentiments expressed by the *Townsman*, Woodstock wasn't doing too badly. Certainly, the recently opened plaza and the multiple stores within wasn't on the verge of abandonment. Twine's Catskill Bookshop on Mill Hill Road had been joined by a new bookstore, the Juggler, owned by Jean and Jim Young. Opening its doors on Tinker Street next to the Cafe Espresso, the Juggler, in addition to books and magazines, offered "Great Records—Mono and Stereo—$2.00 each."[24] A little further up Tinker Street, the Weathervane presented antiques and fabrics directly across from Anderson Hardware while, opposite the Woodstock Library, the Gilded Carriage, under Marie Basil, had begun its long run as one of Woodstock's more beloved establishments. The Historical Society of Woodstock, thanks to an agreement with the National Bank of Orange and Ulster Counties, began to occupy the historic Longyear home on Rock City Road, while, further up Rock City Road, Nina Kincaid's Folk Art (which for a period boasted a talking parrot) opened daily. Further out of town, in Bearsville, Kevin Sweeney had opened Simulaids, a unique manufacturing operation that produced realistic reproductions of actual wounds to be used in first aid instruction. Sweeney had brought the business to Woodstock in part due to its reputation as an art colony. As Sweeney told the *Kingston Daily Freeman*, "Painting them as wounds really look was one of the big problems. Here we don't have that problem. . . . There are many artists capable of doing it well around here."[25] Bearsville, in addition to Albert Grossman's burgeoning complex, also welcomed the newly constructed Overlook Methodist Church, complete with fully occupied pews on Sunday.

Meanwhile, long-established businesses continued to anchor commercial operations along the town's main thoroughfare, including Deanie's Restaurant, Cousins Home Appliance, and H. Houst & Son. Rotron was doing well, too, announcing a two and a half million dollar loan for the construction of a new plant in the town of Olive. And for those seeking to join the more established, "civil" element of Woodstock, a Woodstock split-level home with a mountain view consisting of four bedrooms, two and a half bathrooms, fireplace, dining room, and two-car garage could be had for thirty-four thousand dollars.[26] In short, Woodstock's economy was showing few signs of being driven asunder by the number of young people arriving in town.

Not all established Woodstockers took the same approach as their neighbors when it came to how they felt or treated newcomers. As Happy Traum once noted regarding his early years in Woodstock, despite his awareness of tensions in town:

> I have to say, some of the locals, the longtime locals, were extremely good to us, extended us credit when we didn't have any money. Art Peper [Peper's Garage] was a sweetheart of a guy and Joe Forno, who ran the local pharmacy when it was right in town, one time opened up at night because one of our kids had an earache. So, it wasn't universally a conflict. . . . I think a lot of the townspeople also were used to this Bohemian artist thing going back to the beginning of the twentieth century. So, they knew they had a bunch of eccentrics in town anyway.[27]

Still, an uneasiness persisted, and it was further exacerbated by an unexpecting Woodstock over Labor Day weekend in 1967. As the headline in the *New York Times* read on September 4, 1967, "Hippy Festival Upstate Is Cool amid the Bonfires."[28] Something called a *Sound-Out* had come to town—or at least just over the town line Woodstock shared with Saugerties. Despite all that was happening in Woodstock during the summer of 1967—including a full slate of nine productions at the Woodstock Playhouse that included the comedies *Barefoot in the Park* and *Luv* and the musical *Oklahoma*; Maverick Concerts launching its fifty-second season; the Turnau Opera presenting Rossini's *Barber of Seville* and *Pagliacci*; classes offered by the Woodstock Guild of Craftsmen in jewelry and metalwork as well as weaving taught by Berta Frey; and the Woodstock Artists Association opening its forty-eighth season with an exhibit titled "Black and White"—the so-called Hippy Festival not only became the talk of the town that post-Labor Day summer but also aided in laying the cornerstone for what was on the horizon.

Small towns are often notorious as communities where most not only know your name but your business as well. As a result, one of the unique aspects surrounding the staging of the Sound-Out in 1967 was the fact that relatively few Woodstockers knew of the plans to hold such a gathering in an open field at Pan Copeland's farm—the same property that the Vos family had once called home following World War II. Despite a lack of advertising, except for some flyers, Jocko Moffitt, a California import working as both a roofer and a drummer, and friends organized a three-day, three-night event that brought together an "estimated two thousand people" according to the *Woodstock Week* (the *New York Times* estimated more than one thousand) to listen to rock, folk, blues, and jazz music. Some brought tents and sleeping bags, others simply lay beneath the stars as the music moved across the field. Attendance cost for one day was two dollars and fifty cents, seven dollars for all three days.[29]

With the music casually kicking off late in the afternoon, an impressive lineup of both local and nationally known (or soon to be nationally known) musicians took to the stage over the course of the festival. As listed on the hand-drawn poster used to advertise the event, the lineup included Richie Havens, Tim Hardin, Ron McLean, Jim Welch, Jerry Merrick, Bruce Murdock, Eve Otto, Junior Wells, Paul Krassner, Billy Batson, Major Wiley, Elaine White, John Bassett, Andy Robinson, Kenny Rankin, the Group Image, the Blue Light, the Muffins, Woody's Truck Stop, and

Figure 42. Poster advertising the original Sound-Out. *Source:* Historical Society of Woodstock Archives/60s and 70s Music Collection.

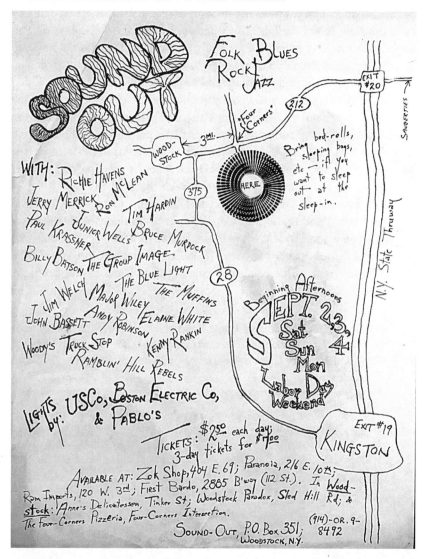

the Rambling Hill Rebels. In addition to the music each evening, light shows produced by USCO, Boston Electric Co., and Pablo's flashed across the field on makeshift screens.[30]

Perhaps because so little publicity had attached itself to Moffitt's plans, the growing cast of anti-anything hippie had little time to form opposition or to voice their objections to the festival. In fact, in published accounts by both the *New York Times* and the *Woodstock Week*, the three days on Pan Copeland's property received a generally positive local reaction. As offered by band manager Jacob Solman in the *Times*, "There was no hysteria, just very orderly people and the police were beautiful, too." Solman added that he "was impressed by the communality" of the event.[31] Similarly, the *Woodstock Week* noted, "There was little disturbance in the proceedings, one man was arrested for using obscenities to a policeman, but other than that there was remarkable order considering the great number of people attending. Each morning all the campers cleaned the meadow and stacked the garbage in heaps to be taken to the town dump."[32]

The first Sound-Out was not the last. Though a disagreement caused a split between Moffitt and Pan Copeland, both produced their own version of a festival in Woodstock in 1968. Moffitt produced his Sound-Out at the Woodstock Playhouse, while Copeland launched the Woodstock Sound Festival, set, as the original Sound-Out had been, on her property.

Figure 43. Under the direction of Edgar Rosenblum, the Woodstock Playhouse promoted numerous musicians and concerts throughout the 1960s, including the 1968 Sound-Out. *Source:* Historical Society of Woodstock Archives/Woodstock Playhouse Collection.

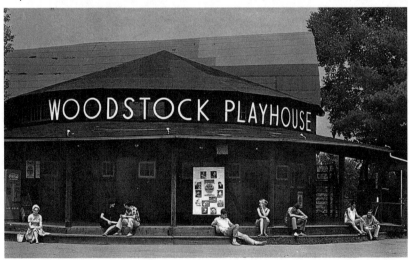

Meanwhile, Woodstock Playhouse proprietor Edgar Rosenblum, in addition to the 1968 Sound-Out, was continuing his midnight concerts and support of the local music scene at the venue, featuring such artists as Tom Paxton, Peter Yarrow, and Tim Hardin. In fact, on the same night the original Sound-Out opened on Copeland's property, the Playhouse hosted a folk concert featuring Billy Faier, Happy Traum, Sonia Malkine, and Linda Masterson.[33] Two years later, The Band settled in at the Playhouse to record their album *Stage Fright*, with Todd Rundgren serving as the album's engineer.

Three days and nights of music, a peaceful crowd sitting in a field listening to music, a summer festival. Sound familiar? While the initial Sound-Out was minus torrential rainfall, its concept gave a certain music promoter by the name of Michael Lang some ideas. As Lang later told *Chronogram Magazine*, "Nineteen-sixty-eight had been a terrible year, with the assassinations of Martin Luther King and Bobby Kennedy, and Vietnam and the violence at the Democratic Convention in Chicago." He continued, "I just thought about how nice it was for someone to be sitting out under the stars in the summer, smoking a joint, and listening to music. I thought, 'I wonder if something like this but bigger could work here.' "[34]

As Woodstockers bid farewell to 1967, unsuspecting of the events yet to come as hinted at by Lang, they did so under new leadership. Bill West had moved on to a seat in the Ulster County Legislature, and the town supervisor's office was now occupied by Milton Houst. They also awoke on the first Sunday of the new year to the news that Clarence Schmidt's multistory architectural structure on Ohayo Mountain had burned to the ground. Originally a simple cabin, Schmidt's twenty-five-year effort at constructing his "mountain art" building—derided by some, praised by others, and the focus of an earlier lawsuit to have the structure demolished—had received national attention and was subject to constant visits by curious Woodstockers. Constructed from almost any material Schmidt could find and haul up the mountain, the edifice rose some seven stories. Unfortunately, it was the assortment of materials coated by tar that caused the structure to burn rapidly. Fully consumed by flames by the time firefighters arrived on the mountain, Schmidt's quarter-century effort was reduced to what reports described as "an open pit."[35] While Schmidt made a second attempt at yet another structure—this time employing a station wagon at its base—it too met a fiery end. Confined to a nursing home in Kingston for many years after, Schmidt could often be seen sitting and waving from the home's front porch to passersby along Kingston's Albany

Avenue. Described in an exhibition of his work by the Woodstock Artists Association in 1976 as "a major figure on the boundary of environmental art and folk art,"[36] Schmidt passed away in 1978.

The year 1968 had not started well, and the outside world was creeping in. While some were already engaging in organized discussions in opposition to the war in Vietnam, a group supporting the candidacy of Eugene McCarthy for president was meeting weeks before Lyndon Johnson announced that he would not seek another term in office. As announced by the group's publicity chairman, Tobie Geertsema, it was the intention of the organizers to "elect three delegates from the 28th Congressional District to go to the national Democratic convention in Chicago this August. . . . And they will be totally and completely committed to Sen. Eugene McCarthy."[37] Meanwhile, across town, the Woodstock American Legion post passed a resolution calling for the "compulsory conscription for all young men between the ages of 17 and 18." While the resolution included the Peace Corps as part of their definition of service, it went on to state as justification, "Surely, the country will benefit from the efforts of our youth in service and the harm caused by race riots, draft protests, drug addiction, school dropouts, youth crime, and the effects of growing up in a welfare [sic] environment will be diminished."[38]

At the same time as lines were being drawn over the war in Vietnam, a more cosmic presence was beginning to filter into Woodstock life, as exemplified by the announcement of a special Woodstock program focusing on the life and teachings of spiritual master Meher Baba. Advertised to be held at the Kleinert Hall on Tinker Street, event organizers promised "elaboration" on Meyer Baba's statements relating to "Existence, the Drug question, Real Mysticism, War, and the evolution of 'Consciousness.'" In announcing the event in the *Woodstock Week*, organizers explained Baba's intent to "bring about a happy blending of the head and the heart" and revitalize "all religions and cults and bring them together like beads on a string."[39]

As the outside world continued to encroach on the lives of Wood-stockers, however, residents were not without concerns that hit closer to home. In 1968, the Onteora School budget saw increased scrutiny as the public repeatedly voted down proposed spending plans offered by the school board. Following the budget's rejection by voters, the board ultimately declared that the following school year would operate under an austerity budget, impacting services across the school system, including the purchase of new textbooks and equipment, while also limiting transportation options and bringing a halt to scholastic sports and field trips.

Crime also entered the picture. A stabbing in June left a victim in critical condition at a hospital in Kingston, while a kidnapping and attempted strangulation of an eleven-year-old Woodstock girl became front-page news and increased tensions throughout the town. Abducting the girl near the Tannery Brook bridge, the kidnapper proceeded on a three-hour drive through the county and at one point attempted to sexually assault his young victim. After the girl was finally released in Kingston, authorities were able to apprehend the suspect based on information the victim had provided.[40]

Crime was also at the center of Woodstock's return to addressing the so-called hippie problem that summer as complaints continued to pour forth at a Town Board meeting in August. Rising to speak, Eric Hiltz, a longtime Woodstock resident, announced, "I'm seriously thinking about moving out of town" unless the town does something about the that "certain element." Another speaker claimed that he had resorted to locking "his three children in their yard for play and finds he would rather shop in Kingston than in Woodstock because of the local 'hippie' population."[41]

While Supervisor Houst reminded the audience that "there is no law against long hair, wearing blankets or going unwashed," he did note that the town had recently hired three part-time constables and that the Board was looking to expand police coverage to twenty-four hours.[42] Still, problems were growing for the newly installed supervisor, as the issue of trespassing was now becoming central to many of the complaints the town was receiving.

On Tuesday evening, September 17, 1968, the Woodstock Town Board met to consider a new law directed at trespassing and directly aimed at the young people who were now among them. While trespassing was an offense already found in town law, the new law under consideration came with a twist, calling "for the arrest of a trespasser without the previously required consent of the property owner."[43] In short, anyone could now file a complaint—anywhere—if they believed the act of trespassing was taking place by simply calling the police. The next Tuesday, a group of local citizens came to question the new regulation. The immediate concern they raised focused on the property rights and the wishes of the owner. "'Can the police assume people do not have the permission to be on property,' a woman asked?"[44] Could police arrest someone simply on the complaint of a person who did not own the property? Could a complaint come from a passing motorist based on the looks of a person or how they were dressed? Others wondered if a deer hunter walking through unposted lands could be arrested, or a truck driver pulled over because he was tired and needed to rest. Supervisor Houst believed not, stating that he "thought the local constabulary was lenient and educated enough not to arrest a person under such circumstances."[45]

Supporters of the new law countered with their own concerns. According to the reporter covering the meeting for the *Kingston Daily Freeman*, their complaints centered on hippies entering seasonally occupied homes during the winter. As noted by one part-time resident, "The trouble is discovered when the owners return in the spring and find their homes were lived in and ransacked. Then it is too late to do anything about the trespassers." Yet another woman, described as "angry" by the newspaper's reporter, put it more bluntly, "I do not want people on my property that have not been invited."[46] As the rhetoric began to rise, one Woodstocker shouted, "Let's clean up this town, it's not safe for my children." A mother in attendance concurred, "My children were chased from the pump house by nude swimmers."[47]

Pushing back against these complaints and the proposed law, a member of the audience brought the real issue of the meeting to a head by asserting, "Let's stop pussyfooting around. What you are really talking about is, 'Let's get the hippies.'" Yelling back in retort, another in attendance asked, "Why don't you put up a sign, 'Hippies invited?'"[48] Despite the opposition and the rancor of the evening, the Town Board passed the new law. True to the law's intent, the number of arrests for trespassing rose accordingly.

And yet, despite the many challenges of a challenging year, something new was stirring that fall along Woodstock's Millstream Road that gave rise to the promise that only art can bring. Reinforcing and expanding upon the ideals and beliefs of the art colony's founders, the newly formed Woodstock School of Art announced that it would open its doors on October 6. Behind the new school were its four founders: Robert Angeloch, Franklin Alexander, Lon Clark, and Jerry Jerominek. It was, in fact, Jerominek's building along the Sawkill where the school first welcomed students. Once a sawmill, the two-story structure that housed Jerominek's Tatra Prints was a building steeped in Woodstock lore. In addition to a mill once operated by Dan Sully and his wife, the building later housed a general store and stagecoach stop, was home to female students attending the Art Students League summer program, and, at one time, was an emporium of sorts hosted by Louise Hellstrom. With a jazz band and furnishings that included red carpets and zebra-striped chairs, Hellstrom's Woodstock Lodge often played host to various local and visiting notables, including, on occasion, muckraking author Sinclair Lewis.

Purchased several years later by Jerominek and his wife Rosemary, Tatra Prints occupied the first floor. There, the couple produced graphic art and silk-screened Christmas cards. The second floor of the building, as well as some outbuildings on the property, became home to the first classes offered by the new art school. They included silk-screen classes with Jerominek as instructor, portrait painting by Alexander, and drawing and painting classes conducted by Angeloch and Clark.

On Sunday, October 6, 1968, more than three hundred people crowded into the school's studios to celebrate its opening. Press reports indicate that those in attendance "feasted" on everything from potato chips to pickled herring and a "potent punch that seemed to get stronger as the afternoon hours passed." Looking down from the studio's walls were the works of the school's founders, landscapes that "seemed to bring summer back" and portraits that "came to life as localites Jane Axel, Cornelia and Edgar Rosenblum and Arnold Blanch walked in front of the paintings they had sat for."[49]

In some respects, by reclaiming the original principles of the founding members of the art colony, the newly established school offered Woodstockers' reflection on the fact that the town had known dramatic transitions in prior years. And, though many in town preferred that Woodstock simply go its quiet way, the legacy of change within the pages of Woodstock's story and the town's natural attraction to outside forces could not be ignored. Much as the earlier artists had found, there was a certain sense of freedom and creativity unleashed by the landscape that now attracted a new wave of those seeking the same. In many respects, the confluence of multiple artistic possibilities, intertwined with the physical environment of the Woodstock valley, remained an attraction to many.

Speaking, years later, on a similar theme at a forum hosted by the Historical Society of Woodstock in 2019, Barbara Pickhardt—musician, composer, and artistic director and conductor of the chorale ensemble Ars Choralis—reflected on her arrival in Woodstock and the relationship to the landscape that surrounded her: "There's kind of a connection to the earth, a connection to something beyond us that is manifested in the landscape and the mountains—there's a mysticism, there's something in the vibe I pick up and I don't know how it really effects my music, I know it effects my life and therefore it would affect everything. It has a power, there's a power beyond us."[50] As the sixties moved on, however, there were many in Woodstock who failed to see such connections and the power it held for the newly arrived. To them, the newcomers in town represented more than a passing wave. Rather, it was becoming a tsunami, and it was time for them to push back further against the oncoming flood. The year 1969 and the years that followed bore witness to that attempt.

# Chapter 10

# Woodstock

## What's in a Name?

Simply put, the 1969 Woodstock Festival was not held in Woodstock; it was held in Bethel, New York, about seventy miles southwest of the town. That said, the fact that tourists—even today—still arrive in town asking where the festival was offers an indication of how the town's name became a flashpoint in 1969 and furthered the influx of newcomers and the debate that centered on how the town should respond.

As the festival approached in the summer of 1969, it seemed that the pressures brought upon the town by the added attention and the further influx of young people grew almost daily. Writing in the *Kingston Daily Freeman*, Tobie Geertsema offered her perspective on the "Scene at Woodstock":

> The hippies sprawl on street corners, rap, and ogle back at the oglers whose eyes are cemented on them. Tinker Street has been dubbed "the strip" almost overnight and, as a main playground of psychedelic '60s youth looking for the action, is becoming crammed with hip clothing haberdasheries, coffee shoppe collage, discotheques and rive-gauche cafes pouring their electronic music into the street with the aroma of a summer thunderstorm.
>
> But if it's a fun scene for the kids (in spite of the hucksters hustling, the old guard tourists hassling over the unhappy

changes, and the establishment sometimes harassing), it is frightening to the local gentry.[1]

That same, so-called frightened gentry, as referenced by Geertsema, was not sitting idly by, however. The swimming hole at Big Deep remained closed due to its use by nude bathers and a persistent "herbal aroma" in the air. Town constables continued to respond to reports of trespassing to comply with the law passed the previous year. Constables also continued their vigil over the Village Green and town center. One individual was arrested twice in the same evening, a not uncommon occurrence. At 7:30 p.m. a man feeling no pain was arrested for carrying "an open container of alcoholic beverage upon a public street." A short time later, that same individual was charged with a second offense when he obstructed "vehicular traffic on Tinker Street by stepping into the flow of traffic and waving his arms at an oncoming car, causing the car to stop." Proceeding from the center of Tinker Street, the subject then walked "over to the Village Green and climbed upon the [war] monument and placed his hands into the flowers therein."[2] Such incidents, incidents that were becoming increasingly problematic, underscored the growing hostility townspeople were beginning to voice when it came to the town's newcomers. As one Woodstocker put it at a meeting in a private home called to address the hippie problem, "Our women who walk our streets swallow the filth and dirt that these people exude."[3]

Recognizing the fact that the summer of 1969 was not heading, to say the least, in a positive direction, Woodstockers from various corners began offering efforts at moderation. In June, the Chamber of Commerce hosted a meeting promoted as a discussion on "The Hippie Impact on Woodstock as a Community." Seated among a panel that included the head of the Chamber, Christopher Morris, Dr. Norman Burg, Onteora school superintendent Dr. Harold Snyder, Rotron's, Charles Weidman, and author Jean Martin was Michael Green, a self-declared, vocal member of the hippie community and the first representative of that certain element to be include in such a town-wide discussion. Saying that the "hippie phenomenon was conceived in non-violence, love of nature, humanity and God," Green argued "that the answer will not be found in more strictly enforced laws, curfews, or more police control—all of which lead to more violence, more name calling, more separation into battlefields of we and they."[4] The more established members of the panel did not disagree. Noting that Woodstock is a "unique community," Dr. Snyder stated that the town should avoid "overreacting to the point where we destroy this kind of climate." Others on the panel concurred that a major part of the problem centered on a certain criminal and drug-related element, as well as a lack of community resources for the town's youth.

As if on cue, Sara Mulligan, long behind efforts in support of a youth center in town, rose to charge that there were those in town, including the "town fathers," who "wanted to keep Woodstock the way it was, year after year, when the town was not the way it was, and when there have been changes." Woodstock physician, Dr. Frederick Elias, followed by not only criticizing the town's closing of recreational facilities such as Big Deep but also pushing back over the denigrating language that some in town were using. "This is the cry of wolves for blood," he announced, adding, "hate does not unify a town." Identified in the press only as a "Glasco Turnpike resident," a woman rose to remind Woodstock of its connection to its bohemian past, stating, "The hippies were always here since I came and since I can remember." As a result, she could not "understand the cries of 'THEY are coming . . . THEY are going to get us!'" She asked, in conclusion, "What is the crisis? Are THEY advancing down Route 375?"[5]

Longtime Woodstock resident Howard Koch, screenwriter and Academy Award winner for the film *Casablanca* as well as author of Orson Welles's radio drama *War of the Worlds*, also lent his considerable voice to what he viewed as a town going too far in the attacks that were being launched. Koch, no stranger to the harm accusations can unleash, having been blacklisted during the Red Scare of 1947–1957, wrote in a lengthy letter to local newspapers, in part:

> As a person who chose to make his home in Woodstock because it seemed to me one of the most friendly towns in the country, I am puzzled and dismayed by the outbreak of hostility among some of my fellow residents toward young people whose style of life and dress does not conform to their own. There is a growing tendency to lump all non-conforming youths under the convenient label "hippies" and make them the scapegoat for our own fears and frustrations. I believe we should face the fact, unpleasant as it is, that the things which are deeply wrong with our society—poverty, racism, injustice, corruption and war to name a few—stem from our own past generations, not theirs.[6]

Koch agreed with Sara Mulligan and Dr. Norman Burg that what was needed was a "citizens committee to organize a youth advisory center in Woodstock where we can deal with problems such as drugs and recreation." Concluding, he submitted, "There is a war, overt or covert, in much of the world. In our own community at least, let us live in peace with one another."[7]

Peace, however, was getting hard to find. Less than a day after Koch's letter appeared in the *Kingston Daily Freeman*, attacks against the hippie element escalated, underscoring the possible danger lurking beneath the public discourse. In what was described by the local paper as a "vigilante action" against a local hippie group, a campsite and meditation center located in Mink Hollow was burned to the ground. Speaking that same evening at a prearranged meeting held by the Woodstock Republican Club, local attorney Gerald Wapner characterized the attack as a "complete outrage," noting that the group had received permission from state rangers to camp on the property.[8] A nearby camper, Herbert Grubb, later described the aftermath to the *Daily Freeman*, "One large tent was burned, a big jungle hammock torn to shreds and thrown in the creek, a month's food supply dumped on the ground, cups and plates broken, books and artwork burned and tarpaulins, raincoats and tools stolen." Grubb also noted that prior to the incident, campers had seen a red pickup truck "in the area and a group of youths carrying guns near the campsite."[9]

Although the alleged actions of a roaming group of local young people did not a crisis make, their elders were not beyond adding fuel to the simmering fire. While one demanded that any arrested newcomer be "deloused and have their heads shaved to clean them up,"[10] another referred to the hippies as "abominations to the aesthetic," as well as accusing "them" of "overrunning the town like maggots."[11] Meanwhile, as summer moved to a crescendo in Bethel, New York, multiple headlines in the *Kingston Daily Freeman* continued to focus on what was happening in the actual Woodstock, including "The Theme in Woodstock—How to Get Our Town Back," "Deny Wittenberg Park to Woodstock Hippies," "What Is a Hippie—Disagreement in Woodstock," "Woodstockers Face Problem—Search for Sane Solution," and, from the *New York Times*, "Woodstock's a Stage, but Many Don't Care for the Show."

While much of the concern expressed in town was directed at the physical presence of certain individuals who, according to some, did not meet Woodstock standards (whatever they were), change continued to impact Woodstock's economic and cultural scene as well.

With the Cafe Espresso holding forth on Tinker Street as home to those more aligned with the more bohemian side of Woodstock nightlife (while Deanie's Restaurant on Mill Hill Road offered a more traditional Woodstock setting), a new establishment had opened its doors on Rock City Road: the Elephant. The Elephant was once home to Dick Stillwell's S.S. Seahorse, a drinking bar where no questions were asked and none expected. The history of the Seahorse comes complete with its own stories, the least of which is the night Stillwell died. As the story has made its way down through the years—no doubt with some embellishments—Stillwell, no fan of providing free drinks to his customers, collapsed behind the bar one night. Carried out from behind the bar by patrons and placed on a ping-pong table, those gathered around him quickly realized he was dead. While trying to figure out what to do next, the realization dawned on those assembled that drinks were now on the house. And so, for the next couple of hours, the life of Dick Stillwell was celebrated by his "loyal" customers as they helped themselves to an abundance of free liquor.

The Elephant proved to be a much different place. Also known as the Purple Elephant, it opened in 1969 and was a changing combination of coffeehouse, restaurant, and miniboutique. With clothing designed by Melinda Lubinsky, including vests, capes, and dresses, the Elephant also offered traditional fare such as burgers and a brunch menu, while also introducing humus, pita bread, and some vegetarian offerings to Woodstockers.[12] Although initially without a liquor license, it was home to music as well. In addition to local musicians, one might, on any given night, catch Tim Hardin, Jerry Jeff Walker, or Richie Havens as light boxes created by Billy Faier pulsed at the periphery. Fred Neal, living for a time at the Millstream Motel, recorded there and, as musicians rolled through Woodstock before and after the Woodstock Festival, Santana arrived one night, down from a rented home on Glasco Turnpike.

Shops along Woodstock's main streets were also changing, as was the self-sufficiency the town once pointed to with pride. As noted by *Freeman* journalist Tobie Geertsema, the shoe repairman near the Village Green was now gone, replaced by a trinket shop where "amulets, incense, chimes, flutes, feathers, Buddha prayer candles, banners, posters, rabbit skins, beads, pipes and prisms" were sold to "square customers by hippie merchants." Nearby, the corner bakery had been replaced by "a store offering relatively high-priced mod clothing and some other lightheadedness from the new gypsies." A leather shop, Hapiglop, had arrived on Tinker Street, and along the same stretch was a porch "on which an elderly lady

Figure 44. Poster announcing the appearance of Jerry Jeff Walker and Bob Gibson at the Elephant on Rock City Road. *Source:* Author's collection.

lulled herself to sleep every summer afternoon in a rocking chair for more than a decade, [where a new shop] purveys psychedelic pantsuits, long skirts and gadgetry of an antique guise." In obvious reference to the Elephant, Geertsema also offered her opinion on the changing nature of dining in Woodstock: "A bar that once provided a ping-pong table giving beer guzzlers a chance to work off their sudsy buzz in athletics is now a typical coffee house landmark. If the food and espresso are meritorious, it is sometimes difficult to enjoy them when the couple at the next table is trying to find God or discover Self while floating on a cool sea of warm Jello by burning incense through lunch."[13] Change, too, was visiting Woodstock's cultural landscape. While the Woodstock Artists Association was celebrating its fiftieth anniversary in 1969 with a series of three exhibits spanning its history, something quite different was unfolding at a gallery near the Woodstock Playhouse. In July an art exhibition titled "Transcendental Art" opened in Woodstock.

While up the road the works of such noted Woodstock artists as Milton Avery, Reginald Wilson, Walter Plate, Anton Refregier, and Judson Smith were being hung by the Woodstock Artists Association, the new Transcendental Art exhibition was presented to the public as an illustration of "energy flow from the Buddha-Realm." Featuring works by a group calling themselves the Woodstock Evolutionary Council, the exhibit included pieces from several individuals who associated themselves with the "hippie movement" in Woodstock, including Michael Green, Billy Faier, Herbert Grubb, Isaac Abrams, Ernest Rivera, and others. While their belief that the exhibition's appeal derived from "the internal unity dance of beautiful ecstatic wave-length consciousness" may have left some Woodstockers shaking their heads, some of the colony's early founders—such as Hervey White—just might have appreciated it.[14]

Meanwhile, at the Woodstock Playhouse, Edgar Rosenblum and director Harold Baldridge were making waves of their own. Under Baldridge's direction, the Playhouse brought to the stage the off-Broadway production of *In White America*. A production that challenged the majority white attendees usually found at the Playhouse, *In White America*, drawing on diaries and letters as well as official documents, took the audience through the Black experience in the United States—from slave ships to the more recent challenge of racial segregation in Little Rock, Arkansas.

The Tinker Street Cinema—having opened in the former Methodist Church—was also stretching out to include different genres, bringing to the local screen *You Are What You Eat*. Although centered on youth along the Sunset Strip in California, the eclectic film—not shy in its efforts to "bombard the eye and the ear"[15]—presented Woodstockers with a glimpse at what they were experiencing daily: hippies, flower power, and a sometimes too close look at the life of the younger generation. Directed by Barry Feinstein and produced by occasional Woodstocker Peter Yarrow of Peter, Paul and Mary fame, the film also offered appearances by a host of Woodstock-connected musical and cultural luminaries, including John

Herald, Paul Butterfield, Clarence Schmidt, and members of The Band: Garth Hudson, Rick Danko, Richard Manuel, and Robbie Robertson.

Public poetry readings were making inroads into Woodstock's cultural milieu as well. On Friday evenings, the Reformed Church on the Village Green opened its doors to local poets.[16] Toward the end of the year, the Cafe Espresso began a series of weekly readings featuring resident poets Janine Pommy Vega, Carol Berge, and George Montgomery.[17] More a throwback to the days of the Cheats and Swings than a new age innovation, folk dancing and square dancing were also becoming a part of Woodstock's weekly cultural scene. Each Friday evening at Woodstock's Town Hall, Ron Sanders offered Woodstockers of any age instruction in traditional dances from around the world.

And yet, even as a festival bearing the town's name unfolded miles away—and as newspapers and other media coverage flashed the name Woodstock across their headlines—the Town of Woodstock still needed to go about the business of being a town. And, despite the attention the festival continued to bring, Woodstock's populace managed to find issues that occupied their attention beyond hippies and the contempt some held for Jimi Hendrix's version of the "Star Spangled Banner."

Directly in the spotlight for many townspeople was enforcement of elements in the town's zoning law. Adopted a few years earlier, the law included a provision relating to the regulation of signage in Woodstock, focusing on oversized signs, neon signs, improper lighting of signs, and the placement of signs. Initially, a grace period had been offered to bring establishments within the code. By 1969, however, that grace period had ended and, with an estimated ninety businesses in violation, a newly appointed building inspector was intent on forcing compliance.

While some businesses, such as Peper's Garage, complied almost immediately by taking down a large Chevron sign that loomed over their brick structure on Mill Hill Road, a little further down the hill compliance wasn't coming so easy. There, the Humble Oil and Refinery Company refused to remove their oversized sign advertising Esso gasoline at Ken Reynold's gas station. Not only did they refuse, but the company let the Zoning Board of Appeals understand that they were willing to "go to the Supreme Court" to fight the determination that they were in violation of the law. Not to be cowed by the oil company's threats, zoning enforcement officer Harold Martin responded that "the major oil companies who oppose the sign ordinance are, in actuality, 'absentee landlords,' attempting to tell

Woodstock what to do." Ben Webster, chairman of the Planning Board, put it a bit more bluntly by noting that Woodstock is "very familiar with the law" and that Woodstockers "are not a bunch of hicks up here!"[18] Ultimately, the Town of Woodstock was not hauled before the learned justices of the Supreme Court and the sign was removed.

Similarly, the Atlantic Richfield Company, which had purchased the former Woodstock Garage from Lou Wilson, also requested a variance for their planned signed on Mill Hill Road. Following an appearance before the Zoning Board of Appeals and a roomful of Woodstockers urging the Board to enforce the law, the company relented and joined both Chevron and Esso in the decision not to challenge the ordinance.

Some good news for those fearing further development in Woodstock—as well as those who chased a golf ball over nine holes—reached townspeople in 1969, as an easement agreement was accepted by the Woodstock Town Board to keep the golf course at the entrance to town "forever open." Negotiated by attorney Marin Comeau on behalf of the golf club at the end of 1968 and with the acceptance of the easement by the Town Board in the spring of 1969, fears were allayed that the property would one day find itself in the hands of developers. As described in the easement, "The Premises will not be developed for any residential, commercial or industrial purposes and the existing scenic and esthetic features of the Premises will not be destroyed, mutilated or concealed so that they may be preserved for the benefit of the public."[19]

With enforcement of the new zoning law and the example set by the golf course easement, Woodstock, acknowledging changing attitudes toward the environment, was beginning to assert increasing control over both its natural resources and town aesthetics. In a snapshot of where town sentiment lay at the beginning of 1969, the Woodstock Association for the Conservation and Improvement of the Township released the results of a survey they had conducted the previous year. Although the town remained split on the prospect of introducing a sewer system in town (42% in favor, 41% against), 95% favored "enforcement of regulations to counter stream pollution." As was evident during the debate over gas station signage, a large majority of the one thousand respondents to the survey believed that not only should neon signs be prohibited but "all signs should be limited in size and brightness." Further, the majority surveyed opposed construction "of high-rise and garden apartments" in town while also favoring the creation of a "design advisory board" to review commercial and public buildings. On the same question of a design board reviewing private property, however, "48 percent drew the line at any advice on their own home, while 35 percent would accept such advice."[20]

As the decade began to wind down and a new one approached, several Woodstockers continued to turn their attention to embracing causes that were increasingly advancing to the fore. While some 400,000 had managed to bestow a peaceful legacy on three days of peace, love, and music at the Woodstock Festival in Bethel, it may have been equally surprising, considering the building tensions in town surrounding the hippie problem, that approximately six hundred Woodstockers from various stations in life—young and old—peacefully came together in October to express their opposition to the war in Vietnam. Coinciding with the nationwide moratorium to end the war, townspeople gathered near the post office on Tinker Street and proceeded to march to the Woodstock Playhouse on the far side of town. With Holley Cantine's Woodchuck Hollow Band in the lead, marchers proceeded without interference past the war memorial on the Village Green bearing signs reading "We Shall Overcome," "Stop the Slaughter in Vietnam," and "Bring Our Men Home from Vietnam." Following the march, a capacity crowd packed the Playhouse for "A Concert for Peace," featuring an eclectic range of music from folk to jazz to rock. It was a day, journalist Tobie Geertsema observed, in which, "Hundreds mobilized in peaceful, lawful protest as they had never done before."[21]

The true reality of the Vietnam War, however, was brought front and center as news arrived months later that a son of Woodstock had been killed in action. Serving as a medic in Vietnam, Richard Quinn was ordered forward during a firefight in Phuoc Long Province to help save a fellow medic who had been hit by enemy fire. Placing himself between the gunfire and his wounded comrade, Quinn too came under fire. Both were killed. Today, Richard Quinn's name can be found on the Vietnam Veteran's Memorial in Washington, DC, and at home his name is the last to be etched in stone at the Woodstock Veterans' War Memorial, now located in the Woodstock Cemetery.

Beginning in the spring of 1970, the environment received increasing notice in Woodstock as celebration of the first Earth Day neared. In April, discussions were held on the damage rock salt—used on town roads in the winter—was doing not only to roadside trees but to fish in local streams as well. In the center of town, the storefront window for Houst's displayed cans of DDT as the business announced it would no longer be selling the poisonous pesticide.

Figure 45. Marker at the current site of the Woodstock Veterans' War Memorial honoring the sacrifice and service of Sergeant Richard Quinn. *Source:* Image by author.

Finding an additional area many in town could agree on, several Woodstockers joined together to form LIFE (Living in a Fulfilled Environment) to further educate the public on environmental issues. Of particular concern to many was the deteriorating conditions of local streams and, more specifically, Tannery Brook as it passed through the center of the village. As the result of a laundromat, village homes, businesses, and restaurants discharging into inadequate septic systems, Tannery Brook, especially during warm summer days, made its presence well known to the olfactory senses of those who passed by.

While efforts turned to enforcement through such means as dye tests for septic systems—at one point, one-third of structures in the village tested failed this test—talk also turned to creating a sewer system for the village. In 1974 under Supervisor Vern May, a referendum was called to determine if the Town Board should move ahead on a 2.5 million dollar engineering report for a sewer system. Even though the county's health commissioner called the situation "serious" in Woodstock, concerns rose over the cost of a bond spread out over a number of years and the fear that such a system would "serve as a magnet for larger residential and industrial developments, not all in character with Woodstock's semi-rural and pristine nature."[22]

Although the initial vote on the proposed referendum failed, the push for a system continued in the years that followed. Added focus was given to the issue when, in both 1974 and 1975, the Woodstock Town Board, following the recommendation of the Ulster County Health Department, closed the Big Deep swimming hole in the Sawkill Creek, not because of hippies and nude swimmers but due to "an unusually high bacteriological count."[23] Not coincidently, parents with knowledge of the possible health risks involved had, for some time, forbidden their children to swim in the Sawkill along the portion of the stream that passed through or was downstream from the village.

Ultimately, a sewer system came to Woodstock through the efforts of multiple supervisors. Trimmed down from initial plans, the town sewer system was centered in the village proper. Under a revised proposal by the town's sewage consultant C. T. Male, the district was not extended to Bearsville or Glasco Turnpike; rather, it covered Mill Hill Road, Tinker Street, Rock City Road, and their associated side streets. While design and construction issues further delayed completion of the system—along with a certain level of politics—the eventual completion of a system in the village encompassing an estimated six hundred structures began an essential step in diminishing the environmental impact an aging system of septic tanks was having on local waterways. Big Deep would open again.

In 1970, the human needs of Woodstockers, including the newly arrived, were also addressed. In February, the Overlook Methodist Church announced that it would join the Office of Economic Opportunity in sponsoring a new preschool program for Woodstock children between the ages of three and five. The first of its kind in Woodstock, the program primarily offered services to the "children of working mothers and children who do not have as many advantages as others to prepare them adequately for school." Operating under the banner of the federally funded Head Start program, the Overlook preschool opened five days a week from 8:00 a.m. to 4:00 p.m. while also providing transportation for children who needed it.[24]

By June 1970, the problem of young people flocking to Woodstock continued almost one year after the festival held in Bethel. As noted by the *New York Times*, Woodstock "for many young people throughout the country, is this village that symbolizes the mood and magic of those three days last August when more than 250,000 overcame rain, mud, snarled traffic and bad trips to come together."[25] While those who continued to arrive may have been in search of the magic associated with the festival, what they found upon arrival was something quite different. Almost daily, as the Trailways bus arrived or hitchhikers were deposited in the center of town, the influx continued unabated. "You see them arrive at the Village Green," said Lynda Sparrow, who managed the leather goods shop called Hapiglop. "They come in here and say, 'You mean this is it?' 'This is all there is?' They expect a festival and all they find is a town with no facilities for them."[26] With a lack of public facilities such as restrooms, the closing of recreational sites, enforced trespassing laws, and, equally important, no support clinics offering medical, drug-related, or psychological services, Woodstock was not necessarily a welcoming place for those without financial means or a personal connection to the community.

Ironically, at about the same time the film documenting the Wood-stock Festival opened at the Tinker Street Cinema, an important step in providing for the very needs of those still arriving in Woodstock was, unexpectedly, taken by an audience member attending a town meeting. At that meeting, Gael Varsi provided her home phone number to chief of police, William Waterous, offering that anyone arriving in Woodstock who needed assistance could call her. Such was the simple beginnings of Family of Woodstock. Operating from her home on Library Lane, Varsi instituted what became a round-the-clock hotline for anyone in need or in crisis. It was a singular operation at first, advising young people on where they might stay and what services might be available to them and talking down those in crisis.[27] But Family grew, often without the support of many in town, who believed such assistance only encouraged even further migration to Woodstock by those without a means of support. As word spread of Varsi's efforts at assistance, additional Woodstockers began to step forward to offer their time as volunteers, working to refer those in need to the services that might aid them. Support also came through various fundraisers, featuring local musicians and such local groups as the Catholic Churches in Woodstock, West Hurley, and Shokan through their support of a switchboard and accruing phone bills.

A year later, Family continued to grow. Eventually moving to head-quarters on Rock City Road, an open house was celebrated in November 1971 with a blessing offered by local clergy and the Woodstock Elementary Band playing.[28] With a Board of Directors now in place and drawing on the efforts of some sixty volunteers working three-hour shifts, Family had begun to solidify its place within the Woodstock community.

As a result of those early efforts, Family's influence and reach only continued to expand throughout the 1970s. Becoming a contract agency with the New York State Narcotics Commission in 1972, Family established an emergency housing facility in 1973 and the Seedling childcare group and Free Store in 1974. By 1975, Family had received United Way funding and was designated by Ulster County as the official hotline for the county. As the decade moved on, the organization expanded beyond Woodstock to communities such as New Paltz and Ellenville.[29] And yet, throughout its remarkable growth, the mission of Family of Woodstock remained much the same as originally outlined in 1970: caring about people through volunteers willing to give of their time and energies in service to all.

In many respects, the creation of Family, though perhaps not recognized by many at the outset, represented a turn in how Woodstock was beginning to view the postfestival years. While Woodstock had not asked for the attention given to it by having its name attached to not only a music festival but an entire generation, it still had to adjust to its new reality. And, although additional battles between locals and newcomers continued as the seventies moved on, many in Woodstock understood the need to accept that reality—a reality that reflected a changing population, a changing economic base, and a changing accommodation with the outside world.

Figure 46. Although Family's work has expanded throughout Ulster County over the years, its home on Woodstock's Rock City Road since the 1970s continues to serve the Woodstock community. *Source:* Image by author.

## Chapter 11

# The Seventies

## Turning toward Home

Within the mix of young people who had arrived in Woodstock in both the pre- and postfestival years, there were certainly those who wandered into Woodstock with little thought given to where their journey might take them. And yet, while the issues relating to trespassing, occupying the Village Green, drug use, and runaways continued to impact the town, others arrived who would form a more lasting connection with the town. Although their lifestyles, dress, political opinions, and values did not necessarily align with the town's more conservative establishment, their arrival began to shape the future direction of Woodstock. Roots began to take hold, families were started, homes were purchased, and new businesses were established. In many respects it was the beginning of an assimilation not too dissimilar from what the early artists had undertaken so many years ago. That similarity was underscored by one community elder who had arrived during the art colony's early days, Adolph Heckeroth. The owner of the longstanding business Heckeroth Plumbing remarked as he watched the latest "invasion" of Woodstock, "Now they call them hippies. Then they called us anarchists."[1]

Hippies they may have been, but when their kids start attending the local elementary school and there are PTA meetings to attend, when a new business provides a need that grows in demand, or when an unmistakable talent lends its gift to the community, elements begin to merge and directions slowly shift.

When Karyn Bevet arrived in Woodstock in October 1969, she spent her first night at the Cafe Espresso listening to the Jerry Moore Work Band. She had first encountered the "Woodstock scene" through her earlier attendance at the Sound-Outs on Pan Copeland's farm: "I loved the Sound-Outs. I met a lot of nice people. The music was great. There was one night there when we thought we saw a flying saucer, Jerry Jeff Walker was singing, and he kept singing while we're all looking up. Everyone was so stoned having this group experience watching a flying saucer."[2] Early on, Bevet worked at many of the restaurants in town, including the Woodstocker, where she became the manager and where Mark Black's music could be heard on a variety of Friday evenings. She also found employment at the Bear Cafe, serving eggs over easy to Albert Grossman on many Woodstock mornings. While studying for a nursing degree, she also found employment at the Espresso, the Watering Troff, Joyous Lake, and Duey's, home to buckets of Wing Ding Chicken. In time, Bevet eventually joined several of the newly arrived who found a permanent home and a personal connection to Woodstock, establishing a long and distinguished career as a registered nurse and community volunteer.

Figure 47. The Woodstocker restaurant in Bradley Meadows Plaza. *Source:* Courtesy Karyn Bevet.

Similarly, Jim Hanson arrived in 1969, selling flowers on the street and forming the band the Warblers. As he recalled, he often set up his flower operation outside a Woodstock bar so late-departing male patrons—who were now probably in trouble with their wives—could assuage their guilt by arriving home with flowers in hand. Hanson eventually moved on to work with troubled youth during a lengthy career as a social worker while also rising to the position of captain of the Woodstock Fire Police.

Jim Hanson wasn't the only musician who arrived in Woodstock during the halcyon days of the late sixties and seventies to take up life in a newly adopted hometown. Certainly, Happy and Artie Traum were a part of that list and over the years gave back to the community in countless ways through various benefits and community events. John Herald, Paul Butterfield, and John Sebastian can easily be added to that list as well. One other musician also became central to Woodstock as the years moved on, rising in appreciation to the level of having a local road named after him—Levon Helm Boulevard.

Helm, of course, as a member of The Band, had arrived in Woodstock as part of the group's time at Big Pink, just across the town line. Ultimately, following The Band's dissolution, Helm endeavored to take on a future property located along Woodstock's Plochmann Lane, property that eventually became home to his Midnight Ramble. The future, however, had other plans before the Rambles impacted Woodstock's music scene to the extent that it has.

Though fire took the barn he had purchased and a diagnosis of throat cancer and bankruptcy combined to get in his way, Helm fought back and began what has been described as a second act for the ages. The barn was rebuilt and became a home not only for Helm but also for the Rambles. And though it was thought he would never sing again, Helm pushed through his cancer diagnosis to reclaim his voice. Eventually, the Rambles became a must attend Woodstock evening, and as the years unfolded Woodstockers began to welcome the boy from Turkey Scratch, Arkansas, as one of their own.

As a result of that strengthening connection with Woodstock, Helm lent his talents to a variety of fundraising benefits: more specifically, concerts closely aligned with the local school district. In 2006, for example, he brought his music to Onteora on behalf of the school district's music program. Later, he hosted an "Acoustic Ramble" for Woodstock's elementary school music program, only to be followed by a benefit for the Onteora arts program.

Along the way, other benefits followed for such agencies as the Woodstock Rescue Squad. When Hurricane Irene brought its destruction to the area, Helm, as he often did on such occasions, called upon his close associates in the musical world, including Natalie Merchant, Donald Fagan of Steely Dan, Graham Parker, and others, to support a benefit for grassroots Hurricane Irene relief efforts. On this occasion, beneficiaries of his efforts included the Phoenicia Rotary/Sharp Committee Flood Relief, the Prattsville Relief Fund, the MARK Project, and Ulster County Habitat for Humanity Flood Relief.[3]

With all the trials that Helm fought through over the years, he increasingly recognized and found the importance of community. And as Woodstock embraced him, he returned that embrace whenever he could. As Barbara O'Brien, Levon Helm's manager and the one who, with a close-knit team around her, is credited with seeing Helm through his second act, later said regarding Helm's sense of what was important to the four-time Grammy winner and member of the Rock and Roll Hall of Fame:

> As time went on, as the separation from The Band found distance, Levon saw himself more as a member of the community and I guess in the south where they come from the biggest thing you could ever achieve is being a member of your local Chamber of Commerce. So, once we got established, we joined the Ulster County Chamber of Commerce and every year they give you this plastic plaque that every year you replace the year with. So here we have his basement, we started to collect all his gold records that he had given away over the years, all the awards, the Grammys that he had won, we had everything on display. But, if somebody came to visit, and I was there, he [Helm] didn't send me downstairs to get a gold record or a Grammy, he said go get that Chamber of Commerce thing—and I'd bring the Chamber of Commerce plaque up to whoever was visiting because in Levon's mind, if you could be a member of your local Chamber of Commerce that's what means you made it. So that's what I learned from him, aside from everything else, all the gold records and the Grammys, he still was a local guy who wanted to be recognized by his community.[4]

Figure 48. L-R: Larry Campbell, Levon Helm, and Barbara O'Brien announcing 2008 Grammy Award for Helm's *Dirt Farmer* album. *Source:* Image by Paul LaRaia. Courtesy Barbara O'Brien.

Cindy Cashdollar concurred. Cashdollar is perhaps one of Woodstock's finest homegrown musicians. Not only did her Dobro and steel guitar talent lead her to work with Helm and fellow members of The Band, but as a member of Asleep at the Wheel she also found herself collaborating with such legends as "Willie Nelson, Merle Haggard, Dolly Parton and Lyle Lovett." Additionally, she contributed to the efforts of other music stalwarts such as Leon Redbone, Van Morrison, John Sebastian, and Bob Dylan.[5] Reflecting on her friendship with Helm over the years, Cashdollar offered:

> Levon to me was—he could have been a native of Woodstock—he was just so ensconced in the community, I mean he was the rock star, but he was also the local guy that did a lot of things for the community. When he met people, I think it made everyone feel like they were special and part of Woodstock and certainly part of the Ramble and part of his life. I think he was a southern gentleman, a Woodstock person—a man of the universe.[6]

Yet another musician made his way to Woodstock in the summer of 1974. Though familiar with musicians who had begun to call Woodstock home—including Happy Traum, who Ed Sanders had first seen in 1961, and the Paul Butterfield Blues Band, having shared gigs with the group at the Cafe Au Go Go—it wasn't music that brought Ed Sanders to Woodstock, but his writing.

Sanders, a driving force in 1960s counterculture as leader of the Fugs and a Beat poet, was also a nonfiction author whose book on the Manson family in 1971 drew widespread attention and mainstream sales. In their review of *The Family—the Story of Charlie Manson's Dune Buggy Attack Battalion*, the *New York Times* praised Sanders's work as "the first complete, authoritative account of the career of Charlie Manson."[7] As the book continued to find an increasingly wide audience, Sanders himself became the subject of death threats from Manson devotees. He recalled, "I used to get pictures of myself all cut up with the words 'piggies' and 'snitch.' I was one of the founders of the Youth International Party, which is the Yippies, and there grew up within the group a counter-Yippie movement, and they were very angry with me. So . . . this group kept breaking the windows of [my] Land Rover."[8] As a result, Sanders understood that it was probably time to leave the confines of New York's Lower East Side "to escape this cult, this Yippie faction, and my upsetness over the Manson family. I had a friend here [in Woodstock] who . . . had a chicken coop on Sickler Road, so we rented a chicken coop, and I moved all my stuff up here. We didn't know if we would go back to New York or stay here. . . . At the end of the summer, we decided to stay."[9]

With money from royalties and the sale of some of his archives to the University of Connecticut, Sanders and his wife, Miriam, eventually settled along Woodstock's Meads Mountain Road. He recalled, "I had, like, enough money and so in 1977 we bought the last cheap house in Woodstock for twenty-eight thousand dollars."[10]

And yet, despite his radical background and his knowledge of all Woodstock had been through in the late sixties and early seventies, Sanders's reception in Woodstock belied the notion of an unwelcoming town for newcomers. "I knew the town had a lot of old traditional conservatives but that they allowed people like me (a radical, even socialist, I was never a Communist); the town extended protection. I could call the police up at any time and get a response even though I was pretty controversial."[11]

As Sanders settled into Woodstock, his background in organizing was soon called upon. It was not a role he was unfamiliar with. In addition to his varying efforts organizing against the war in Vietnam and nuclear power, the Fugs, as part of the 1967 antiwar march on Washington, lent their performance energies to an exorcism of the Pentagon. Sanders later joined antiwar activists Jerry Rubin and Abbie Hoffman in organizing the Festival of Life concert in Chicago during the 1968 Democratic National Convention. After learning of a proposal to construct a Sheraton Inn and Conference Center on the site of Woodstock Estates (currently the location of the Woodstock Post Office), Sanders joined others in Woodstock—including Cornelia Rosenblum, Robin Delisio, musician Robbie Dupree, Robert Haney, Murray Prosky, and Rob Baumstone—to form the Friends of Woodstock Committee in an effort to push back against such a large-scale development near the center of town.[12] As Sanders later recalled, "They wanted to build an onsite septic system where, like, three hundred guests would pump their sewage, so people became alarmed. My first thing was, I printed a bumper sticker "Stop the Sheraton," then we started having meetings."[13] Over the course of their opposition, hundreds of Woodstockers joined Sanders and the committee in the battle against the Sheraton proposal and ultimately prevailed.

The Sheraton experience led Sanders further into the world of Woodstock zoning. As the LaValle administration neared its end in the 1980s, and following the tabling of multiple attempts to revise Woodstock's zoning law, Sanders, under the incoming administration of Brian Hollander, chaired a new committee aimed at revising the town's outdated law. By 1989, the former Fug and author of *Tales of Beatnik Glory* and *The Poetry and Life of Allen Ginsberg* had, even while working with Republicans, delivered the law that as of this writing remains in place.

In ways similar to Jim Hanson, flowers played a role in bringing Jay Sadowitz and Rita Sands to Woodstock. Jay Sadowitz was employed by IBM in New York City when he was transferred to Kingston. Not long after, no longer satisfied with working within the corporate structure of Big Blue, Sadowitz hooked up with a partner selling flowers from a street cart in Albany. Eventually, that led to him and his wife Rita opening Jarita's Florist on Tinker Street in a shop carved out of the former Mower's Market by owners Ann and Perk Gentilin. As Sadowitz recalled, if you wanted to open a business at that time you needed only a small business loan, some rent, and a down payment. Now, he reflected, it would cost you a million dollars.[14] Today, Jarita's remains one of the longest-running businesses on Tinker Street.

JoAnn Margolis arrived in Woodstock in 1969 to visit her brother. There she met Ken Traub and, after a three-month courtship, married and eventually opened Woodstock Craft Tools, providing implements for jewelry making, pottery, and the like. Woodstock Craft Tools morphed into the Jewelry Store on Tinker Street, which remained in business for twenty-six years. In the 1980s, Margolis also headed the Woodstock Chamber of Commerce.[15]

In 1970, Robin and Mike Kramer made their way to Woodstock and eventually opened a small clothing business behind what was then the Cafe Espresso. Initially selling "Eskimo coats for kids" and posting "homemade advertisements all around town," the couple then opened the Woodstock Trading Post on Tinker Street in 1974 to sell "jeans, cowboy shirts, denim jackets. . . . We'd have a deal where you could trade in two pairs of jeans for one of ours." The Trading Post became Woodstock Design and, underscoring the longevity that grew from many of the newcomers during the not-so-tranquil hippie years, the business was eventually led by their daughter.[16]

By 1973, much of the commercial landscape that dotted Tinker Street had changed once again. Joining establishments such as Hapiglop, Joshua's, the Espresso, and the Gilded Carriage was a series of businesses unimagined not many years before, many of which were dedicated to the arts and crafts sensibilities that the early art colony had fostered: Free-wheel Pottery, Annie's Down Home Stitchin' (new and remade clothing and alterations), Lee's Ceramics, Ruth Pawelka Jewelry, Stephen Robin Furniture, Jim Warren Silversmith, the Fabric Shop, Phrugg (needlecrafts, yarn, macrame), and Loretta Klein's.[17] Rounding out the new collection of businesses along Tinker Street was something that the more conservative side of Woodstock might have never imagined: Vidakafka, a lingerie shop that arrived in the early seventies via the imagination of Nancy Kafka.

Additionally, in 1972 as Woodstockers began to turn to healthier eating, Barry Ballister found a home in Bearsville for his Sunfrost Farms, a vegetable and fruit stand and juice bar. And a bit later in the decade, Bob Whitcomb opened the doors to his Sunflower Market in 1978. In that same year, in the space that once housed Joe Forno's Colonial Pharmacy, Ellen Shapiro and Barry Samuels brought their independent bookstore to town under the name of the Golden Notebook.

In 1968, by virtue of a T-shirt purchased for 50 cents on the Lower East Side, a commune that soon came to Woodstock found its name: the True Light Beavers. The commune, located in the Riverby section of Wittenberg, not only served as home for upward of seventeen people at its height but also brought to the area a cohort of individuals who had a lasting impact on the town. They were a family, some married, some not. Some were related—the Careys: Tobe, Alan, and Marty—some not. There were children. There were chickens, gardens, and pets. There was Woodstock's first dome structure designed and built by the Rinzlers: Curry and Cinnamon. More importantly, as Cinnamon Rinzler once told the *New York Times*, there was within the whole "a sense of purpose, continuity and progress."[18]

As a result of that purpose, the True Light Beavers launched the Woodstock Free School and produced *Feast—A Tribal Cookbook*, which, according to the *Woodstock Times*, was promoted widely with "full-page advertisements in *Rolling Stone* and the *New York Times Book Review*."[19] Yet another volume, *On the Bus*, was also released, documenting what *Kirkus Review* described as "a traveling road show, a family going from Woodstock (N.Y.) to the Yucatan, getting off on 'truckin' consciousness, reaching out to shake hands with planet brothers and sisters."[20]

Like a number of those who became permanent residents of Woodstock, many of the commune's members took up a—somewhat—more conventional lifestyle as the years passed. The Careys, by example, continued their involvement in Woodstock. Tobe Carey established himself as a video documentarian while Marty Carey pursued his work in fine art. Meanwhile, brother Alan became a photographer for the *Kingston Daily Freeman* and *Woodstock Times* while also establishing with Mark Antman, Image Works, a stock photography agency. And yet, the core principles that many in the collective had arrived with remained, as those who stayed continued to hold reverence for what they found in Woodstock: "the simple quality of life, the emphasis on individual freedom and the unspoiled surroundings."[21]

Meanwhile, on the corner of Mill Hill Road and Deming Street, yet another impactful change was underway, in a building that once housed Charlie's Ice Cream Parlor. After coming to town, Ron Merians and his wife Valma purchased the former ice cream parlor, where they established the legendary Joyous Lake. The Merians, later joined by Richard Fusco and others, began the work required to open an "alternative style restaurant" on the corner opposite Woodstock's best-known restaurant at the time, Deanie's. At first, Merians admitted in an interview given to the *Woodstock Times* in 1975, "I didn't know what I was doing." Still, piece by piece, year by year, the Joyous Lake evolved.[22] Merians described the work on the building as a "kinetic sculpture—something I've built with my own two hands."

Joyous Lake, at first, had no bar; rather, in its early days it was noted as having, in addition to its food, a juice bar. Eventually, economics dictated that a bar be added; as Merians told the *Times*, "I didn't want a bar but the Lake couldn't sustain itself without it." As legend has it, when Tim Hardin rose one night to begin singing while standing on what then served as a loading dock, music also found a vital new home there. Whatever the origin, the arrival of music at Joyous Lake not only fundamentally altered Woodstock's night life but also advanced Woodstock's centrality to the music of the 1970s.[23] It would do a disservice to try to list all who performed at Joyous Lake during its heyday. Suffice it to say that when you include names like The Band, Paul Butterfield, Muddy Waters, Van Morrison, John Sebastian, Charles Mingus, Bonnie Raitt, and Vassar Clements on an initial list, you gain a glimpse at why crowds stood outside the Deming Street entrance to pay a relatively painless coverage charge and enter a space, though crowded, that felt like Woodstock should. That intimacy increased even further when neighbors like Happy and Artie Traum, Robbie Dupree, Orleans, NRBQ, or Jerry Moore took to the stage.

As the decade progressed, Woodstock—and the rest of America—discovered disco, and the Lake was no exception. From Andy Robinson to Magic Markie to the eventual reign of the queen of disco in Woodstock, Disco Linda (Linda Sheldon), disco nights at the Lake marked a change in Woodstock's cultural milieu. Perhaps, as some have speculated, it was a pushback against the counterculture elements of the sixties; perhaps it was an advance wave signaling the arrival of the "me generation"; whatever the reason, disco had arrived not only at the Lake but at other venues in the area as well. Eventually, as these things seem to do, the good times at the Lake slowly came to an end. And although the Lake continued to operate following the Merians' departure at the end of the seventies, the heyday of the Joyous Lake will long be remembered as an integral part of a town that served as midwife to a remarkable era of music.

During this period, Woodstock was beginning to see transitions within a larger transition. As newly arrived individuals began to settle into a Woodstock lifestyle—while Woodstockers of longstanding slowly (and grudgingly) moved toward acceptance of the emerging reality—and as new businesses spoke to a changing clientele and changing tastes, Woodstock was beginning to show a fledgling maturity. That said, the road ahead was not without concerns or even conflict; after all, it was still Woodstock. And, as with much that had gone before, the town was not without its share of eccentricities or occasions that became part of town lore in the years ahead.

Figure 49. 1970s Joyous Lake advertisement as it appeared in the *Woodstock Times*. *Source:* Author's collection.

Ronald Merians and

# THE JOYOUS LAKE
## Woodstock

*are proud to present*

*Thurs. June 14*

# THE JERRY MOORE WORK BAND
### Special: Bottled Beer 40 cents

*Fri., June 15*

# DISCOTHEQUE
#### with Linda Sheldon

# LADIES NIGHT
#### Ladies Drink FREE from 9 to 11

*Sat., June 16*

# SONNY TERRY & BROWNIE McGHEE
#### Special Opening Act

# THE EDDIE KIRKLAND BLUES BAND

Just beyond Joyous Lake, evenings and music extended well into the night at Bud Sife's Sled Hill Cafe, where during a rainstorm water flowed across Deming Street and began to flood the floor. And while such an intrusion seldom failed to bring a halt to the evening's good times, as Jim Hanson recalls, it necessitated raising above floor level whatever related equipment that night's entertainment had hauled in.

Up on Rock City Road, across from the town's cemetery, a change of sorts was also taking place as the Village Jug gave way to Rosa's Cantina. Before Rosa's was fully entrenched, however, there was the matter of getting rid of the Jug's piano. The piano was purchased by Jim Hanson and loaded onto his truck one day. Just as Hanson began to drive the piano to its new home in Zena, Wayne Ambrosio jumped in the back and proceeded to entertain those walking through town with a series of piano riffs as the vehicle traveled down Rock City and Mill Hill Road.[24]

Rosa's began as a Mexican restaurant. Eventually, after adding live music and disco, things began to take off. According to "Just Plain Bo," whose experiences as a bartender at Rosa's later formed the basis for an article in the *Woodstock Times*, "At Rosa's it was cooking, it was hot, there was dancing, loud music, lots of smoke, it was a boogie joint, people were hanging around—it was even fun in the parking lot."[25] It was disco, however, in the form of "Disco Enduro" as well as legal issues that, according to "Just Plain Bo," sent Rosa's into the pages of Woodstock memory.

Disco Enduro was the brainchild of both head shop owner Magic Markie and Rosa's proprietor, Carl Fisher. The basic idea was to set a Guinness World Record for the most days of continuous discotheque. The goal was to complete 33 1/3 days of playing nothing but disco music, eclipsing the previous record of twenty-seven days. During the period the attempt was underway, Rosa's was open twenty-four hours a day. Magic Markie entered the booth on July 4, 1975, after arriving at Rosa's in a limousine. Under the rules, Markie was required to play "continuous disco music, fifty percent albums, fifty percent 45s." In addition to maintaining a logbook, a "physician of certification" was required by Guinness. Woodstock doctor Darlyne Pew filled in, providing periodic checkups and, under the rules, was "required to do urinalyses checking to make sure Markie is totally drug-free."[26] Beyond the promotional aspects of the plan, which enhanced business for Rosa's, what was to be gained? Fisher explained to the *Woodstock Times* that, in addition to a possible book, "this could lead . . . to TV appearances such as the David Frost or Johnny Carson shows."[27]

As Markie discoed along physical ailments attempted to, but did not, deter his progress. A sore throat was treated by Dr. Pew. Local dentist Alan Altman "arrived with a portable lab and an assistant to fill a cavity." And, along the way, local chiropractor Joel Auster worked to alleviate back pain.[28] But failure of the physical body wasn't the only threat to the success of Markie's and Carl Fisher's disco mission. That came from Alan Van Wagenen. Van Wagenen, although not acting in his role as a town law enforcement officer at the time, contended that Markie had fallen asleep for "15 minutes" early on Sunday morning, thus negating the record attempt. (Guinness rules allowed for a rest period of five minutes when required.) Van Wagenen's claim was advanced further by Dick Benoit, who stated that, although he was only in Rosa's for about "2 minutes," while there, he didn't "hear any music coming from the bar." Benoit's and Van Wagenen's claims were countered by people in Rosa's at the time. And, while it was believed that Markie may have fallen asleep for a couple of minutes, Markie insisted "that the music was on in the booth."[29]

By the time Markie broke the Guinness record, he wasn't the only one exhausted. The staff was reportedly tired of it all and, according to Fisher, local interest had fallen off. Rosa's owner noted, "Even though some people think I'm making a million bucks, there hasn't been droves of people coming in."[30] Just Plain Bo, who had been no fan of the Disco Enduro plans, recounted, "Rosa's being open 24 hours a day was a joke for the whole 33 1/3 days. If he [Fisher] had stuck with what he had, Rosa's would still be here today." Adding, as 1975 moved on, "The crowd changed—the bathrooms got beat-looking, glasses were broken and stolen, there were cigarette butts in the flowers. It became the type of crowd that can turn you against the business."[31]

Yet another change confronted Woodstockers in the early seventies—not a change over what bar one might choose to stumble out of in the early morning hours but one that appeared on Woodstock television sets. Ken Marsh and Woodstock Community Video had come to town, bringing with him a Sony Portapak and a couple of half-inch, reel-to-reel videotape editing machines. The Sony system, with its relatively affordable cost, instant black-and-white playback, and reliable audio, brought the medium of video within reach of artists, social activists, and community organizations. To introduce townspeople to the medium, Marsh literally first adopted the concept of street video by placing monitors atop trash cans on Tinker Street and in front of the Grand Union supermarket, playing back content of local interest. Eventually, he extended his reach through a relationship with Kingston Cablevision, and programming related to town functions, events, and personalities began appearing in the homes of Woodstockers. At the outset, the effort to simply get programming on the air required hauling playback equipment to Kingston Cablevision's headend, located at California Quarry. There was no studio, no lights, no crew. Rather, it became a matter of plugging the playback deck in, making the proper video and audio connections, and starting the tape. As a result, public access television—minus the frills—had arrived in Woodstock.

Working at the outset from his home off Tinker Street, Marsh later moved operations to Parnassus Square on Lower Byrdcliffe Road. In addition to continuing his efforts in support of public access, he provided an experimental training ground for such video artists and documentarians as Gary Hill and Tobe Carey. Although Ken Marsh eventually left Woodstock, the concept and assistance he provided to several Woodstockers eventually led to the creation of a public access studio in what is now the Mescal Hornbeck Community Center. And, although community video in Woodstock has had its conflicts and periods of turmoil over the years—including accusations of censorship and a thrown punch between two producers with differing views over Woodstock's direction—the vision Ken Marsh brought to Woodstock in the early seventies continues some fifty years later.

In some respects, Woodstock in the 1970s is a more difficult town to describe than its 1960s counterpart. While several newcomers were beginning to offer a more stabilizing influence on their adopted hometown than those who had arrived in Woodstock to explore the hippie lifestyle, the issues that the hippie problem presented to some in the community were still relevant. One example involved the New York Telephone Company. In 1972, the telephone company presented plans to expand a building that housed company equipment on Neher Street. Ultimately the request was heard by the Zoning Board of Appeals and the Civic Arts Council (a precursor to today's Commission for Civic Design). As discussions went back and forth over initial concerns related to the building's design, a representative of the phone company expressed his frustration with what he regarded as the town's excessive concern with design. Referring to the state of Neher Street at the time, the company's representative claimed, "That street is a depressed area, anyway. Hippies all around you. People are asking for things to look beautiful when everything else is falling apart. There are people hanging out windows and music blaring all the time."[32]

While trespassing seems to have drawn less attention, that same year Woodstock's chief of police, William Waterous, addressed his concern over the number of hitchhikers often found on the side of Woodstock's roads with thumb extended. As the *Woodstock Review* reported following a discussion with the chief, "It causes bad traffic situations, and the force receives many complaints about hitchhikers. He says it must stop, or there will have to be arrests."[33]

Meanwhile, the Town Board began to show some—albeit only partial—recognition of the new reality by establishing the Woodstock Narcotics Guidance Council. The newly established group was to be headed by

Walter Van Wagenen, retired Woodstock Elementary School principal. In addition to Van Wagenen, the council consisted of a "minister, an educator, a doctor or two, an attorney, a Town Board member, 'and maybe a gal.'" When audience members David Boyle and Billy Faier expressed their opinion that a former addict should be included in the group's makeup, it was explained that the council "was not going to be doing any 'contact' work where actual drug experience would be helpful."[34]

"And maybe a gal"? Perhaps it was simply a throwaway line; nonetheless, it was a reference undoubtably heard by several Woodstock women, whose voices were increasingly on the rise. In 1972, the Woodstock Women's Project began fundraising activities to secure proceeds that would go toward meeting women's health needs, providing educational literature for women, and establishing a women's health clinic. By summer, the Woodstock Women's Health Project was underway, working in part with Family of Woodstock to offer birth control and abortion referral services.[35]

One year later, the issue of rape was brought front and center at a forum sponsored by the Women's Health Collective and Family. Held at the Overlook Methodist Church in Bearsville, a crowd of 150 people engaged in discussions related to the difficulties for women, both locally and nationally, when it came to prosecuting and achieving a conviction in rape cases.[36] The forum engaged even more Woodstockers the following evening when it was aired by Woodstock Community Video.

In 1974, the Women's Center was launched to provide an opportunity for Woodstock women to engage in "workshops, consciousness raising groups, and informal get-togethers." Offering her thoughts on the need for the Center in Woodstock, spokesperson Christine Potters told the *Kingston Daily Freeman*, "It's a particular kind of place where women can feel they can get the support they need from other women."[37]

While the women's liberation movement was sweeping across the land and into Woodstock, yet another woman's voice rose out of the 1975 election. It was not, however, a voice that would necessarily align with the more progressive declarations of many in Woodstock. In the 1975 election, the first woman was elected as town supervisor: Valerie (Val) Cadden. In a closely fought election, Cadden had defeated her Democratic rival, Bill Kronenberg by some fifty votes. And as Cadden prepared to replace her predecessor, Vern May, there was one last major cultural battle on the horizon: the issue of home relief.

The basic concept behind home relief was to provide temporary (ninety days) support for able-bodied members of the community who were unable

Figure 50. Val Cadden, elected in 1975 as Woodstock's first woman town supervisor. *Source:* Historical Society of Woodstock Archives/People Collection.

to find employment and had no alternative means of income. For towns such as Woodstock, regulations at the time required the town to pay "100 percent of home relief to the county," which later was partially reimbursed by the state and federal governments.[38] That reimbursement equated to returning roughly 50 percent of the town's initial outlay. In years prior to the growth of its population, that cost was bearable in the town's budget. In 1970, for example, the cost to Woodstock was three thousand dollars. With the arrival of so many newcomers, however, the town's expenditure for home relief was rising to exorbitant levels. By 1975 it had grown to seventy thousand dollars.[39] And as the town's budget rose, town officials were not the only ones to take notice: residents began to see their tax bills rise accordingly. As a result, yet another period of animosity between old and new moved to the fore. Festering wounds were being reopened.

For the town of Woodstock officials, the problem was clear: too many newcomers were applying for and receiving benefits they weren't entitled to. As there was no residency requirement, the town in 1976 saw the home relief roll increase to over one hundred individuals. Despite efforts to limit who was deemed eligible, it became clear to Cadden that the town was engaging in a losing battle. She claimed, "These people know how to manipulate the system, they're smart and they know they can beat it. They get on home relief and stay on it."[40]

Cadden's sentiments were not without support in the community. As Chief William Waterous told the *New York Times*, "I don't call them hippies. I call them drifters and bums because that's what they are."[41] Increasingly, town officials also cast blame on Family of Woodstock as an organization that was exacerbating the problem by assisting those arriving in town without resources. Citing the belief that "Woodstock needs more people who can pay their own way," Cadden and the majority of the Town Board were not happy with Family's plans for a facility that temporarily housed runaways, believing that it would "attract many young people to the town who might eventually land up on welfare." [42] In opposition to her fellow Town Board members, Jane Van De Bogart, the lone Democrat on the board at the time, defended Family, stating, "The irony is that they are blaming this problem on the only people in town who are trying to do something about it."[43] Also countering the perceptions some town officials had of Family's operations, Michael Berg, Family director, told the *Woodstock Times* that he believed, "The more conservative elements of the Town Board are making Family the scapegoat for the welfare problem."[44] At one point in the debate, the Town Board—with Councilwoman Jane Van De Bogart proving the lone exception—went as far as denying Family the use of Woodstock's Town Hall for a fundraiser. Although the Board later reversed that decision, the uneasy relationship between the town and Family continued as the issue of home relief managed to capture the attention of both local media and the *New York Times*.

Ultimately, Val Cadden determined that Woodstock could no longer afford—and would no longer pay—the costs accrued in support of the current home relief system. As a result, she suspended payments to Ulster County, refusing to pay a nineteen thousand dollar relief bill due to the county for the last two months of 1975. Cadden had estimated that the total relief costs to the town in 1976 could be as high as 140,000 dollars, for which the town received only half back as a reimbursement. Citing the fact that Woodstock's cost for home relief was the second highest in the county—surpassed only by to the entire city of Kingston—Cadden expressed her fear that the rising costs could eventually threaten "the town with bankruptcy."[45]

Following the refusal to make further payments, Cadden and the Town Board advocated major changes in how the system was implemented. While acknowledging the need to support residents who had fallen on hard times, Cadden and those in support of her stand argued for a residency requirement, equity across the county for home relief payments, and more local control over who met eligibility requirements and who did not, the latter point spurred on by the frustration encountered over the fact that Woodstock could not simply close a case when it determined an individual was no longer eligible for relief. At the time, if such a determination was made by the town, a hearing at the county level was required. In 1975, of the sixty-nine cases Woodstock attempted to close, only four were upheld. "All the rest were reinstated," Cadden told the *New York Times*. "One we won was a young man who was supposed to cut weeds for the town. He said ecology consciousness forbade him to kill a growing thing."[46]

As time moved on, Cadden did not relent in her efforts to see reform come to the established system. In addition to pressing Ulster County to "split the costs equitably over the [county's] entire tax base," Cadden called upon the state's social service commissioner "to mandate county-wide home relief financing as part of the comprehensive welfare reform package which his department is working on for submission to the State Legislature."[47] As she pressed for reform, Cadden's efforts, in part due to the publicity received regarding her fight and Woodstock's efforts to enforce restrictions, eventually saw Woodstock's home relief roll reduced. By the end of 1976, Woodstock counted thirty individuals eligible for assistance. And, while work continued both on the county and state levels regarding welfare reform, it was time for Woodstock and Cadden to move on.

Well, almost. There was, after all, the matter of the Village Green snowman. Under funds from the Comprehensive Employment Training Act established by Jimmy Carter, the town had hired several individuals to undertake maintenance tasks around the village. Following a late winter snowstorm, the employees were instructed to begin removing snow from the center of town, specifically the Village Green. Believing his crew was beginning to suffer psychological strain following their hard work, crew foreman Sam Shirah thought a break was in order. During their break, the crew crafted a twenty-foot snowman in the center of town—with evergreen hair. Objections soon followed from both taxpaying residents and members of official Woodstock, who noted that "over 60-man hours at a cost of $180 had been invested in a snowman."[48] Shirah further stoked the controversy by issuing a press release a short time later, a press release that failed to gain much sympathy from either side of the political aisle. To compound matters, Shirah's release also managed to offend the recently formed Woodstock Gay People organization and their push for the adoption of a gay rights ordinance in Woodstock. As the *Woodstock Times* described the aftermath:

> The release had suggested the Democratic and Republican Town Board members deal with their differences in an invigorating snowball fight. Woodstock Gay People had also taken exception to Shirah's suggestion that WGP [Woodstock Gay People] President Ruth Simpson battle it out with snowballs against Rev. Jeff Williams, Mountain Chapel pastor and gay rights ordinance opponent.[49]
>
> In a bit of irony between two political opposites, the same *Times* article noted responses to Shirah's suggestions from both Councilwoman, Jane Van De Bogart and Supervisor, Val Cadden:
>
> "The next thing you know they'll be giving a harvest festival and asking Val and I to wrestle it out in a pile of leaves," said Van De Bogart.
>
> "You know, that's not a bad idea, Jane," the Supervisor responded.[50]

Finally, as the 1970s neared its end, two opposing Woodstock politicians were close to agreeing on something.

Chapter 12

# The Vanishing Village?

Will Rose came of age during the years the Byrdcliffe Art Colony was under construction and "folks" known as artists were arriving in town. Some sixty years later in his 1963 book *The Vanishing Village*, Rose recalled his life as a boy while the Woodstock he knew was in the throes of a major transition. Through stories constructed around the daily comings and goings at his father's store in the center of Woodstock, Rose grappled with his fears as change began to surround him and his family. What would happen to the small town he had so intimately known as it transformed into something he didn't quite understand? He worried about the new people who were coming to town, changing it from a sleepy hamlet to a home for radical artists: "They are saying that our old Holland Dutch village is going to pass out of the picture. They say that they hear men by the name of Whitehead or White or Brown or something like that have bought up half the side of Overlook Mountain below Mead's Mountain House and they are going to change Woodstock into an art colony. If this is so, it is terrible."[1]

As he reflected years later, Rose recalled a prophecy on the inevitability of change once delivered by a frequent visitor to his father's store, a prophecy that far outlasted the days when the mail—and newcomers—were delivered to Woodstock by coach:

> But I guess we might as well get ready for mighty changes.
> That's what Dominie Park was telling men in front of the
> store when the mule stage from West Hurley came in with

the mail. . . . "Customs change," he said, "as the years and the centuries change and our beloved haunts creep into the foggy past as the future rolls upon us. Fires and new demands will consume our traditions, and the chisel and the saw will orchestrate their symphony."[2]

The store Will Rose knew as a boy is long gone. So are his memories of the "smells of our horses and sweaty leather and the hot iron in Henry Peper's blacksmith shop." Gone too is the air filled "full of ripe apples and plums and pears and grapes in the fall."[3]

By the same token, a boy growing in age during the height of the art colony might also have written of recalling the smell of campfires as Maverick revelers celebrated well into the night. So too might a "child of the sixties"—while not really missing the smell of patchouli oil—lament the loss of music reverberating from inside Joyous Lake on a Saturday night.

In many respects, and for multiple generations, the future has indeed "rolled upon" Woodstock. Some might even say it arrived in the form of

Figure 51. Arriving at Rose's General Merchandise Store at the turn of the twentieth century. Current site of the Woodstock Artists Association and Museum on Tinker Street. *Source:* Historical Society of Woodstock Archives/Town Center Collection.

a steamroller. And while the "chisel and the saw" prophesied by Dominie Park in Will Rose's day may not have dramatically altered Woodstock's physical architecture, chisels and saws of a metaphorical nature have certainly redirected the road Woodstock has attempted to navigate—and continues to do so.

Over the course of half its history, Woodstock and its townspeople have known various incursions upon the order that was. From the early artists' descent upon the natural landscape, to the tourists and economic turns that followed, to an influx of young people seeking much, many have followed a beacon that seemingly emanates from the top of Overlook Mountain.

Following the turmoil and vagaries visited upon the town during the 1960s and 1970s, however, Woodstock, as much as Woodstock could, began to settle into a relative calm. And as the town marked the years that concluded a century of transformation, more hometown changes began to occupy the days of those settled in the Woodstock valley.

With a sewer system for the village finally coming online and a new sidewalk project completed, the town took a major step in ensuring preservation of seventy-six acres in the center of the village. In April 1979 Supervisor Val Cadden delivered a check totaling 256,730.59 dollars to real estate agent Carol Eichhorn, representing the Christian Science Church, owners of the former Comeau Estate.[4] Along with town offices, original plans for the property included various recreational facilities such as a baseball field and a swimming pool, but over time community sentiment regarding its use began to evolve. Following a raucous battle waged by those opposed to placing the town's highway garage on the property, that evolution culminated in the decision to place the property under a conservation easement overseen by the Woodstock Land Conservancy.

While voices were raised in debate over the future of the Comeau property, a diverse collection of voices was also heard over the airwaves as Woodstockers tuned to a new radio station on the dial, Woodstock's own WDST. Founded by Jerry Gillman, the station's origins trace back to 1970, when Gillman first moved to the hamlet of Shady. Unable to find a decent radio station from his new home, Gillman launched a decade-long struggle to fill the void. WDST launched in 1980 and as Brian Hollander, the station's one-time morning voice, later recalled, "When it finally came forth, what a glorious chaos it was, a bursting expression of creativity that carried with it the pent-up voice of a Woodstock that we all believed the world needed to hear."[5]

Within that glorious chaos, WDST's programming rose to meet the needs of an increasingly diverse community. Eschewing a specific format, the station offered an eclectic range of music from classical to country, folk, contemporary, and jazz. Gillman himself became one of the station's more recognized on-air talents as his gravelly voice commanded the air each day reading from a chosen book during the "Bookstall Hour."

At about the same time, Woodstockers were being asked to consider the theories of the town's very own self-proclaimed "assassinologist," Rush Harp. It was Harp's detailed knowledge of guns that led him to believe that the assassination of President Kennedy could not have been carried out by a lone gunman such as Oswald, and therefore Kennedy's death was the result of a conspiracy. Eventually, for anyone driving to Kingston from Woodstock along Route 28, it became increasingly difficult to ignore Harp's theories as a billboard, paid for by Harp, not only confronted conventional belief regarding Kennedy's assassination but expanded to also question the deaths of Robert Kennedy, Martin Luther King, and Mary Jo Kopechne. "Who Killed J.F.K., R.F.K., M.L.K., M.J.K.?" read the billboard.

In 1986, Woodstock's Town Board turned with urgency to addressing a major infrastructure problem that held life-threatening implications. Some thirty-five years after Blanche Hoodes and her son, Michael, celebrated being the first home to connect to the newly created Woodstock Water District, news of a far more ominous nature greeted the six hundred district users when New York State health officials notified the town that water samples revealed asbestos levels twice the proposed federal safety standard. Concern quickly spread among those in the village connected to the water district as the word *cancer* began appearing in the local press in association with the asbestos scare.

With fears both real and imagined sweeping through the village, the Town Board under then supervisor John LaValle moved quickly, putting aside other pressing business. As LaValle told the *Woodstock Times*, "Everything else has gone by the boards. All we're working on right now is asbestos."[6] Ultimately, the town gained the upper hand over the problem as pipes were replaced and system testing continued to ensure that consumers within the district remained safe. Still, to monitor the impact of the asbestos discovery over time, district users were sent a survey to track any increase in cancer for several years.

On the political front, as Woodstock moved through the 1980s, Woodstock Democrats were in the ascendency. Since the inception of the Republican Party prior to the Civil War, Woodstock Republicans had held the reins of governance firmly in their hands. That was about to change. In 1987, Democrats managed to finally wrest control of town government away from Republicans. In what was described by the *Woodstock Times* as "an overwhelming election victory," Democrats elected Brian Hollander as supervisor, two councilpersons, and a town clerk. The lone Republican victor was Bill Harder, Woodstock's incumbent highway superintendent.[7] As Democrats celebrated at Deanie's Restaurant that election evening, those gathered might have been even more overjoyed had they known that election night victories would become commonplace for Democrats well into the twenty-first century.

The year 1987 also marked Woodstock's bicentennial. As the town celebrated its two hundredth year of existence with parades, music, poetry, and, yes, even a Hula-Hoop contest, time was also afforded for reflection. What had Woodstock become as it traveled history's winding road, and where was it heading? Having survived the incursions—or invasions—of the past, what lay before a small town with a large reputation?

Ultimately, as the tie-dye began to fade, assimilation began. New arrivals slowly became longtimers, and as those who had arrived as part of the sixties invasion put down new roots, they also began to raise families, proved adept at opening new and successful businesses, ran for political office, and contributed to the pool of volunteers small town's heavily rely on. And yet, as the 1987 election offered, assimilation in Woodstock didn't necessarily mean a return to the town's conservative ways. The new Woodstockers—as well as native Woodstockers who had come of age in the sixties and seventies—carried with them more progressive views than their predecessors regarding local and national issues.

As a result, as the years moved toward a new millennium, the seemingly inherent trait of opposition often found in the pages of Woodstock history began to assert itself regarding more liberal issues: the environment, politics, social issues, housing, and questions of what constitutes a community. For example, Woodstockers adapted a defiant "no" when it came to two separate issues: "no" in the form of no nukes, and "no" to lights atop Overlook Mountain.

From the mid-1970s on, Woodstockers continually rallied against the spread of nuclear power. As early as 1976, with a petition drive and benefit concert on the Village Green, townspeople gathered in support of New York's efforts to pass the Nuclear Responsibility Act of 1976. Alarmed by the potential sighting of a nuclear plant in nearby Cementon, New York, even the Reformed Church on Woodstock's Village Green

aided in the protest, allowing a concert on the Green featuring the Bea-
verland Band. It was the first time the Church—primary owners of the
Village Green—permitted use of the property for something other than a
"church-related event."[8] With the seeds planted, Woodstockers continued to
actively oppose nuclear power use within the Hudson Valley and beyond
across multiple years and through various means, including "No Nukes"
concerts, marches, and, of course, petitions.

In the mid-1980s, Woodstockers also took to the barricades when
a local television station constructed a transmission tower on the top of
Overlook Mountain. As if the tower itself silhouetted against the sky atop
Overlook wasn't disturbing enough to see, when the station later added
lights to the tower, the organization No Lights-Save Overlook Mountain
was formed to push back against commercial intrusion upon Woodstock's
most important physical landmark.

Speaking before a No Lights gathering in 1988, Alf Evers, reflecting
on past commercial intrusions upon the mountain and the land, reminded
those gathered that "the Indians used the mountain as a hunting ground,
and they apologized to the spirits of the creatures they killed for food,
taking from nature only what they needed. The white people corrupted
this attitude of the Indians with their policy of plunder, actively expressed
in lumbering, burning and quarrying for small monetary gains." Concluding, Evers urged those gathered to "hold together and fight the battles to
save the mountain."[9] Attorney Alan Sussman, a leader of the No Lights
movement, agreed with Evers, adding simply, "A culture which destroys
its sacred places is no culture at all."[10]

Though the legal wrangling that followed went against the No Lights
group and the tower—with lights—remained, a strong message had been
sent to those who would consider future intrusions upon the Woodstock
landscape, a message echoed by jewelry store owner JoAnn Margolis:
"It's a beautiful spot and you don't want to change it. No matter when
you came to Woodstock—whether it was 70 years ago, 20 years ago or
six months ago—you want to close the door behind you."[11] Such was the
sentiment that found its way into the thoughts of many Woodstockers as
the future continued to move upon them.

The year 1988 also saw destruction of a different form visited upon
yet another sacred sight in Woodstock. As Memorial Day dawned upon
Woodstock, townspeople awoke to the Woodstock Playhouse engulfed in
flames. The completely wooden structure burned quickly and ferociously,
lighting up the early morning sky over the village. Unique for its archi-

Figure 52. 1988 advertisement by the No Lights group calling for a celebration of Overlook Mountain and the prevention of exploitation of Overlook by commercial entities. *Source:* Author's collection.

# CELEBRATE
# OVERLOOK MOUNTAIN DAY
## Saturday, April 30     12:30 p.m.
## JOIN IN A PICNIC, GIANT PUPPET SHOW AND WALK TO SUMMIT

Overlook Mountain has been the symbol of Woodstock for hundreds of years, exerting a presence and beauty which everyone recognizes and cherishes.

But, Overlook Mountain has never been as vulnerable to commercial exploitation as it is right now.

Overlook cannot help itself. It cannot protect its woods from being clearcut; or its shoulders from being scarred by roads; and it cannot safeguard its exquisite silhouette from unsightly structures.

Only we can prevent this from happening. We must stop the destruction of our environment.

To celebrate the Mountain's great heritage and to remind us of what we have and what we're losing, NO LIGHTS/SAVE OVERLOOK MOUNTAIN is sponsoring "Overlook Mountain Day."

## THE CELEBRATION

The celebration starts at 12:30 at the Overlook trailhead (top of Meads Mountain Road - across from the Tibetan Monastery) with entertainment and other special events. Then join in a leisurely walk up Overlook accompanied by local musicians for a picnic and GIANT PUPPET SHOW.

Bring a picnic lunch. Bring musical instruments. Dress appropriately. Please arrive early so events can start on time.

**Rain Date: Sunday, May 1 * For More Information: (914) 679-7183/339-3050**

Sponsored by NO LIGHTS/SAVE OVERLOOK MOUNTAIN, P.O. Box 146 Bearsville, NY 12409

tectural presence at the entrance to the village, the Woodstock Playhouse had served as a primary center of professional theater, music, and dance in Woodstock for fifty years. When Woodstock awoke that morning, the collective "colony of the arts" immediately understood that more than a building had been lost. Though arson was suspected, no charges were ever brought in the destruction of one of Woodstock's most venerable landmarks.

As the twentieth century began to wear out its welcome, many in Woodstock also began to revive and attach the "No" label—as in No Music—to an important part of Woodstock's economy and to the town's long-standing calling card. Woodstock's iconic music venues were closing. On January 7, 1999, Woodstockers were greeted with the headline "Venue Leaving—Tinker Street Closes Doors after a Decade as Town's Prime Music Spot."[12] Having evolved from the former site of the Cafe Espresso, the Tinker Street Cafe was—along with the Joyous Lake—one of the last bastions still holding forth as a place where live music could be heard in Woodstock. Gone were the days of the Elephant, the Sled Hill Cafe, and Rosa's Cantina. And as the music faded at the Tinker Street Cafe, so too did the ghosts that once hovered about the building since the early days of the Espresso, from Dylan to Hendrix.

The ghosts surrounding the glory days of the Joyous Lake were also slipping into the ether as the one-time jewel of Woodstock's live music scene began to fall on difficult times. Through multiple owners, legal questions, and diminishing clientele, Joyous Lake eventually closed its doors, leaving Woodstock, as it moved through the first decade of the twenty-first century, without the invitation that once summoned the outside world. Some simply blamed the economy, others pointed to the enhanced enforcement of drunk driving laws, while it was also noted that those baby boomers growing up in the sixties and seventies were now at home with kids and jobs to attend to in the morning. Whichever the case—or the combination of multiple factors—Woodstock was an increasingly quiet town. While one might still find music on a given night at the Watering Troff on the Bearsville Flats, the era of barhopping through town from one venue to another was receding, only to become fodder for oft-repeated stories in the days that lay ahead.

As Woodstock crossed into the new millennium, however, a portion of the town's cultural landscape began to see restoration. In September 2000, the Woodstock Film Festival was launched, leading the *Woodstock Times* to offer the banner headline "At Last! A *Real* Woodstock Festival."[13] The brainchild of cofounder and executive director Meira Blaustein and cofounder Laurent Rejto—with some sixty volunteers lending their talent and energy in support—the first festival screened more than eighty independent films while also offering panel discussions, workshops, and its share of after parties at a variety of Woodstock venues.[14]

In the years to follow, the Woodstock Film Festival only grew in stature, expanding programs throughout the area, offering opportunities to young and underserved filmmakers, receiving attention in the pages of *Variety*, attracting name actors, producers, and directors, and receiving recognition as an Oscar Award festival in the "Short Narrative, Animated Short, and Short Documentary categories."[15]

In 2003, Woodstock's music scene received a needed lift with word that Levon Helm was putting together what became the Midnight Ramble at his home on Plochmann Lane. In an effort to move on from the muddied saga of The Band (the son of Arkansas told the *Woodstock Times*,

"If they would leave me alone, I would leave them the fuck alone."[16]), Helm, while also attempting to put his battle with cancer in the rearview mirror, began to piece together the basic elements of what over the years became yet another chapter in Woodstock's storied music legacy. Beginning with rent parties to avoid foreclosure, Helm and manager Barbara O'Brien undertook efforts to craft the structure that transformed into the Midnight Ramble. With an assembled band behind him that included his daughter Amy, Larry Campbell, Teresa Williams, Little Sammy Davis, and others, the Midnight Ramble was, in 2004, returning a level of music to Woodstock worthy of its past.

Woodstock's music scene was further complemented with the addition of the Woodstock Invitational Luthiers Showcase later in the decade. Originating through the efforts of Baker Rorick, each year the Luthiers Showcase offers the creations of some of the finest craftspeople working in the field. It features handmade acoustic guitars and other string instruments, including though not limited to banjos, mandolins, ukuleles, and twelve-strings. Supplemented by live music, the Showcase, by 2010, only its second year of operation, was attracting upward of fifteen hundred[17] people to view, purchase, and discuss the assembled crafts.

Almost in parallel to the Luthiers Showcase, the Woodstock Playhouse was emerging from the ashes. In November 2010, the Pan American Dance Foundation, a local not-for-profit corporation operating the New York Conservatory for the Arts in neighboring Hurley, New York, stepped forward to purchase and undertake the revitalization of the Playhouse. With executive directors Randy Conti, Douglas Farrell, and President Diane Stein serving as the guiding forces, the rise of the Woodstock Playhouse, upon completion, seemed to bring balance to the colony's entrance, while also returning a year-round venue committed to the arts. The doors of the Woodstock Playhouse reopened in June 2011 with a gala reception and performance of *A Chorus Line*.

Woodstock's cultural landscape, however, was not the only component of town life that was witnessing change as the calendar began to move through the new century. Though slow in its recognition, Woodstock was about to know yet another invasion. Unlike previous experiences with change, however, where the lives of the newly arrived were grounded in the arts—or the attraction others found in that promise—the impending twenty-first-century incursion would have no Ralph Whitehead or Albert Grossman as its architect. Rather, what Woodstock represented (whether grounded in myth or reality), the physical attraction the natural landscape offered, the tragedy of 9/11, the COVID-19 pandemic, a shifting real estate market, improved internet access, and an influx of well-heeled buyers converged to serve as midwife to yet another chapter of change in Woodstock's story. As a myriad of factors impacted those contemplating escape from urban environments, the Catskills beckoned. And while Woodstock had maintained a long history of second-home owners who made their way back and forth between New York City and their local homes over the years, the newly arrived, twenty-first-century version of change brought a different set of challenges to a town not unfamiliar with questioning the meaning of community. People were moving to Woodstock, and in their wake housing costs began to climb dramatically, leaving behind those without the financial means to engage in bidding wars—or pay cash. So dramatic was the change, some wondered if a universal symbol for real estate should be added to the town seal.

Meanwhile, the name *Woodstock* seemed to find new popularity in the minds of visitors wishing to escape for a country weekend. As a result, Woodstock was introduced to the concept of short-term rentals as the once plentiful supply of long-term rentals began to diminish, rentals that had been a main source of housing for town workers, store clerks, some seniors, and young Woodstockers just starting out. And while Woodstock became the first town in Ulster County to offer a short-term rental law attempting to limit the market, the barn doors had been open too long, as several long-term renters were forced to disperse to more affordable locations. Calling upon the town's history with newcomers, some asked, "Where would the young artist or musician arriving in Woodstock today find an affordable place to live and pursue their passion?"

For those engaged in the struggle to maintain some form of affordability in town, an early affordable housing plan offered by the Rural Ulster Preservation Company (RUPCO) appeared to offer, at a minimum, a marginal solution. And yet, Woodstock being Woodstock, no such project goes unchallenged, as objections to the project poured forth, from legal questions surrounding the permitting process, project scale, protection of wildlife, and environmental impact to who would pay for water testing and connection to the town's water system.

Eventually—though it took years—the RUPCO project saw completion (though reduced in size from its original scope). In doing so, however, debate over the project foreshadowed a growing split within the community over affordable housing. Questions were being raised over what constitutes equity within a community, what responsibility falls upon the town itself to provide for all its citizens, and what balance needs to be struck? As longtime housing advocate Susan Goldman related to the *New York* Times regarding the RUPCO battle and the contradiction she viewed at the time, "This is a town where if someone is sick or someone's house burns down, people will come out of the woodwork to be generous and to help. . . . But we don't see people who have a need for housing as part of that community. It's a town full of social progressives, but we don't look at our own community the way we look at the rest of the country."[18] In the paradox offered by Goldman lies the core of debate Woodstockers will face in the days ahead. What does community character mean and what would be—or not be—permitted in Woodstock's backyard?

Woodstock's attraction to newcomers has long been noted by those on the outside looking in. Its physical environment, its cultural history, its diversity of opinion, and its small-town sense of community have all offered a welcome sign over the years. And yet when those core elements and the balance of the original attraction begins to shift, primarily along economic lines and commercially inspired perceptions of Woodstock's past, the question legitimately arises if Woodstock can remain Woodstock? And, as one watches the twenty-first-century version of Holley Cantine's trudgers make their way about Woodstock in increasing numbers, the words of Will Rose and his fears of a vanishing village echo across the years while also introducing the concept of gentrification long before it entered Woodstock's twenty-first-century vocabulary. As Rose wrote over half a century earlier:

> I have overheard it said that some of them are well-to-do and don't have much regard for money, and so they, this kind, will buy up a big patch of mountain land so as to have maybe a little waterfall in a brook on their place. . . . Besides, the artists coming to Woodstock have attracted a good many folks who are not artists, but think it is fine to live in a high, artistic place like Woodstock is getting to be.[19]

Rose, of course, was unsettled by the belief that a way of life was being lost. And in many respects, he was not wrong, as such fears persist every time a consequential change ripples through a community. And yet, while some still hold the legacy of the art colony comfortably in their arms, the 1960s—and its myriad of tangential connections—remain at the forefront for many of the newly arrived, as if walking Woodstock's streets or purchasing acreage grants entry to a unique history in contrast to the pathways other small towns have negotiated.

Unfortunately, the history that is sometimes adopted by those newly arrived seldom includes the full scope of a community's past. Rather, it becomes streamlined, failing to recognize the intricacies behind the complete story. As a result, nostalgia begins to elbow its way in as a substitute. It is true that Woodstock cannot (nor should it) extract itself from the apparitions of the past—Dylan exiting the Cafe Espresso's drive on his motorcycle, The Band fresh from their Big Pink home and ready to take on Woodstock nightlife, the powerful presence of Albert Grossman as he entered a room, the head and bead shops, the retelling of tales about evenings spent in a field as music floated through the air. But these stories are subchapters in a much larger story. Should they become the main theme of Woodstock's story—as some seem to wish and some attempt to capitalize on—then, perhaps, Milan Kundera was correct when he offered, "In the sunset of dissolution, everything is illuminated by the aura of nostalgia."[20] For a town that has witnessed change through progressive eyes over the years, it is ironic that so many continue to view Woodstock's existence by gazing into a mirror that reflects what may have been.

Woodstock is a community with, unarguably, a past that is different. The reality of that history, however, lies in the path its people have chartered over the years. It is found in the early settlers clearing the land in a struggle to build a new life for themselves and their families, while, at the same time, questioning the power their wealthy landlords held over them. It is a road carved by the hard work of those who drew upon the natural resources of the land to sustain a viable community. It is found in the artists crafting homes out of rundown barns while bringing a new way of looking upon the landscape that served as fuel to their creative ways. And it's found in the young people who not only challenged the status quo in the 1960s and 1970s but went on to write new chapters in Woodstock's story. And yet the resulting changes that have impacted Woodstock in more recent years have undoubtedly left several Woodstockers wondering about the security of that foundation and what the days ahead might bring.

With housing and rental costs rising beyond the reach of those who serve the food and lattes in Woodstock's multiple restaurants, while also impacting those who offer their time as volunteers for essential town services—from a fire department, to multiple town committees, to its Meals on Wheels program, to a vanishing Little League—and with the once hotly debated Onteora School District closing elementary schools due to a decrease in enrollment from 2,470 in the late 1990s to 1,100 students today,[21] many are left with the same concern a young Will Rose once voiced, "Is there a vanishing Woodstock?"

It is a delicate—and sometimes tricky—balance when change comes to a small town. There are of course, those who desire no change, who wish to keep a community as it was, where doors aren't locked at night and where neighbors look out for each other without the need to raise a fence marking their territory. And yet, it is possible to view some newly arrived changes as actual additions to what once was, such as the more recent boost to Woodstock's music scene. Where "Ruth Brewer and her RKO Artists—offering Sparkling Dance Rhythms and Close Harmony" once entertained guests during the Great Depression, the new life given to the Colony on Rock City Road has returned more currently inspired rhythms of its own to Woodstock's nightlife. Additionally, the revitalization of Albert Grossman's Bearsville complex by social entrepreneur and music and history lover Lizzy Vann is attempting to return the magic that seemed to surround the site during the days of the Baron of Bearsville.[22] Wrapped in reminders of a time when music burst forth from Bearsville—including album covers, posters, and rooms dedicated to Dylan, Janis Joplin, and Van Morrison—Vann's restoration of the theater and restaurants is an endeavor to link past and present. And while her purchase of other sites in town have left some to wonder where her entrepreneurship might be headed, there is a certainty to the fact that, whatever the future holds, the landscape once meticulously overseen by Albert Grossman is once again filled with music. At the same time, however, battle lines continue to be drawn by those who challenge growth in the form of expanded development. As quickly as developers offer proposals for primarily upscale housing projects, opponents marshal efforts to block such plans with environmental and zoning objections.

In all respects, a small town such as Woodstock is only as good as the accommodation found among its citizens. It is a lesson that Woodstock has learned on more than one occasion, ultimately finding balance with both the artists and young people who came to stay. As Woodstock moves forward, it remains to be seen if such a balance can be found within its new reality. And while each new transition has attached its own chapter to Woodstock's story, Woodstock life, even for the newly arrived, has ultimately rested on the ability to manage integration into small-town existence, joining in a shared connection in preserving both the physical landscape and its history, respect for community character, and active participation in the issues of the day (as messy as that might seem at times). And though Woodstock has stumbled at times—sometimes badly—it is a compact that over the years has anchored those who have called Woodstock home, while, at the same time, recognizing that the underlying creativity newcomers can bring to that compact is—and has been—an integral element of moving forward.

Some forty years ago, Woodstock historian Alf Evers similarly contemplated that inherent nature of Woodstock life as he looked to the future: "It is unlikely that the distinctive unit of social life we call Woodstock can be easily rooted out. It has survived many blows and after each one has risen in added strength. And because of the creative vitality that has kept the Woodstock spirit alive, future observers looking out from the Village Green and from the top of Overlook may find what they see stirring to their imagination and emotions in ways we cannot dream of."[23] Perhaps that is what a young Will Rose, like those of us focused too closely on the present, could not understand. Unforeseen by Rose was the century that stretched out ahead and the creative contributions Woodstock would deliver to the world far beyond its own borders. Nor could he see that, despite the changes on the horizon, Woodstock would continue to build on the same foundation that underscored its earlier years—a foundation upon which individual stories, though unique in their own telling, ultimately merge and a community rises, rising with the knowledge that as a people we are never separate from our past but are an integral part of a combining experience that builds upon what has been.

And so, the future stretches out before a new era in Woodstock's long journey. If history is to be our guide, change will continue to come to Woodstock. That it will be met with opposition and challenges is a given—challenges that will test newcomers and old timers alike and their ability to find common ground. If those challenges are met with a true knowledge of Woodstock history and an authentic understanding of the road Woodstockers have traveled through the years—as opposed to those who would market what they think Woodstock was—Woodstock will meet the trials that most assuredly lie ahead. And in doing so, those whose future homes are destined to lie within the shadow of Overlook Mountain will not only embrace the uncommon history laid at their doorstep but will carry forward the creative and independent spirit that has embedded itself into Woodstock life for more than two centuries.

Figure 53. Woodstock's Overlook Mountain. *Source:* Image by author.

# Notes

## Woodstock: By Way of Introduction

1. Florence Peper, January 1, 1914, Diary, ed. Carl Van Wagenen, Historical Society of Woodstock Archives, Florence Peper Collection.

2. Peper, November 30, 1921, Diary.

3. Peper, September 1, 1939, Diary.

4. Anita M. Smith, "History and Hearsay—The Down Rent War," in *Publications of the Historical Society of Woodstock Volume IV* (Woodstock, NY: Historical Society of Woodstock, July 1931), 12.

5. "100 Assert Right to Swim in City's Drinking Water," *Kingston Daily Freeman*, June 10, 1922.

6. "100 Assert Right to Swim in City's Drinking Water."

7. Bolton Brown, "Early Days at Woodstock," in *Publications of the Woodstock Historical Society Volume XIII* (Woodstock, NY: Historical Society of Woodstock, 1937), 5.

8. Henry Morton Robinson, "The Maverick," in *Publications of the Historical Society of Woodstock, Volume II* (Woodstock, YN: Historical Society of Woodstock 1933), 4.

9. Robinson, "Maverick," 7.

10. Peper, November 5, 1918, Diary.

11. Bill Kovach, "Woodstock a Stage, but Many Don't Care for the Show," *New York Times*, July 9, 1969.

12. Louise Hasbrouck Zimm, "Pioneer Life in Woodstock," in *Publications of the Historical Society of Woodstock* (Woodstock, NY: Historical Society of Woodstock, 1930), 12.

13. Rene Cappon, "Artists Like in Fish Bowl at Once-Secluded Colony," *Victoria Advocate*, September 25, 1958.

# Chapter 1

1. "Mrs. Roosevelt Officiates at Woodstock NYA Center as Cornerstone is Placed," *Kingston Daily Freeman*, June 27, 1939.

2. Alf Evers, *Woodstock—History of an American Town* (Woodstock, NY: Overlook, 1987), 569.

3. Colony Club, advertisement, *Kingston Daily Freeman*, September 1, 1934.

4. Hungarian Inn, advertisement, *Kingston Daily Freeman*, June 8, 1938.

5. Evers, *Woodstock*, 570.

6. Richard Heppner, "Mother of Invention: Augusta Allen and the Woodstock Dress," *Woodstock Times*, March 24, 2016.

7. Dyrus Cook, letter to the editor, *Kingston Daily Freeman*, February 1, 1939.

8. "Ku Klux Klan Gets More Members," *The Woodstock Weekly*, September 20, 1924.

9. Evers, *Woodstock*, 493.

10. Evers, *Woodstock*, 490.

11. Alf Evers, *The Catskills—From Wilderness to Woodstock* (Woodstock, NY: Overlook, 1982), 633.

12. "Woodstock Playhouse Opens," *The Overlook*, July 8, 1938.

13. "No Depression Felt by Woodstock Artists," *Kingston Daily Freeman*, April 12, 1932.

14. *Woodstock Artists and the Federal Art Projects of the WPA Era* (Woodstock, NY: Historical Society of Woodstock, 1985), catalog of an exhibition at the Historical Society of Woodstock, August 24–October 5, 1985, 4.

15. Evers, *Woodstock*, 594.

16. Bill Grolty, Interview with Eugene Ludins, *WPA in Woodstock*, Historical Society of Woodstock/Interview Collection.

17. *Woodstock Artists*.

18. "The Woodstock Story Told in Paintings, Photography, Sculpture and Ceramics," D. Wigmore Fine Art, http://dwigmore.com/woodstock_essay.html, accessed March 13, 2021.

19. "Woodstock Has Measles Outbreak," *Kingston Daily Freeman*, April 1, 1940.

20. Marguerite Hurter, "Art Manager," *Kingston Daily Freeman*, August 8, 1940.

21. Marguerite Hurter, "Woodstock," *Kingston Daily Freeman*, July 16, 1940.

22. "Maverick Festival Personalities," the Maverick Festival, Woodstock, 1915–1931, https://www.newpaltz.edu/museum/exhibitions/maverick2007/, accessed February 14, 2023.

23. Marguerite Hurter, "Gaston Bell Is Writing Plays," *Kingston Daily Freeman*, June 20, 1940.

24. During this era, newspapers seldom published the first names of married women, preferring instead to use Mrs. followed by their husband's first and last name.

25. "Group Organizes and Pledges Aid to Foes of Nazis," *Kingston Daily Freeman*, August 6, 1940.

26. "Aid Anti-Fascist Refugees Aim of Fair at Woodstock," *Kingston Daily Freeman*, August 15, 1940.

27. "20 Recruits Sign for Enlistment in 156th Field Units," *Kingston Daily Freeman*, September 17, 1940.

28. "Woodstock," *Kingston Daily Freeman*, November 13, 1940.

## Chapter 2

1. "Judge Conway Tells Memorial Day Crowd U.S. Already at War," *The Overlook*, June 6, 1941.

2. "W.F. Terwilliger Found Dead in Country Club Woodshed," *The Overlook*, February 21, 1941.

3. "Hungarian Inn Burns; Ex-Owner Is Called Suicide," *Kingston Daily Freeman*, January 19, 194.

4. "Carl Eric Lindin Has Retrospective Exhibit at Bard," *Kingston Daily Freeman*, March 31, 1941.

5. "Demand Congressional Investigation of Federal Arts Project in New York," *The Overlook*, March 7, 1941.

6. "Audrey McMahon of W.P.A.," *New York Times*, August 28, 1981.

7. "Woodstock," *Kingston Daily Freeman*, March 8, 1941.

8. "Record Crowd Saw Toboggan Races at Woodstock Sunday," *Kingston Daily Freeman*, February 17, 1936.

9. Heckeroth, Bill, interview by Janine Mower, *Growing Up in Woodstock*, Woodstock Library Forum, October 9, 2004.

10. "County 'Pro Hitler' Mrs. Whitney Says, Mrs. Schoonmaker Declines War Debate," *Woodstock Press*, August 8, 1941.

11. "County 'Pro Hitler.'"

12. "County 'Pro Hitler.'"

13. "County 'Pro Hitler.'"

14. Alf Evers, *Woodstock—History of an American Town* (Woodstock, NY: Overlook, 1987), 605.

15. "Infantile Paralysis Closes School Health Officer Advises Parents," *Woodstock Press*, September 26, 1941.

16. Hubert W. Blade and Jocelyn Blade, letter to the editor, *Woodstock Press*, October 3, 1941.

17. "F.Y. Hall Forecast U.S. War Entrance," *Woodstock Press*, December 21, 1941.

18. "150 Attend Film Opening," *Woodstock Press*, December 5, 1941.

19. "Christmas Eve on Green to be Held," *Woodstock Press*, December 12, 1941.

20. Florence Cramer, Diary, December 28, 1941, Historical Society of Woodstock Archives, Cramer Family Collection, 87.

# Chapter 3

1. Florence Ballin Cramer, Diary, December 28, 1941, Historical Society of Woodstock Archives, Cramer Family Collection, 91.

2. "Legion Lists Town's Arms for Defense," *Woodstock Press*, December 24, 1941.

3. "Mass Meeting Elects Comeau Woodstock Defense Chairman," *Woodstock Press*, December 24, 1941.

4. "Entire Town Urged to Enroll," *Woodstock Press*, December 24, 1941.

5. "Many Appointments to Defense Tasks Announced by Chairman," *Woodstock Press*, December 31, 1941.

6. "Many Appointments to Defense Tasks Announced by Chairman."

7. "Lindin Named to Distribute County Tires," *Woodstock Press*, January 9, 1941.

8. "Red Cross Thermometer on Village Green," *Woodstock Press*, January 9, 1941.

9. "Blackout Test Called Perfect," *Woodstock Press*, January 20, 1941.

10. "Bombs Fall in Bearsville," *Woodstock Press*, May 8, 1941.

11. "Red Cross Tops Campaign Goal," *Woodstock Press*, February 20, 1942.

12. "WWII Years 1939–1945, Online Gallery of the Artistic Journey of Yasuo Kuniyoshi," Smithsonian American Art Museum, https://americanart.si.edu, accessed July 17, 2022.

13. "Kuniyoshi Loyal to America Artists and Students Attest," *Woodstock Press*, December 31, 1941.

14. "U.S. Navy May Use Byrdcliffe as Retreat for Disabled Sailors," *Woodstock Press*, May 20, 1942.

15. "Local Family Servant Unmasked as Nazi Spy," *Woodstock Press*, June 17, 1942.

16. "To Form AWVS Chapter Here," *Woodstock Press*, February 20, 1942.

17. "Victory Garden at the National Museum of American History," Smithsonian Gardens, https://gardens.si.edu/gardens/victory-garden/, accessed September 12, 2022.

18. "Victory Garden Starts, Dowd Urges All to Register," *Woodstock Press*, April 10, 1942.

19. "Victory Garden Starts."

20. "Victory Garden Starts."

21. "Baker Tells Salvage Need," *Woodstock Press*, February 6, 1942.

22. "Attention!! Traitors!!," *Woodstock Press*, August 7, 1942.

23. "Hundreds at Saugerties Cheer Woodstock Draftees Departure," *Woodstock Press*, April 17, 1942.

24. "Gladys Hurlburt Tells Story of the Observation Post," *Woodstock Press*, April 24, 1942.

25. "Woodstock Observation Post; Swing Shift," *Woodstock Press*, June 5, 1942, Historical Society of Woodstock Archives, Anita M. Smith Collection.

26. "Woodstock Is about the Same Size as Lidice," *Woodstock Press*, July 18, 1942, Historical Society of Woodstock Archives, Anita M. Smith Collection.

27. "Fourth Crowds Hears Shotwell Say War Is to Save Our Ideals," *Woodstock Press*, July 10, 1942.

28. "French Dance Profits $500," *Woodstock Press*, July 17, 1942.

29. Marion Bullard, "Sparks," *Ulster County News*, May 21, 1942.

30. "Record Trout Bagged Here," *Woodstock Press*, April 10, 1942.

31. Richard Heppner and Janine Fallon Mower, *Legendary Locals of Woodstock* (Charleston, SC: Arcadia, 2013), 96.

32. "One Sailor Killed, Another Missing in War at Sea," *Woodstock Press*, December 4, 1942.

33. "Eric Carl Lindin, 73, Dies Helped Found the Art Colony," *Woodstock Press*, November 13, 1942.

34. "Larry Elwyn Dies," *Woodstock Press*, April 17, 1942.

35. "The Why of It," *Woodstock Press*, August 21, 1942.

36. "Woodstock Stages Successful Drive," *Kingston Daily Freeman*, October 10, 1942.

37. "Woodstock," *Kingston Daily Freeman*, December 12, 1942.

38. "Woodstock," *Kingston Daily Freeman*, February 11, 1943.

39. "Bastille Day Is Held at Woodstock," *Kingston Daily Freeman*, July 19, 1943.

40. Heppner and Mower, *Legendary Locals*, 101.

41. Anita M. Smith, *Woodstock History and Hearsay* (Woodstock, NY: WoodstockArts, 2006), 221.

42. "Russian General Will be Speaker at Town Hall," *Kingston Daily Freeman*, September 25, 1942.

43. "Prince to Speak," *Kingston Daily Freeman*, October 10, 1943.

44. "Russian War Relief Launches Book Drive," *Kingston Daily Freeman*, June 2, 1945.

45. "Sonia Malkine," interviewed by Mike Russert and Wayne Clarke, New York Military Museum, January 18, 2002, https://museum.dmna.ny.gov/application/files/7915/9464/5518/Malkine_Sonia_May.pdf, accessed September 15, 2022.

46. "Manuel Bromberg," https://www.manuelbromberg.com/WW-II-finalYES.html, accessed October 3, 2022.

47. Heppner and Mower, *Legendary Locals*, 94.

48. Martin Schutze, "Hervey White—Spoken at His Funeral," funeral program, October 23, 1944, Historical Society of Woodstock Archives, Maverick Collection.

# Chapter 4

1. "Woodstock Plans War Memorial on Village Green," *Kingston Daily Freeman*, September 9, 1947.

2. "Woodstock Plans War Memorial on Village Green."

3. "Woodstock Plans War Memorial on Village Green."

4. "Officers Selected for War Memorial," *Kingston Daily Freeman*, October 10, 1947.

5. "Officers Selected for War Memorial."

6. "Officers Selected for War Memorial."

7. "Design Selected for War Memorial," *Kingston Daily Freeman*, October 25, 1947.

8. Merrill Mecklem Piera and Sarah Greer Mecklem, "Marianne Greer Mecklem, 1913–1988," in *Gathering Woodstock Women* (Woodstock, NY: Historical Society of Woodstock, 2012), 17–18.

9. Piera and Mecklem, "Marianne Greer Mecklem," 18.

10. "Design Selected for War Memorial."

11. "Officers Selected for War Memorial."

12. "Woodstock Club Votes Playground Action for Village," *Kingston Daily Freeman*, December 9, 1947.

13. "Woodstock Club Votes."

14. "Woodstock Club Votes."

15. "Woodstock Club Votes."

16. "Woodstock Legion Gives Support to Memorial Group," *Kingston Daily Freeman*, December 13, 1947.

17. Wilna Hervey Is Honorary Head of Memorial Group," *Kingston Daily Freeman*, March 15, 1948.

18. "Village Memorial Is Dedicated at Special Ceremony," *Kingston Daily Freeman*, June 2, 1948.

19. "Military Burial Held Here for Pacific Warr Veteran," *Kingston Daily Freeman*, June 19, 1948.

20. "Affiliation with Third Party Voted," *Kingston Daily Freeman*, January 30, 1948.

21. Peg Hard, "Democracy Fails Clergyman Says, Blames Truman," *Kingston Daily Freeman*, March 24, 1948.

22. "Weaver, Kingsbury Address 100 at Wallace Meeting," *Kingston Daily Freeman*, August 4, 1948.

23. "Weaver, Kingsbury Address 100."

24. "The People's Songs Archive," Sing Out, https://singout.org/ps-archive/, accessed December 19, 2022.

25. "Weaver, Kingsbury Address 100."

26. Alf Evers, *Woodstock—History of an American Town* (Woodstock, NY: Overlook, 1987), 629.

27. "John Kingsbury, Lecturer, Dead," *New York Times*, August 4, 1956.

28. Evers, *Woodstock*, 629.

29. "U.S. Security is Seriously Threatened," *Kingston Daily Freeman*, August 30, 1948.

30. "U.S. Security Is Seriously Threatened."

31. "U.S. Security Is Seriously Threatened."

32. "Woodstock Agog over Burning of Cross Near Bird's," *Kingston Daily Freeman*, August 31, 1948.

33. "New York Attorney Gives Threat to Woodstock Board; Some Resentment Is Voiced," *Kingston Daily Freeman*, September 16, 1948.

34. "New York Attorney Gives Threat."

35. "New York Attorney Gives Threat."

36. "Vote in County Districts," *Kingston Daily Freeman*, November 3, 1948.

# Chapter 5

1. Eva Beard, "Background and History," in *Publications of the Historical Society of Woodstock*, Vol. XVII (Woodstock, NY: Historical Society of Woodstock, 1955), 6.

2. Rose Oxlander, "Woodstock Years," in *Publications of the Historical Society of Woodstock* (Woodstock, NY: Historical Society of Woodstock, 1955), 14.

3. Oxlander, "Woodstock Years," 15.

4. Oxlander, "Woodstock Years," 14.

5. "Hoodes Get First Water Supply from New Village System," *Kingston Daily Freeman*, August 19, 1950.

6. "The Start of the Woodstock Water District Project," Republican Campaign Literature, 1949, Historical Society of Woodstock Archives, Town Government Collection.

7. Florence Peper, September 14, 1950, Diary, ed. Carl Van Wagenen, Historical Society of Woodstock, Florence Peper Collection.

8. "Girl Cagers Get Aid from Village," *Kingston Daily Freeman*, January 31, 1950.

9. "Winners of 19 Games This Year," *Kingston Daily Freeman*, January 31, 1950.

10. "Webster Students Familiar Sight on Village Streets," *Kingston Daily Freeman*, August 8, 1950.

11. "Ties Result at Horse Show for Two Top Trophies," *Kingston Daily Freeman*, June 25, 1950.

12. "Chairmen Named for Library Fair; Set for July 27," *Kingston Daily Freeman*, July 10, 1950.

13. "Engagement of Hughes Is Denied by Kenneth Wilson," *Kingston Daily Freeman*, August 23, 1950.

14. "Engagement of Hughes."

15. "Local Artists Picked for Gotham Exhibit," *Kingston Daily Freeman*, November 27, 1950.

16. "Woodstock to Dedicate Elementary School at Rites," *Kingston Daily Freeman*, December 28, 1950.

17. "Quite a Career and Quite a Way to Remember It," *Woodstock Times*, August 9, 1979.

18. "Woodstock to Dedicate."

19. Oxlander, "Woodstock Years," 16.

20. "Marion Bullard Dies in Woodstock," *Kingston Daily Freeman*, December 19, 1950.

21. Florence Peper, May 17, 1952, Diary, ed. Carl Van Wagenen, Historical Society of Woodstock Archives, Florence Peper Collection.

22. Richard Heppner and Janine Fallon Mower, *Legendary Locals of Woodstock* (Charleston, SC: Arcadia, 2013), 46.

23. "Governor Speaks at Thruway Ceremony, Predicts New Superhighways to Chicago," *Kingston Daily Freeman*, October 26, 1954.

24. "IBM in Kingston Timeline," Hudson River Valley Heritage, https://omeka.hrvh.org/exhibits/show/kingston-the-ibm-years/ibm-in-kingston-timeline, accessed October 14, 2022.

25. "Bearsville Flats Site of 36 Home Development," *Woodstock Townsman*, February 3, 1954.

26. John Ebbs, "J. C. van Rijn Reminiscences," unpublished manuscript, August 22, 1992, Historical Society of Woodstock Archives, People Collection.

27. Ebbs, "J. C. van Rijn Reminiscences."

28. Ebbs, "J. C. van Rijn Reminiscences."

29. Heppner and Mower, *Legendary Locals of Woodstock*, 37.

30. Ebbs, "J. C. van Rijn Reminiscences."

31. "A Time for Growth," *Woodstock Townsman*, November 11, 1953.

32. "Woodstock Opening in Full Force for Summer Trek," *Woodstock Townsman*, May 26, 1954.

33. "Tourists Go Home," *The Wasp*, July 10, 1954.

34. "Tourists Go Home."

35. "Tourists Are You Still Here?" *The Wasp*, July 31, 1954.

36. "Tourists Are You Still Here?"

37. "Holdridges Chosen as Real American Family for Holiday," *Kingston Daily Freeman*, November 20, 1951.

38. "Holdridges Chosen."

39. "Holdridges Chosen."

40. "Holdridges Chosen."

41. "Johtje Vos, Who Served Wartime Jews, Dies at 97," *New York Times*, November 4, 2007.

42. "Johtje Vos."

43. Sarah G. Mecklem and Barbara Moorman, "Johanna Hendricka Kuyper (Vos)," in *Gathering Woodstock Women* (Woodstock, NY: Historical Society of Woodstock, 2012), 95.

44. Mecklem and Moorman, "Johanna Hendricka Kuyper (Vos)," 96.

45. Mecklem and Moorman, "Johanna Hendricka Kuyper (Vos)."

## Chapter 6

1. Mary Lou Paturel, "Interview with Alf Evers," Woodstock Public Access Television, n.d., Historical Society of Woodstock Archives/Mary Lou Paturel Collection, 41:40.

2. "Project Started to Build Parish on Donated Land," *Kingston Daily Freeman*, May 1, 1954.

3. Alf Evers, *Woodstock—History of an American Town* (Woodstock, NY: Overlook, 1987), 537.

4. Mark Anderson, *For All the Saints* (Bloomington, IN: Authorhouse, 2006), 26–28.

5. Anderson, *For All the Saints*, 223–224.

6. "First Church of Christ, Scientist, Woodstock," Christian Science New York State, https://christiansciencenys.com/first-church-of-christ-scientist-woodstock/, accessed March 28, 2022.

7. Clarence Bolton, "Science and Art," Clarence Bolton Collection, Historical Society of Woodstock Archives.

8. Richard Heppner and Janine-Fallon Mower, *Legendary Locals of Woodstock* (Charleston, SC: Arcadia, 2013), 57.

9. "Our Parish History," 150th Anniversary St. John's Parish, https://d2h4p
72yjb3hg1.cloudfront.net/28726/documents/2022/1/St.%20Johns%20150%20
Anniversary%20book-1.pdf, accessed April 16, 2022.

10. Heppner and Mower, *Legendary Locals of Woodstock,* 45.

11. Evers, *Woodstock,* 580–583.

12. Evers, *Woodstock,* 501.

13. Washy Wilber, interview by John Mower and Terry Breitenstein, June
2015, video recording, Historical Society of Woodstock Archives.

14. US Department of the Interior National Park Service, National Register
of Historic Places, George Bellows House, December 19, 2017, p. 12, https://
npgallery.nps.gov/GetAsset/33dcbc82-b6b7-4041-868c-f576344c9da7, accessed
April 17, 2022.

15. "Andrew Lee, 17, Dies from Accidental Shot," *Kingston Daily Freeman,*
January 9, 1956.

16. "Woodstock Board Votes to Dedicate Field to Andy Lee," *Kingston Daily
Freeman,* January 12, 1956.

17. "Little League Dinner Scheduled October 5," *Kingston Daily Freeman,*
September 27, 1957.

18. 1957 Woodstock Festival, The Woodstock Festival Committee, summer
1957.

19. "Ruling Is 26 Voted Illegally," *Kingston Daily Freeman,* July 7, 1957.

20. "Ruling Is 26 Voted Illegally."

21. "Machine versus Child," The Committee of 500 for Centralization with
Onteora, advertisement, *Kingston Daily Freeman,* August 16, 1957.

22. "Children versus Machine," Mothers against Onteora, advertisement,
*Kingston Daily Freeman,* August 19, 1957.

23. "Pro-Onteora Vote May Be Appealed Again," *Kingston Daily Freeman,*
August 21, 1957.

24. "Appeal of Deckleman Ruling to Follow Receipt of Order," *Kingston
Daily Freeman,* October 8, 1958.

25. Democratic political advertisement, *Kingston Daily Freeman,* November
1, 1957.

26. Lesley Geertsema, "Tobie Geertsema," in *Gathering Woodstock Women*
(Woodstock, NY: Historical Society of Woodstock, 2012), 69.

27. Richard Heppner, *A Woodstock Fire Department Journal* (Woodstock,
NY: Woodstock Fire Department, 2006), 31–33.

28. "Town Board Receives Data on Proposed Community TV," *Kingston
Daily Freeman,* January 13, 1958.

29. "Hans Schimmerling," Wikipedia, https://en.wikipedia.org/wiki/Hans_
Schimmerling, accessed March 12, 2022.

30. Lisa Tiano, "Spring Music Festival Huge Success at School," *Kingston
Daily Freeman,* May 26, 1958.

31. Lisa Tiano, "Arts Students League School Opens in Woodstock June 2," *Kingston Daily Freeman*, May 12, 1958.

32. "Purse Totaling $3625 Is Presented to Rev. Todd."

33. "Tobie Geertsema's Proposal for Planning Board Hailed," *Kingston Daily Freeman*, December 29, 1958.

34. Lisa Tiano, "Pick Five Woodstock Artists for National Academy Show," *Kingston Daily Freeman*, February 16, 1959.

35. "Library Fair Program Complete for July 30," *Woodstock Press*, July 23, 1959.

36. "Prizes Awarded for Best Hats at Annual Party," *Woodstock Press*, August 20, 1959.

37. " 'Bettina's Promise' Hilarious Woodstock Foundation Play," *Kingston Daily Freeman*, September 15, 1959.

38. "Two Walk Out as Board Okays Budget Estimate," *Woodstock Press*, October 8, 1959.

39. "Two Walk Out."

40. "Two Walk Out."

41. "Torchlight Parade Opens Giant Republican Rally," *Woodstock Press*, September 17, 1959.

42. "Molyneaux Is New Supervisor as Republicans Score Sweep," *Kingston Daily Freeman*, November 4, 1959.

43. "Press among 6 Spots Hit by Vandals," *Woodstock Press*, September 9, 1959.

44. "Juvenile Delinquency," *Woodstock Press*, September 19, 1959.

45. "Jay-Teens Selling Christmas Trees," *Kington Daily Freeman*, December 14, 1959.

# Chapter 7

1. "Set Woodstock Folk Festival at the Estates," *Kingston Daily Freeman*, September 14, 1962.

2. Brian Hollander, "Remembrance: Eric Weissberg," *Hudson Valley One*, April 10, 2020.

3. Ed Sanders, "Huckleberry Festivals," email message to author, April 21, 2022.

4. "An Appreciation of Alf Evers," Woodstock Journal.com, http://www.woodstockjournal.com/appreciationofalf.html, accessed April 21, 2022.

5. Happy Traum, "Music from Home," *Woodstock Years*, Vol. II (Woodstock, NY: Publication of Historical Society of Woodstock, 2007), 14.

6. Woodstock Association, *Woodstock Speaks-Up, A Public Opinion Survey* (Woodstock, NY: Woodstock Association, 1960).

7. Woodstock Association, *Woodstock Speaks-Up*.

8. Woodstock Association, *Woodstock Speaks-Up*.

9. "Town Board Establishes Planning Board," *Kingston Daily Freeman*, February 17, 1960.

10. Miss Mary, advertisement, *Kingston Daily Freeman*, May 5, 1965.

11. Olivia Twine, "Twine's Catskill Bookshop and the Art of Growing Up in Woodstock," in *Remembering Woodstock* (Charleston, SC: History Press, 2008), 99.

12. Twine, "Twine's Catskill Bookshop," 102.

13. Richard Heppner, "Before the Deluge II," *Woodstock Times*, September 19, 2019.

14. Mary Lou Paturel, "The Sixties," Woodstock Public Access Television, n.d., Historical Society of Woodstock Archives/Mary Lou Paturel Collection, 54: 29.

15. "Pageant Ladies Using Destroyer, Horse to Travel," *Kingston Daily Freeman*, July 2, 1960.

16. Dorothy Nadel, "Sandra June Andrade Is Talent Winner in JCC Pageant; Repeats Tonight," *Kingston Daily Freeman*, July 8, 1960.

17. "Pike Opens First Major Art School Since League," *Kingston Daily Freeman*, July 23, 1960.

18. "Memorandum on Discipline Given Strong PTA Backing," *Kingston Daily Freeman*, January 19, 1961.

19. "Memorandum on Discipline."

20. "Woodstock Youth Center Report," *Ulster County Townsman*, May 17, 1962.

21. "Woodstock Youth Center Report."

22. "Woodstock Youth Center Report."

23. "League Urges Public Support Youth Center," *Kingston Daily Freeman*, June 1, 1962.

24. Lisa Tiano, "Rec Committee Will Assume Operation of Youth Center, *Kingston Daily Freeman*, June 13, 1962.

25. Lisa Tiano, "How to Finance Youth Center Divides Board," *Kingston Daily Freeman*, June 22, 1962.

26. Richard Heppner, "Four Days in November: Woodstock, 1963," *Woodstock Times*, April 24, 2017.

27. Heppner, "Four Days in November."

28. Heppner, "Four Days in November."

29. Florence Peper, November 24, 1963, Diary, ed. Carl Van Wagenen, Historical Society of Woodstock Archives, Florence Peper Collection.

## Chapter 8

1. "Let's Stop Blaming Our Police," *Ulster County Townsman*, August 20, 1964.

2. "Woodstock Constables Are Cleared of Brutality," *Kingston Daily Freeman*, February 18, 1965.

3. "Woodstock Constables."

4. "Citizens Group Will Press for Police Hearing," *Kingston Daily Freeman*, August 17, 1964.

5. Sonia Rice, letter to the editor, *Kingston Daily Freeman*, August 8, 1964.

6. Rice, letter to the editor.

7. Lisa Tiano, "Board Inquiry into Alleged Police Brutality Thursday," *Kingston Daily Freeman*, August 26, 1964.

8. Lisa Tiano, "Board Hears 24 Witnesses in Woodstock Police Inquiry," *Kingston Daily Freeman*, August 28, 1964.

9. "Woodstock Clears Officers for Time," *Kingston Daily Freeman*, November 5, 1964.

10. "Woodstock Clears Officers."

11. "Woodstock Clears Officers."

12. "Woodstock Clears Officers."

13. "Woodstock Constables."

14. "Woodstock Constables."

15. "Woodstock Historian Starts Action for $25,000 Damages in Arrest Case," *Kingston Daily Freeman*, April 21, 1965.

16. "Board Sets Tuesday Hearing," *Kingston Daily Freeman*, March 8, 1965.

17. "Board Sets Tuesday Hearing."

18. "Board Sets Tuesday Hearing."

19. "Woodstock Historian Starts Action."

20. Ed Sanders, *Alf Evers—Life of an American Genius* (Woodstock, NY: Meads Mountain Press, 2021), 140.

21. Lisa Tiano, "Zoning Battle in Perpetuity Is Prediction by Evers," *Kingston Daily Freeman*, January 22, 1965.

22. "Crowds Turn Out by Hundreds for Bradley Meadows Opening," *Kingston Daily Freeman*, February 10, 1966.

23. "Town Will Lease Cashdollar Dump," *Kingston Daily Freeman*, October 27, 1965.

24. Lisa Tiano, "Seek Legal Action to Force Compliance with Dump Laws," *Kingston Daily Freeman*, October 5, 1964.

25. "Molyneaux Asks Legislation to Aid Narcotic Enforcement," *Kingston Daily Freeman*, June 8, 1965.

26. "Fight Begins against Stigma in Woodstock," *Kingston Daily Freeman*, June 19, 1965.

27. "Molyneaux Asks Legislation."

28. "Fight Begins."

29. "Fight Begins."

30. Charles M. McCarthy, "School Is Prime Targeting Area Probe of Drugs," *Kingston Daily Freeman*, March 18, 1964.

31. McCarthy, "School Is Prime."

32. McCarthy, "School Is Prime."

33. "Doctors, Lawyer, Detective Split on Narcotics Control," *Kingston Daily Freeman*, March 20, 1964.

34. "Doctors, Lawyer, Detective."

35. "Doctors, Lawyer, Detective."

## Chapter 9

1. Maria Logendyke Elwyn, Personal Journal, May 13, 1966, Historical Society of Woodstock Archives, Maria Logendyke Journals.

2. "Young America's Answer to Walt Whitman Finds a Haven on Woodstock's Byrdcliffe," *Kingston Daily Freeman*, February 8, 1968.

3. Laurie Ylvisaker, interview by author, January 14, 2023.

4. Bob Dylan, *Chronicles: Volume One* (New York: Simon and Schuster, 2004), 116.

5. Paul Smart, "Bearsville's Baron," *Woodstock Times*, February 24, 2011.

6. "Bearsville's Baron."

7. "Woodstock Wants Moves to Limit Drinking, Noise," *Kingston Daily Freeman*, July 21, 1966.

8. "Woodstock Wants Moves."

9. "Reasons for Benches Removal 'Now Suspect' Petition Says," *Kingston Daily Freeman*, September 9, 1966.

10. "It's High Time," *Ulster County Townsman*, October 13, 1966.

11. "It's High Time."

12. "Board Studying Possibility of Inaugurating a Curfew; Says Kids Out Until 4 A.M.," *Kingston Daily Freeman*, June 23, 1966.

13. "Board Studying Possibility."

14. "Woodstock Sets Strong Ordinances," *Ulster County Townsman*, August 4, 1966.

15. "Woodstock Sets Strong Ordinances."

16. "Woodstock Sets Strong Ordinances."

17. "Woodstock Sets Strong Ordinances."

18. "Woodstock Sets Strong Ordinances."

19. "Historian's Report Says '66 Good Year Here; Hopeful for Arts, Recreation in Future," *Kingston Daily Freeman*, January 23, 1967.

20. "Season Opened on Boom Note; Holiday Weekend Successful," *Kingston Daily Freeman*, May 28, 1966.

21. Jeremy Wilber, "Woodstock Meets the Sixties," in *Remembering Woodstock*, ed. Richard Heppner (Charleston, SC: History Press, 2008), 117–118.

22. R. L. Duffus, "An Eden of Artists Fights a Serpent," *New York Times*, August 25, 1929.

23. "It's High Time."

24. "Spend a Day in Woodstock," *Kingston Daily Freeman*, December 14, 1967.

25. "Woodstock Firm Reproduces Wounds of Every Type to Help Save Lives," *Kingston Daily Freeman*, January 21, 1967.

26. "Wonderful Woodstock," advertisement, *Kingston Daily Freeman*, April 26, 1967.

27. Happy Traum, "The Impact of Music on Woodstock Culture," Historical Society of Woodstock Panel Discussion, Applehead Studio, recorded July 13, 2019.

28. "Hippy Festival Upstate Is Cool amid the Bonfires," *New York Times*, September 4, 1967.

29. "Sound-Out," *Woodstock Week*, September 7, 1967.

30. Sound-Out Poster, 1967, Historical Society of Woodstock Archives/60's and 70's Music Collection.

31. "Hippy Festival Upstate."

32. "Sound-Out."

33. Woodstock Playhouse, "Folk Concert," advertisement, *Kingston Daily Freeman*, August 31, 1967.

34. Peter Aaron, "Michael Lang on the Woodstock Festival," Chronogram, August 1, 2019, https://www.chronogram.com/hudsonvalley/we-were-half-a-million-strong/Content?oid=8820311, accessed September 14, 2022.

35. "Fire Tragedies Hit the Area," *Kingston Daily Freeman*, January 8, 1968.

36. "A Tribute to Clarence Schmidy," *Woodstock Times*, April 8, 1976.

37. "McCarthy Group Pens Resolutions," *Kingston Daily Freeman*, February 14, 1968.

38. "Woodstock Post Says Draft All Youths 17 to 20," *Kingston Daily Freeman*, April 1, 1968.

39. "Mystic to Be Topic on 29th," *Woodstock Week*, March 22, 1968.

40. "Bail Denied Kidnap Suspect," *Kingston Daily Freeman*, July 29, 1968.

41. "Woodstock People Talk about Hippies," *Kingston Daily Freeman*, August 21, 1968.

42. "Woodstock People Talk about Hippies."

43. "Woodstock Oks Trespass Law; Buys Dump," *Kingston Daily Freeman*, September 18, 1968.

44. "Woodstock Oks Trespass Law."

45. "Woodstock Oks Trespass Law."

46. "Woodstock Oks Trespass Law."

47. "Woodstock Oks Trespass Law."

48. "Woodstock Oks Trespass Law."

49. "A Sunday Kind of Scene," *Kingston Daily Freeman*, October 19, 1968.

50. Barbara Pickhardt, "The Impact of Music on Woodstock Culture," Historical Society of Woodstock Panel Discussion, Applehead Studio, recorded July 13, 2019.

## Chapter 10

1. Tobie Geertsema, "The Scene at Woodstock," *Kingston Daily Freeman*, June 19, 1969.

2. Woodstock Police Department Reports, September 14, 1969, Historical Society of Woodstock Archives, Town Government Collection.

3. Tobie Geertsema, "Woodstockers Face Problem—Search for Sane Solution," *Kingston Daily Freeman*, June 25, 1969, 1.

4. Geertsema, "Woodstockers Face Problem."

5. Geertsema, "Woodstockers Face Problem."

6. Howard Koch, letter to the editor, *Kingston Daily Freeman*, June 26, 1969.

7. Koch, letter to the editor.

8. Tobie Geertsema, "Woodstock Situation—A Touch of Violence," *Kingston Daily Freeman*, June 27, 1969.

9. Geertsema, "Woodstock Situation."

10. Bill Kovach, "Woodstock's a Stage, but Many Don't Care for the Show," *New York Times*, July 8, 1969.

11. Geertsema, "Woodstock Situation."

12. Tobie Geertsema, "Going Gourmet," *Kingston Daily Freeman*, May 17, 1969.

13. Geertsema, "Scene at Woodstock."

14. "Energy Flows from Buddha-Realm," *Kingston Daily Freeman*, July 12, 1969.

15. "You Are What You Eat," *Kingston Daily Freeman*, March 13, 1969.

16. "Poetry Readings," *Kingston Daily Freeman*, July 12, 1969.

17. "Diversion for a Winter's Night—Poetry Readings," *Kingston Daily Freeman*, December 20, 1969.

18. "Oil Firm to Board: Zoning Law Illegal," *Kingston Daily Freeman*, March 14, 1969.

19. "Woodstock Golf Club Conservation Easement," 1969, Historical Society of Woodstock Archives, Woodstock Country Club Collection.

20. Tobie Geertsema, "The Questionnaire in Woodstock—Some Are Happy, Others Critical," *Kingston Daily Freeman*, January 29, 1969.

21. Tobie Geertsema, "600 Parade in Woodstock," *Kingston Daily Freeman*, October 16, 1969.

22. "Woodstock Vote Set on Sewage Proposal," *Kingston Daily Freeman*, October 24, 1974.

23. Jon Powers, "Big Deep Closed, Marbletown Open in Pollution Crisis," *Kingston Daily Freeman*, August 22, 1974.

24. "Head Start in Woodstock," *Kingston Daily Freeman*, February 16, 1970.

25. Michael T. Kaufman, "Woodstock Uptight as Hippies Drift In," *New York Times*, June 16, 1970.

26. Kaufman, "Woodstock Uptight."

27. "Early Days at Family of Woodstock," WoostockArts, https://woodstock arts.com/early-days-at-family-of-woodstock/#more-2500, accessed September 12, 2022.

28. "Open House Slated for Center," *Kingston Daily Freeman*, November 11, 1971.

29. "Timeline," Family of Woodstock, https://www.familyofwoodstockinc. org/who-we-are/timeline/, accessed September 13, 2022.

## Chapter 11

1. Michael Kaufman, "Woodstock Up Tight as Hippies Drift In," *New York Times*, June 19, 1970.

2. Karyn Bevet, interview by author, Woodstock, October 5, 2022.

3. "Musicians' Benefit Helps Irene Victims," *Times Herald Record*, November 20, 2011, https://www.recordonline.com/story/news/2011/11/20/musicians-bene-fit-helps-irene-victims/49829091007/, accessed August 22, 2023.

4. Barbara O'Brien, Historical Society of Woodstock Forum—"John W. Barry Discussing His Book *Levon Helm: Rock, Roll & Ramble—The Inside Story of the Man, the Music and the Midnight Ramble*," taped August 19, 2023, Historical Society of Woodstock Archives.

5. Brian Hollander, "Cindy Cashdollar," https://cindycashdollar.com, accessed August 21, 2023.

6. Cindy Cashdollar, Historical Society of Woodstock Forum—"John W. Barry Discussing His Book *Levon Helm: Rock, Roll & Ramble—The Inside Story of the Man, the Music and the Midnight Ramble*," taped August 19, 2023, Historical Society of Woodstock Archives.

7. Robert Christgau, "The Family—the Story of Charlie Manson's Dune Buggy Attack Battalion," *New York Times*, October 31, 1971.

8. Ed Sanders, interview by author, August 22, 2023.

9. Ed Sanders, interview by author, August 22, 2023.

10. Ed Sanders, interview by author, August 22, 2023.

11. Ed Sanders, interview by author, August 22, 2023.

12. Tinker Twine, "Friends Speak Out," *Woodstock Times*, September 13, 1984.

13. Ed Sanders, interview by author, August 22, 2023.

14. Jay Sadowitz, interview by author, December 21, 2022.

15. JoAnn Margolis, interview by author, December 12, 2022.

16. Paul Smart, "Woodstock Design Passes from Robin and Mike to Daughter Daisy," *Woodstock Times*, February 13, 2017.

17. The New Woodstock Merchant's Association, advertisement, *Woodstock Times*, May 31, 1973.

18. Enid Nemy, "Intellectuals Learn to Use Their Hands as Well as Their Minds," *New York Times*, October 9, 1973.

19. "The True Light Beavers," *Woodstock Times*, November 22, 1972.

20. "On the Bus," *Kirkus Review*, March 1, 1973.

21. Jacques Steinberg, "Woodstock Nation, and Address," *New York Times*, July 17, 1994.

22. "The Joyous Lake—An Interview with Ron Merians," *Woodstock Times*, November 20, 1975.

23. "The Joyous Lake."

24. Jim Hanson, interview by author, November 22, 2022.

25. "Whatever Happened to Rosa's?" *Woodstock Times*, June 17, 1976.

26. "And the Beat Goes On," *Woodstock Times*, July 10, 1975.

27. "And the Beat Goes On."

28. "Snag Hits Disco Enduro," *Woodstock Times*, July 24, 1975.

29. "Snag Hits Disco Enduro."

30. "Markie Makes It," *Woodstock Times*, July 31, 1975.

31. "And the Beat Goes On."

32. "Civic Arts Council Reverses Stand," *Woodstock Times*, September 28, 1972.

33. "Police Chief Supports Home Rule," *Woodstock Review*, January 27, 1972.

34. Town Board News," *Woodstock Review*, February 10, 1972.

35. Marguerite Culp, "Local Abortion Counseling," *Woodstock Times*, July 27, 1972.

36. "Rape—Not a Problem Peculiar to New York City," *Woodstock Times*, July 12, 1973.

37. Dorothy A. Narel, "Men Are Not Allowed in New Center Recently Opened in Woodstock, *Kingston Daily Freeman*, December 15, 1974.

38. Molly Ivans, "Welfare Ends in Woodstock as a Response to Drifters," *New York Times*, September 11, 1976.

39. Ivans, "Welfare Ends."

40. Ivans, "Welfare Ends."

41. Ivans, "Welfare Ends."

42. "Two Worlds Collide," *Woodstock Times*, April 22, 1976.

43. Ivans, "Welfare Ends."

44. "Two Worlds Collide."

45. "Support for Cadden," *Woodstock Times*, April 29, 1976.

46. Ivans, "Welfare Ends."

47. "Home Relief Costs Going Down," *Woodstock Times*, November 11, 1976.

48. Andrea Barrist Stern, "Might Make White," *Woodstock Times*, March 2, 1978.

49. Stern, "Might Make White."

50. Stern, "Might Make White."

## Chapter 12

1. Will Rose, *The Vanishing Village* (Woodstock, NY: Twine's Catskill Bookshop, 1963), 11.

2. Rose, *Vanishing Village*, 16.

3. Rose, *Vanishing Village*, 16.

4. "Remembrance of Things Gone," *Woodstock Times*, May 3, 1979.

5. Brian Hollander, "A Life Well Lived, Jerry Gillman Passes at 81," *Woodstock Times*, December 25, 2008.

6. Andrea Barrist Stern, "Crocidolite Tears," *Woodstock Times*, January 2, 1986.

7. Marguerite Culp, "Changing of the Guard," *Woodstock Times*, November 5, 1987.

8. "Nuke Plants Protested," *Kingston Daily Freeman*, June 6, 1976.

9. Spider Barbour, "A Mountain Worth Saving," *Woodstock Times*, May 5, 1988.

10. Barbour, "Mountain Worth Saving."

11. Kirk Johnson, "Toasting a Legacy of Eccentricity," *New York Times*, June 5, 1987.

12. Todd Paul, "Venue Leaving," *Woodstock Times*, January 1999.

13. "At Last! A *Real* Woodstock Festival," *Woodstock Times*, September 28, 2000.

14. Andrea Barrist Stern, "Flick Fever," *Woodstock Times*, September 14, 2000.

15. "History of the Woodstock Film Festival," Woodstock Film Festival, https://woodstockfilmfestival.org/history#:~:text=The%20inaugural%20Woodstock%20Film%20Festival,from%20all%20over%20the%20world, accessed October 24, 2023.

16. Bob Margolis, "Levon's Midnight Ride," *Woodstock Times*, November 25, 2004.

17. "Interview with Baker Rorick from the Woodstock Invitational Luthiers Showcase," Vintage and Rare, https://www.vintageandrare.com/blog/2011/09/interview-with-baker-rorick-from-the-woodstock-invitational-luthiers-showcase/, accessed October 25, 2023.

18. Peter Applebome, "In Woodstock, Values Collide over Housing," *New York Times*, September 13, 2011.

19. Rose, *Vanishing Village*, 338.

20. Milan Kundera, *The Incredible Lightness of Being* (New York: Harper Collins, 2004),

21. Maria M. Silva, "Onteora School Board Votes to Close Phoenicia, Woodstock Schools," *Times Union*, May 4, 2023.

22. "Lizzie Vann," Bearsville Theater, https://bearsvilletheater.com/profile/lizzie-vann/, accessed October 28, 2023.

23. Evers, Alf, *Woodstock—History of an American Town* (Woodstock, NY: Overlook, 1987), 676.

# Selected Bibliography

Anderson, Mark. *For All the Saints*. Bloomington, IN: Authorhouse, 2006.

Beard, Eva. "Background and History." In *Publications of the Woodstock Historical Society*. Vol. XVII, 6. Woodstock, NY: Historical Society of Woodstock, 1955.

Blelock, Weston, and Julia Blelock. *Roots of the 1969 Woodstock Festival*. Woodstock, NY: WoodstockArts, 2009.

Brown, Bolton. "Early Days at Woodstock." In *Publications of the Woodstock Historical Society*. Vol. XIII, 5. Woodstock, NY: Historical Society of Woodstock, 1937.

Cramer, Florence Ballin. Diary, 1906–1947, Historical Society of Woodstock Archives, Cramer Family Collection.

Dylan, Bob. *Chronicles*. Vol. 1. New York: Simon and Schuster Paperbacks, 2005.

Ebbs, John. "J. C. van Rijn Reminiscences." Unpublished manuscript. Historical Society of Woodstock Archives, People Collection, August 22, 1992.

Elwyn, Maria Logendyke. Diary, Personal Journal. Historical Society of Woodstock Archives, Maria Logendyke Elwyn Journals, 1944–1970.

Evers, Alf. *The Catskills—From Wilderness to Woodstock*. Woodstock, NY: Overlook, 1982.

———. *Woodstock—History of an American Town*. Woodstock, NY: Overlook, 1987.

Gaede, Jean. *Woodstock Gatherings: Apple Bites and Ashes*. Woodstock, NY: Broken Madonna, n.d.

Geertsema, Lesley. "Tobie Geertsema." In *Gathering Woodstock Women*, 69. Woodstock, NY: Historical Society of Woodstock, 2012.

Heppner, Richard. *A Woodstock Fire Department Journal*. Woodstock, NY: Woodstock Fire Department, 2006.

Heppner, Richard, and Janine-Fallon Mower. *Legendary Locals of Woodstock*. Charleston, SC: Arcadia, 2013.

Historical Society of Woodstock. *Woodstock Artists and the Federal Art Projects of the WPA Era*. Exhibition catalogue. Woodstock, NY: Historical Society of Woodstock, 1985.

Hoskyns, Barney, *Small Town Talk*. Boston, MA: Da Capo Press, 2016.

Kundera, Milan. *The Incredible Lightness of Being*. New York: Harper Collins, 2004.

Knutson, K. Eric, and Janine Fallon-Mower. "A View from the Sixth—The Story of Woodstock's Golf Club, 1929–2004." Woodstock, NY: n.p., 2004.

Lewis, Sinclair. *It Can't Happen Here*. New York: Penguin, 2005.

Mecklem, Sarah G., and Barbara Moorman. "Johanna Hendricka Kuyper (Vos)." In *Gathering Woodstock Women*, 96. Woodstock, NY: Historical Society of Woodstock, 2012.

Oxlander, Rose. "Woodstock Years." In *Publications of the Woodstock Historical Society*. Vol. XVII, 14. Woodstock, NY: Historical Society of Woodstock, 1955.

Peper, Florence. Diary. Edited by Carl Van Wagenen. Historical Society of Woodstock Archives, Florence Peper Collection, 1914–1984.

Piera, Merrill Mecklem, and Sarah Greer Mecklem. "Marianne Greer Mecklem, 1913–1988." In *Gathering Woodstock Women*, 17–18. Woodstock, NY: Historical Society of Woodstock, 2012.

Rose, Will. *The Vanishing Village*. Woodstock, NY: Twine's Catskill Bookshop, 1963.

Sanders, Ed. *Alf Evers—Life of an American Genius*. Woodstock, NY: Meads Mountain Press, 2021.

Schlesinger, Arthur M. Sr., and Dixon Ryan Fox, eds. *A History of American Life*. New York: Simon and Schuster, 1996.

Shotwell, James T. *The Autobiography of James T. Shotwell*. Indianapolis, IN: Bobs-Merrill, 1961.

Smith, Anita M. *Woodstock History and Hearsay*. Woodstock, NY: WoodstockArts, 2006.

Traum, Happy. "Music from Home." In *Woodstock Years*. Vol. II, 14. Woodstock, NY: Historical Society of Woodstock, 2007.

US Department of Interior National Park Service. National Register of Historic Places, George Bellows House, December 19, 2017. https://npgallery.nps.gov/GetAsset/33dcbc82-b6b7-4041-868c-f576344c9da7.

Woodstock Association. *Woodstock Speaks-Up, A Public Opinion Survey*. Woodstock, NY: Woodstock, 1960.

# Index

Ruth Pawelka Jewelry, 198